Let's talk

How the tax system works and how to change it

Edited by Jonathan Bradshaw

CPAG • 30 Micawber Street • London N1 7TB

Child Poverty Action Group works on behalf of the more than one in four children in the UK growing up in poverty. It does not have to be like this. We use our understanding of what causes poverty and the impact it has on children's lives to campaign for policies that will prevent and solve poverty – for good. We provide training, advice and information to make sure hard-up families get the financial support they need. We also carry out high-profile legal work to establish and protect families' rights. If you are not already supporting us, please consider making a donation, or ask for details of our membership schemes, training courses and publications.

Published by the Child Poverty Action Group
30 Micawber Street
London N1 7TB
Tel: 020 7837 7979
staff@cpag.org.uk
www.cpag.org.uk

The views expressed are those of the authors and do not necessarily represent the views of the Child Poverty Action Group.

© Child Poverty Action Group 2019. Contains public sector information licensed under the Open Government Licence v3.0. Crown Copyright 2014

This book is sold subject to the condition that it shall not, by way of trade or otherwise, be lent, resold, hired out or otherwise circulated without the publisher's prior consent in any form of binding or cover other than that in which it is published and without a similar condition including this condition being imposed on the subsequent purchaser.

A CIP record for this book is available from the British Library
ISBN: 978 1 910715 48 2

Child Poverty Action Group is a charity registered in England and Wales (registration number 294841) and in Scotland (registration number SC039339), and is a company limited by guarantee, registered in England (registration number 1993854). VAT number: 690 808117

Cover design by Colorido Studios
Cover illustration by sketchpadstudio.com
Typeset by Devious Designs
Printed in the UK by CPI Group (UK) Ltd, Croydon CR40 4YY

About the authors

Fran Bennett is Senior Research and Teaching Fellow, Department of Social Policy and Intervention, University of Oxford. She is a former director of the Child Poverty Action Group and is an active member of the Women's Budget Group.

Jonathan Bradshaw CBE FBA is Emeritus Professor of Social Policy at the University of York, a board member of Child Poverty Action Group and Chair of its policy committee.

Alan Buckle is Chair of the board of Child Poverty Action Group and formerly Deputy Chair of KPMG International until 2013.

David Eiser is Research Fellow in the Fraser of Allander Institute at the University of Strathclyde.

David Finch is Senior Research Fellow at the Resolution Foundation.

Antonia Keung is Lecturer in Social Policy at the University of York.

Andy Lymer is Professor of Accounting and Taxation at the University of Birmingham Business School.

Alan Marsh is Emeritus Professor of Social Policy at the University of Westminster and a member of the Child Poverty Action Group board.

Stephen McKay is Professor of Social Research at the University of Lincoln.

Tony Orhnial CB is a board member of the Child Poverty Action Group and formerly Director of Personal Tax and Welfare Reform at HM Treasury.

Michael Orton is Senior Research Fellow in the Institute for Employment Research, University of Warwick.

Adrian Sinfield is Emeritus Professor of Social Policy at the University of Edinburgh and a member of Child Poverty Action Group's policy committee.

Andrew Summers is Assistant Professor of Law and Associate Member of the International Inequalities Institute at the London School of Economics.

Acknowledgements

In 1988 the Child Poverty Action Group (CPAG) published a book by John Hills called *Changing Tax: how the tax system works and how to change it*. Now Professor Sir John Hills, he is not the author of this new version, but he has been consulted throughout the production and we are grateful for the model he left us to work with, for his willingness to be fairly closely plagiarised in parts and for his advice throughout. When CPAG decided that it needed to tackle taxation, it decided to call on the services of board members, members of our policy committee and academic and other supporters. We are grateful to them all for their entirely pro bono efforts on our behalf.

Thanks are also due to Alison Key for editing and managing the production of this book, and to Kathleen Armstrong for proofreading the text.

This volume has been produced by individuals who are responsible for the content of each chapter. It should not be assumed that every author agrees with the views expressed in all chapters, including the recommendations.

Foreword

In a recent Tweet, I expressed disgust that millions now rely on parish relief in the form of food banks, despite the fact they have paid good taxes for a decent social security system. In response, an aghast Tweeter told me off for mentioning the negative word 'tax'. I had mentioned it to draw attention to the fact that benefit claimants are taxpayers too – we all both contribute and claim at different stages in our lives. And sometimes at the same time. But a fellow campaigner regarded this as too toxic to mention. This started me thinking, if we can't talk about tax, how can we campaign successfully for an end to child poverty? We cannot will the ends without talking about the means. So, here we go: *Let's Talk About Tax* tackles this head on.

The Office for Budget Responsibility 'welfare' report[1] shows that spending on social security has been more or less flat as a proportion of GDP for the past 30 years. Yet the public debate suggests there is a spiralling bill running out of control. Cuts announced since 2010 are now delivering huge savings to the Treasury, and by 2021/22 we will be spending around £40 billion a year less on social security than in 2010.[2] Justified as deficit reduction, it was never explained why 85 per cent of savings were to come from cuts to benefits and services compared with a mere 15 per cent in tax rises. Given the fact that the Child Poverty Act had been passed with all-party agreement in March 2010, there could have been little doubt back then what the impact of cuts this size would mean for child poverty numbers.

This narrative has been highly toxic indeed. On this view, reducing tax is seen as protective while spending on social security is wasteful. In our view, social security should be seen as an investment in the people of the UK – a principle also expressed in the recent Social Security Act in Scotland. And rightly so. Spending on social security should be seen as an investment, as protective and as a way to prevent poverty among other things. Yet it is hardly ever referred to in this way by government. No wonder the debate and support for social security has become so toxic in recent years. We need to change this.

Both tax and social security are also about redistribution. The amount taken through tax is broadly flat as the progressive impact of income tax is cancelled out by the regressive impact of indirect taxes like VAT. By contrast, social security is broadly redistributive across the income distribution as well as across the life cycle. Both tax and social security play a big role in determining child poverty rates across countries. Across the European Union (EU), two countries stand out as having higher child poverty rates than others before the tax and benefits system kicks in – the UK and Ireland. After tax and benefits, the UK child poverty rate falls to around the middle range in the EU. So our tax and benefits system does most of the heavy lifting in bringing down high child poverty rates to middling ones. And incomes are particularly sensitive to changes in taxes and benefits here, as are poverty rates.

Before the Budget each year, we comment on direct and indirect taxes, national insurance contributions, forms of local taxation and the interaction between the social security and tax systems. It is increasingly hard to isolate the discussion of particular policies that help poor families from the chosen method of financing them. We are chiefly concerned with fairness – for example, we have always argued for a more progressive tax system, which takes a higher proportion of the incomes and capital of the better-off compared with the worse-off – vertical redistribution. We have also argued that we need to recognise the higher needs of families with children at whatever level of income – horizontal redistribution. We have also always argued for fairness in the treatment of men and women, which we believe should lead to independent taxation of individuals, regardless of gender or marital status.

Unfortunately, recent developments in tax policy have tended to increase inequality and unfairness, with means testing and benefit cuts taking a far higher proportion of income from low-income families compared with higher earners who are better able to escape tax. And billions have been spent in recent years increasing the level of the personal tax allowance, the majority of which goes to the richest half of the income distribution. This money could have been much better spent protecting the poorest families from the ravages of austerity.

But those of us who advocate more generous levels of benefits and better quality public services are always asked where the money is going to come from. So the chosen methods of funding improvements must be seen to be fair and more rational in order for the solutions to be accepted as fair and rational. In this book, we conclude that it is possible to devise a more progressive tax system which can finance more generous spending on social security and spending that is more poverty reducing. And more comprehensive restructuring is needed to achieve change rather than just looking to a few extremely rich individuals.

Let's hope this book enables us to make better propositions that will be poverty reducing. Campaigners are often criticised for putting forward policy solutions without costing them out, or telling policy makers how they can be paid for. So we need to talk about tax to be able to answer these questions. I hope this book can provide a starting point for better thinking on the subject.

Alison Garnham
Chief Executive
Child Poverty Action Group

Notes
1. Office for Budget Responsibility, *Welfare Trends Report*, CM 9341, 2016, p32, chart 3.1
2. T Waters, *Personal Tax and Benefit Measures*, Institute for Fiscal Studies, 2018, Budget analysis slides

Contents

	Introduction Jonathan Bradshaw	xi
1	**How the tax system fits together** Jonathan Bradshaw	1
2	**The poor and the rich** Jonathan Bradshaw and Antonia Keung	11
3	**What has happened to the tax system since 2007** Jonathan Bradshaw and Tony Orhnial	22
4	**International comparisons** Jonathan Bradshaw	29
5	**The structure of income tax rates and allowances** Tony Orhnial	39
6	**Raising income tax rates: what we knew then and what we know now** Tony Orhnial	50
7	**National insurance** Stephen McKay	59
8	**Taxation, couples and children** Fran Bennett	70
9	**Tackling tax reliefs** Adrian Sinfield	79
10	**Tax and social security** David Finch	89
11	**Direct taxes and cash benefits: effects and reforms** Alan Marsh	101

12	**Taxing wealth: an overview** Andrew Summers	115
13	**Taxes on inheritances and gifts** Andrew Summers	123
14	**Taxes on investment income and gains** Andrew Summers	135
15	**Taxes on property and net wealth** Andrew Summers	150
16	**Value added tax** Andy Lymer	162
17	**Drinking, driving and smoking** Alan Marsh	171
18	**Council tax** Michael Orton	179
19	**Taxing companies** Andy Lymer	188
20	**Escaping tax** Alan Buckle	201
21	**Devolved taxation: Scotland** David Eiser	224
22	**A strategy for reform** Alan Buckle	236
	Appendix Summary of recommendations	242

Introduction
Jonathan Bradshaw

The tax system is a complex mystery to many people and much misunderstood. The first objective of this book is to provide a straightforward description of how the tax system works, for people without specialist knowledge of the subject. Each chapter that follows provides a self-contained briefing on each element of the tax system.

A second objective related to CPAG's main cause is to explore where the money might be raised if we are to reverse the cuts for low-income families with children.

A third objective is to examine each component of the system to see how its operation could be made more progressive (vertically, horizontally, spatially, over the life cycle, generationally and by gender) – ie, shift the tax share from those on low incomes with children towards those with higher incomes and without children – while simultaneously removing anomalies and inconsistencies in its existing structure. Horizontal equity – in this case, in relation to those with the additional costs of bringing up children – is for us a key objective for the tax and benefits system. Changes in this system can also affect the distribution of resources within the household in a positive (or negative) direction in terms of what share is received by its members.

The Child Poverty Action Group (CPAG) exists to eradicate child poverty. Yet according to the *Households Below Average Income* series, the relative child poverty rates have increased both before and after housing costs between 2010/11 and 2017/18, the latest year for which we have data.[1] The Institute for Fiscal Studies estimates that child poverty rates will now rise rapidly to 2021 and beyond, effectively sweeping away all the gains made in poverty reduction after 1999.[2] Wages at the bottom of the distribution have been rising more rapidly than average, thanks to improvements in the minimum wage, and the unemployment rate at 3.8 per cent is at near record low.[3] So, it is not wages or unemployment driving up poverty. It is austerity policies.

After the banking crisis began in 2008, the Labour government's response was admirably anti-cyclical – benefit upratings were maintained and brought forward, taxes were increased on the better off. Child poverty continued to fall, despite a sharp increase in unemployment. When the coalition came to power in 2010, it protected child tax credit for two years, then reversed these measures and set out to reduce the deficit and cut public expenditure as a proportion of GDP. The measures were initially designed to take 80 per cent from spending and 20 per cent in increased taxation, but in the event almost all of it has been taken from spending because the coalition chose to raise personal tax allowances, including raising the higher rate threshold (though the basic rate limit was frozen).[4]

Some benefits were abolished, working-age benefits were uprated by the Consumer Price Index rather than the Retail Price Index. The Child Poverty Act was abandoned (but now admirably rescued and strengthened in Scotland). Limits to housing benefit were imposed, including the 'bedroom tax'. Public sector pay was frozen. Huge cuts were made in services, particularly local government services. Having won the 2015 general election, the Conservatives announced a whole new raft of cuts, including freezing working-age benefits, eviscerating universal credit, lowering the benefit cap and introducing the 'two-child limit'.

About £39 billion will have been taken out of the social security budget by 2021. There have been many analyses of the cumulative distributional consequences of these measures, most recently by Reed and Portes for the Equality and Human Rights Commission (EHRC).[5] The conclusions are clear: the lowest income decile groups have had the biggest losses; the poorest local authorities have suffered the biggest revenue losses; and the cuts have hit the incomes of families with children most. Poor lone parents are the biggest losers and rich pensioners have hardly been touched. While most analysis is done by households, both the EHRC and the House of Commons Library have also shown that women have lost out in particular, in part because of their generally lower incomes and in part because of being conduits of benefits for others (including children).[6] There is more to come. Many of the cuts have only begun to be rolled out.

It is clear to CPAG that the only hope of eradicating child poverty is to stop the freeze in working-age benefits, reverse the cuts to universal credit, abolish the bedroom tax, two-child limit and benefit cap and lift local rent limits. Given the pressures on public expenditure, this can only be achieved by increased borrowing, quantitative easing or raising taxes.

We do not set out to make the philosophical case for a more equitable distribution of the country's resources; there is already plenty of material available for those who need to be convinced. Our aim is rather to provide a manual for those who want to achieve that aim.

Also, we do not engage with the macro-economic arguments around the austerity policies that have been pursued since 2010. We only point out that, as well as those with children at the bottom end of the distribution having borne the main burden of austerity, the cuts have not yet been successful in eradicating the deficit in the public finances. The Office for Budget Responsibility now forecasts a borrowing requirement of £13.5 billion in 2023/24.[7] One important reason why they did not achieve more deficit reduction is that the public expenditure cuts were offset by cuts in income and other taxes. Nor has the strategy been successful in raising economic growth – the economy has been growing but by only 0.4 per cent in the second quarter of 2018. The Office for Budget Responsibility revised its GDP growth forecasts down to 1.2 per cent for 2019.[8]

Outline of this book

This book updates *Changing Tax: how the tax system works and how to change it*, written by John Hills and published by CPAG in 1988, and references are made to this throughout.

Chapters 1 to 4 are all introductory. **Chapter 1** is a summary of the whole system and concludes with an analysis of the distributional impact of direct and indirect taxes. **Chapter 2** takes that further showing how the distributional impact has changed over time and exploring the scope for higher income taxes on the rich. **Chapter 3** is a brief introduction to how the tax system has changed since 2007, though there is more detail in many of the subsequent chapters. **Chapter 4** presents some basic comparisons of the UK tax system compared with other rich countries.

Chapters 5 focuses in more detail on income tax rates and allowances and **Chapter 6** reviews what is known about the impact of increasing income tax rates. **Chapter 7** covers the other main direct tax on income – national insurance contributions.

When John Hills wrote *Changing Tax* there was a great deal of debate about the married man's tax allowance, which was being reformed at the time. **Chapter 8** covers the tax treatment of couples and children, and the critical contribution of child benefit for horizontal equity.

Chapter 9 is focused on perhaps the most neglected element of tax policy – the resources we do not tax and the huge sums of potential revenue lost through these tax reliefs or expenditures.

Taxation interacts with the social security system and most redistribution is achieved by benefits rather than taxes. **Chapter 10** explores this interaction and the marginal tax rates of social security and taxation together. **Chapter 11** discusses possible ways of integrating taxes and benefits, including the basic income proposals.

Chapters 12 to 15 are devoted to wealth taxation. **Chapter 12** reviews the system. **Chapter 13** discusses the taxation of inheritances and gifts, **Chapter 14** the taxation of investment income and gains from wealth and **Chapter 15** the taxation of property and net wealth.

Then Chapters 16 to 18 cover the main indirect taxes. **Chapter 16** covers value added tax, **Chapter 17** covers duties on fuel, alcohol and tobacco, and **Chapter 18** covers local council tax (and, briefly, business rates).

Chapter 19 reviews the case for taxing companies.

Chapter 20 explores the problem of tax avoiders and evaders.

Chapter 21 outlines the extent to which Scotland has used its devolved powers to vary the UK tax system.

Finally, **Chapter 22** outlines a strategy for reform.

Notes

1   Department for Work and Pensions, *Households Below Average Income 1994/95 to 2017/18*, 2019
2   A Hood and T Waters, *Living Standards, Poverty and Inequality in the UK: 2017/18 to 2021/22*, Institute for Fiscal Studies, 2019
3   Office for National Statistics, *Labour Market Overview, UK: July 2019*, 2019
4   R Lupton and others (eds), *Social Policy in a Cold Climate: policies and their consequences since the crisis*, Centre for Analysis of Social Exclusion Research at London School of Economics, Policy Press, 2016
5   J Portes and H Reed, *The Cumulative Impact of Tax and Welfare Reforms*, Equality and Human Rights Commission, 2018
6   R Cracknell and R Keen, *Estimating the Gender Impact of Tax and Benefits Changes*, House of Commons Briefing Paper SN06758, 2017
7   Office for Budget Responsibility, *Economic and Fiscal Outlook*, CP50, March 2019
8   Office for Budget Responsibility, *Economic and Fiscal Outlook*, CP50, March 2019

One
How the tax system fits together

Jonathan Bradshaw

In the tax year starting in April 2019 (2019/20) the government planned to raise £810 billion in tax revenue, about a third of Britain's national income.[1] The way this is broken down between the various taxes is shown in Table 1.1. This is divided into two parts. Direct taxes, which depend on the circumstances (mostly the incomes or profits) of individual taxpayers or companies, account for more than half the total, with income tax the single biggest contributor. Indirect taxes are charged on particular kinds of spending; the most important of these is value added tax (VAT).

Table 1.1:
Sources of tax revenue, 2019/20

Direct taxes	£ billion
Income tax	193
National insurance contributions	142
Corporation tax	60
Capital gains tax	9
Inheritance tax	6
Stamp duty	13
Indirect taxes	
Value added tax	156
Council tax	36
Business rates	31
Fuel duty	28
Tobacco duty	9
Alcohol duty	13
Vehicle excise duty	6
Other taxes	54

Source: HM Treasury, *Budget 2018*, HC 1629, 2018

Income tax (see Chapters 5 and 6) not only remains the most important tax in revenue-raising terms, but is also the most important in determining the distributional effects of the tax system (ie, how people at different income levels are affected), as the amounts charged may be tailored to individual circumstances. Independent taxation has existed since 1990.

The tax is charged on all regular forms of income – wages and salaries, interest, dividends, the profits of self-employed people, rent received – and most 'benefits in kind' like the use of a company car. It is not applied to owner-occupiers' 'imputed rent' – ie, the cash equivalent of the value of living in their own homes rent free.

The amount of tax depends on the total income from all sources over the whole year. For people with earnings, the tax due is worked out by their employer and is withheld from their wages or salary each week or month under the pay as you earn (PAYE) system.

These arrangements mean that most people automatically pay the right amount of tax without HM Revenue and Customs (HMRC) (which collects income tax) having to have any direct contact with them. Only a minority of taxpayers (fewer than 25 per cent of employees, or around one-third of personal taxpayers), those with relatively complicated affairs, must complete a tax return giving details of their income once the tax year has ended so that HMRC can work out their final tax bill. In many other countries, a much greater proportion of taxpayers must go through this process – in some cases, such as the USA, all taxpayers must complete a tax return.

Income tax is paid at one of three rates on incomes above a personal allowance. The basic rate is 20 per cent, the higher rate is 40 per cent, and there is an additional rate of 45 per cent on incomes over £150,000. The personal allowance has been increased from £6,475 in 2010/11 to £12,500 in 2019/20 and the higher rate threshold has been increased from £43,875 to £50,000 over the same period, both a year earlier than originally planned. They will remain at this level in 2020/21 and then be linked to the Consumer Price Index (CPI). As we will see in Chapters 5, 6 and 21, there are slightly different arrangements in Scotland.

There used to be children's tax allowances in the UK, in addition to benefits known as 'family allowances', for those with children. Since the late 1970s, these were combined into child benefit, which is the main way in which the tax and benefits system achieves horizontal equity between those with and those without children. Child benefit is paid to the mother by default.

National insurance contributions (see Chapter 7) are a contribution to social security benefits like the state pension, contribution-based job-seeker's allowance, contributory employment and support allowance, maternity allowance and bereavement benefits. Also, an increase in funding for the National Health Service from 2002 was partly funded by an increase in national insurance contributions.[2] However, although you must meet certain contribution conditions to qualify for contributory benefits, the link between contributions and the level of benefits no longer exists. The national insurance fund:[3]

> ...is separate from all other revenue raised by taxation. The fund is used exclusively to pay for contributory benefits, and operates on a 'pay as you go' basis: broadly speaking, this year's contributions pay for this year's benefits...The government has no powers to use national insurance contributions to fund anything else.

Employees pay national insurance contributions of 12 per cent on earnings of more than £8,632 a year, up to £50,000 a year (in 2019/20); the rate drops to 2 per cent on earnings over £50,000 a year. Employers and self-employed people also pay national insurance contributions.

Corporation tax (see Chapter 19) is charged on profits of incorporated businesses (unincorporated businesses pay income tax). Companies pay tax on their profits at the same rate (currently 19 per cent – it was 35 per cent in 1988), whether or not they retain them for reinvestment or distribute them as dividends to shareholders. The rate is due to be reduced to 17 per cent in 2020. Some 'ring-fenced' companies with profits from oil extraction pay a higher rate of 30 per cent on profits over £300,000.

Inheritance tax (see Chapter 13) currently has a minor role in the tax system. It raises 3 per cent of the amount raised by income tax; 70 years ago, the equivalent proportion was more than 12 per cent. The tax is levied on the estates of those who have died. The estate is taxed at the rate of 40 per cent if it is valued at over £325,000 (although this threshold is now effectively £650,000 for married couples).

Capital gains tax (see Chapter 14) is charged on the nominal difference between the price at which an asset is bought and sold (an indexation allowance for inflation used to apply, but was removed in 1998). Owner-occupied housing is exempt. The rate of tax depends on the individual's income tax band, but is significantly lower than the rate applied to income.

Basic rate taxpayers pay 10 per cent on gains above the allowance (or 18 per cent on residential property). Higher or additional rate taxpayers pay 28 per cent on gains from residential property and 20 per cent on gains from other chargeable assets. In 2019/20, the tax-free allowance was £12,000.

Value added tax (VAT) (see Chapter 16) is paid every time something is sold, apart from certain exempt items like rent or 'zero-rated' items like some foods and children's clothes. The tax is collected at each stage of production or distribution, but the amount eventually adds 20 per cent (up from 17.5 per cent in 2011) to the final purchase price. There is a reduced rate of 5 per cent on, for example, children's car seats and home energy.

Council tax (see Chapter 18) is levied by local authorities on domestic properties. The amount paid depends on the rateable value of the property, the amount the local council charges for that tax band and whether there is an entitlement to discounts or exemptions. There are discounts for single occupancy, for students and for disabled people. There is also a means-tested council tax reduction scheme (previously council tax benefit), administered by the local authority and which varies from place to place.

Business rates (see Chapter 18) are charged on most non-domestic properties, like shops, offices, pubs, warehouses, factories, holiday rental homes and guest houses. The rate depends on the rateable value of the business. Business rate relief may be available – for example, for small businesses, rural businesses or charitable businesses.

Excise duties (see Chapter 17) are charged on items such as petrol, alcohol and tobacco and are the most important of the other indirect taxes. They are charged not only as a percentage of the price but as a charge per item, such as a pint of beer, bottle of wine or a packet of 20 cigarettes. Excise duties are not only expected to raise revenue, but also to have regulatory effects on behaviour, such as discouraging smoking or drinking. Fuel duty has been frozen since 2011, which was costing the Exchequer £840 million in 2019/20.

Box 1.1:
Characteristics of tax systems

Looked at as a whole, the UK's tax system comprises a number of components, each designed to raise revenue from different forms of income or capital – such as income tax, corporation tax or capital gains tax – or on different types of transactions or other activities – such as stamp duty, VAT or insurance premium tax. Each part of the tax system has its own structural features which determine the extent to which it can be regarded as:

- **neutral** in its effect on the efficient working of the economy. A tax is said to be neutral if it does not create incentives or disincentives that influence or distort the consumption, investment and other decisions of taxpayers. It is a general principle of good tax design (for economists, at least) that tax systems should keep distortionary effects to a minimum. But it is important to note that some distortions may reflect a policy intention – so, for example, tobacco taxes are clearly intended to change behaviour as well as raise revenue;

- **horizontally** equitable in producing the same tax outcomes for taxpayers in broadly similar circumstances, or in producing different outcomes for taxpayers in different circumstances – for example, those with and without children (in the UK, this is now achieved via child benefit); and

- **vertically equitable or progressive** in the sense that as an individual's income rises, the average rate of tax levied on that income also rises. Generally speaking, the progressivity of a tax system is determined as much by the amount of any tax-free allowances as by the number of marginal tax rate bands. The structure of the tax system can also be used to affect the relative resources of different individuals *within* the household – for example, by incentivising or disincentivising earning.[4]

And the extent to which it can be regarded as:

- **administratively fair** in its treatment of different taxpayers or groups of taxpayers. This refers to the extent to which different groups receive equal treatment from the tax authorities;

- **administratively efficient** in the sense that it keeps to a minimum the costs of administering and complying with the system. Good tax design requires a system to be as simple and transparent as possible to facilitate compliance by taxpayers and ease of administration by the tax authorities. (In general, the greater the variety of tax bands and allowances and reliefs, the more complex the system.)

It is tempting to make judgements about different parts of a country's tax system separately, and for some features (for example, its complexity or administrative efficiency) this can work well enough. But for others it does not. For a tax to be regarded as 'progressive' it is not necessary for the marginal rate of tax to increase continuously with income. Nor is it necessary for every tax that is part of the tax system to be progressive – it is the overall effect that matters. Likewise, the extent to which a country's tax system redistributes income cannot be gauged simply from the structure of its personal income tax system without taking into account the mechanisms whereby tax and other revenues are transferred between income or wealth groups through expenditure on social security benefits, tax credits and public services, which are more important to certain groups, including families with children and women, for example.

The combined effect of taxes

One of the great problems in analysing tax systems is working out their true incidence – ie, who really pays them. For example, there is some evidence that employers' national insurance contributions are borne, at least partly, by employees on lower wages.[5]

The best source of data on the incidence of direct and indirect taxes is the Office for National Statistics series *Effects of Taxes and Benefits on Household Income*, produced each year since 1977. Note that this analysis is at the household, not individual, level (and so does not give a distributional picture by gender).[6] Figures 1.1 to 1.6 show the percentage of gross income paid in taxes by each decile group (from the poorest 10 per cent of households to the richest 10 per cent of households). The figures are presented for three years: 2007/08 just before the financial crisis, 2010/11 at the change of government and 2016/17. Comparisons are made for two household groups: non-retired households without children and non-retired households with children. A distinction is made between direct taxes – income tax, national insurance contributions and council tax – and indirect taxes – VAT, duties and intermediate taxes.[7]

Figure 1.1:
Percentage of gross income paid in tax, non-retired households with no children, 2007/08

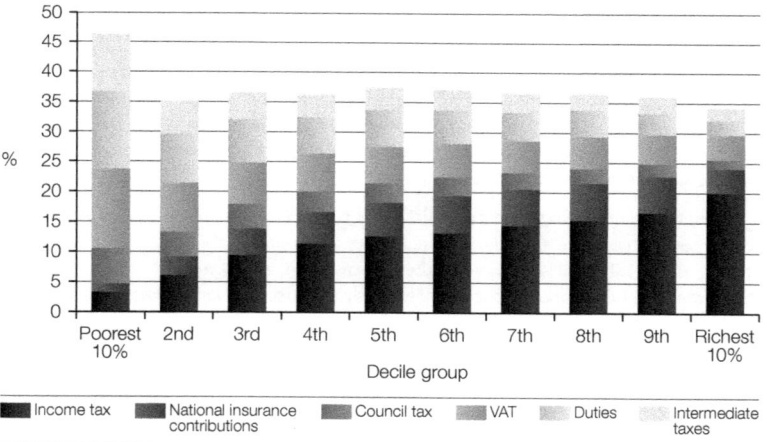

Source: Office for National Statistics, *Effects of Taxes and Benefits on Household Income: historical household-level data sets*, June 2018

Figure 1.2:
Percentage of gross income paid in tax, non-retired households with no children, 2010/11

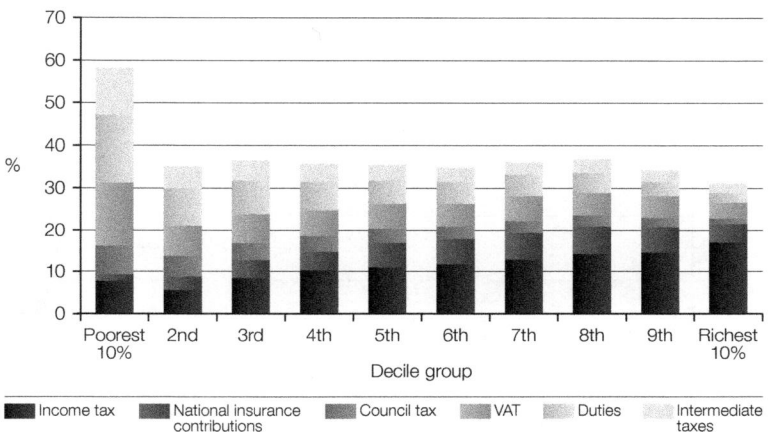

Source: Office for National Statistics, *Effects of Taxes and Benefits on Household Income: historical household-level data sets*, June 2018

Figure 1.3:
Percentage of gross income paid in tax, non-retired households with no children, 2016/17

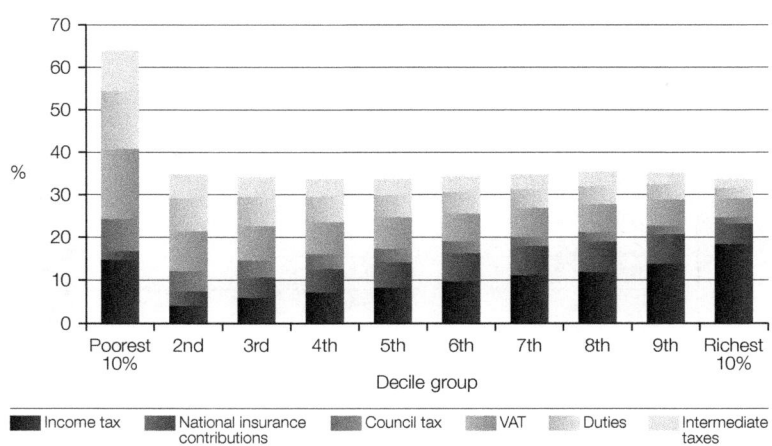

Source: Office for National Statistics, *Effects of Taxes and Benefits on Household Income: historical household-level data sets*, June 2018

Figure 1.4:
Percentage of gross income paid in tax, non-retired households with children, 2007/08

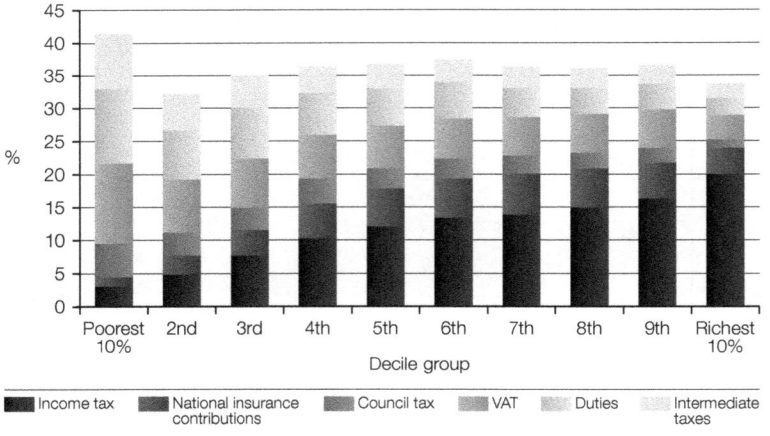

Source: Office for National Statistics, *Effects of Taxes and Benefits on Household Income: historical household-level data sets*, June 2018

Figure 1.5:
Percentage of gross income paid in tax, non-retired households with children, 2010/11

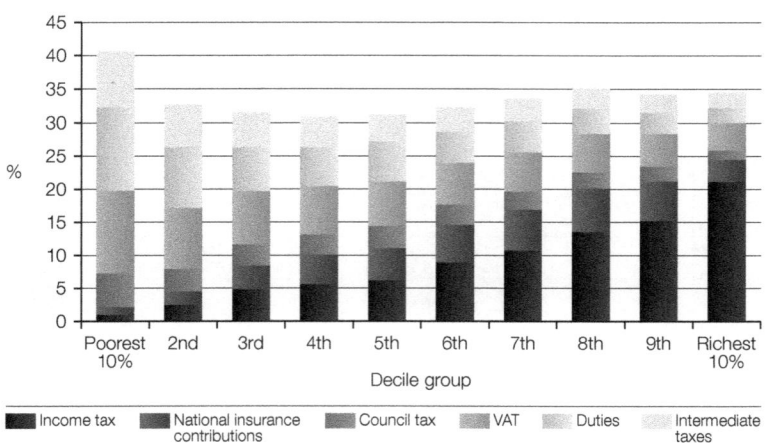

Source: Office for National Statistics, *Effects of Taxes and Benefits on Household Income: historical household-level data sets*, June 2018

Figure 1.6:
Percentage of gross income paid in tax, non-retired households with children, 2016/17

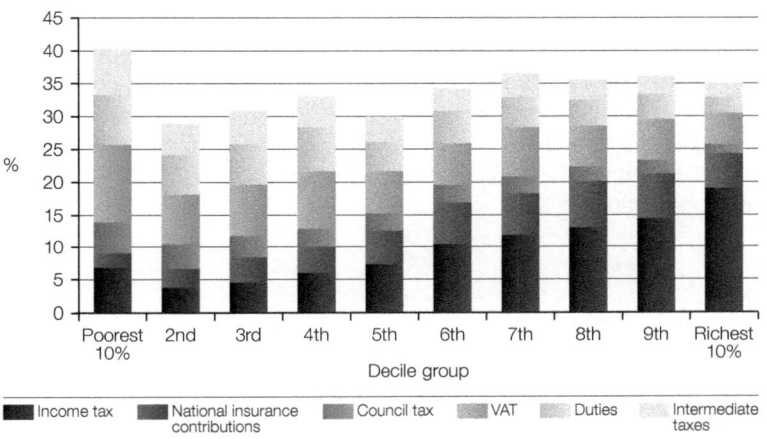

Source: Office for National Statistics, *Effects of Taxes and Benefits on Household Income: historical household-level data sets*, June 2018

The first thing to note is how flat the distribution is – beyond the first decile, households are paying about the same proportion of their gross income in tax regardless of their income. The tax system in the UK is proportional, rather than vertically progressive. (The results for the first decile are possibly misleading for two reasons – first, income is not reliably reported at the bottom end of the distribution, and second and related, there are self-employed households under-reporting their incomes but having higher levels of consumption, hence paying more in indirect taxes.)

The second thing to note is that income tax and national insurance contributions are progressive taxes (income tax more than national insurance) and council tax and the indirect taxes are regressive taxes. The two types of taxes' redistributive efforts cancel each other out.

The third thing to note is that there are no differences in the incidence of taxes paid by households with and without children – children are no longer recognised in the tax system (except for the high-income child benefit charge. The benefits and tax credits system carries that responsibility (see Chapters 10 and 11).

Finally, there is very little evidence here of changes in the incidence of the tax system over the 10 years – despite the many changes in tax rates and allowances made in successive Budgets over the period. A household without children would pay an average of 36 per cent in tax in 2007/08, 35 per cent in 2010/11 and 35 per cent in 2016/17. For households with children, the numbers are 36 per cent in 2007/08, 34 per cent in 2010/11 and 35 per cent in 2016/17. There is evidence of a very slight shift from direct to indirect taxation as a proportion of the tax paid. A household without children would pay an average of 56 per cent of total tax in income tax and national insurance contributions in 2007/08, 54 per cent in 2010/11 and 54 per cent in 2016/17. For households with children, the numbers are 55 per cent in 2007/08, 53 per cent in 2010/11 and 52 per cent in 2016/17.

Notes

1. HM Treasury, *Budget 2018*, HC 1629, October 2018
2. It had been the intention when the NHS was introduced that around 20 per cent of its cost would be funded from the national insurance fund. In 2002/03 about 10–12 per cent was, in fact, funded in this way. In any case, that link between the NHS and the national insurance fund provided a platform for the 'penny for the NHS' increase in national insurance contributions.
3. A Seely, *National Insurance Contributions (NICs): an introduction*, House of Commons Briefing Paper SN04517, p10
4. See analyses by Women's Budget Group of successive Budgets and fiscal/ social policies: www.wbg.org.uk.
5. S Adam, D Phillips and B Roantree, '35 years of reforms: a panel analysis of the incidence of, and employee and employer responses to, social security contributions in the UK', *Journal of Public Economics*, 171, 2019, pp29–30
6. The Institute for Fiscal Studies, however, has suggested how the government might do a gender analysis (see www.ifs.org.uk/publications/5611), including analysis by gendered households – for example, female-headed versus male-headed lone-parent households.
7. Indirect taxes on intermediate goods and services include: rates on commercial and industrial property; motor vehicle duties; duties on hydrocarbon oils; employers' contributions to national insurance, the NHS, the industrial injuries fund and the redundancy payments scheme; customs (import) duties; stamp duties; VAT (on the intermediate stages of exempt goods); Independent Commission franchise payments; landfill tax; Consumer Credit Act fees; bank levy. For more information on the methodology, see Office for National Statistics, *The Effects of Taxes and Benefits on Household Income: financial year ending 2017 – technical report*, 2018

Two
The poor and the rich
Jonathan Bradshaw and Antonia Keung

The tax system has not only to raise revenue, but also to do this both *efficiently* (without heavy administrative costs or damaging the operation of the economy) and *equitably*. While equity is the major concern of this book, the constraints of efficiency must also be considered. As we shall see in this and subsequent chapters, equity and efficiency are not the sole responsibility of taxation. Benefits and services also play a vital part. But our main concern here is taxation.

A key argument about the equity of taxation is about 'equality of sacrifice' – when raising taxes, the burden imposed by taking £1 from a high income is clearly less than that imposed by taking the same amount from a low income. More strongly, the burden imposed by taking 1 per cent of the former will be less than that of taking 1 per cent of the latter. Such arguments imply that the tax system should be progressive – ie, the proportion of income taken in tax should rise with income. As the figures in the previous chapter showed, much of the limited progressivity of the direct tax system is wiped out by indirect taxes.

A tax which takes a greater proportion of low income than high income is regressive. Most indirect taxes are regressive.

A tax which takes the same proportion of all incomes is proportional. The overall impact of direct and indirect taxes in the UK is proportional, as we have seen in Chapter 1. One complication of tax analysis is that taxes can be progressive over one income range but proportional or regressive over another, so that they cannot always be neatly placed into one category.

Taxes and fiscal systems as a whole can also be judged by other criteria, including horizontal equity (for example, between those with and those without children) and also gender equity.[1] But here we focus on vertical progressivity (or the lack of it).

Trends in income distribution

The extent to which one would want taxes to be progressive will depend on the scale of pre-tax inequality. If pre-tax incomes were evenly distributed, the tax system would not have much of a role. By contrast, where pre-tax incomes are unequally distributed, the tax system could be a key weapon for those who want to see a fairer distribution of living standards (but by no means the only one). The rest of this chapter therefore examines what Britain's income distribution looks like.

Figure 2.1 shows what has happened to pre-tax incomes of households (including cash benefits like pensions) since 1977.[2] Note that this analysis is carried out on the basis of household, rather than individual, incomes.[3] Throughout the 1980s, the share of total income of the bottom 40 per cent fell and the share of income of the top 20 per cent increased. Since the end of the 1980s, the shares of the top and bottom have fluctuated, but have overall remained fairly stable, though never recovering the respective shares they had in 1977.

Figure 2.1:
Share of total gross income, 1977 to 2016/17

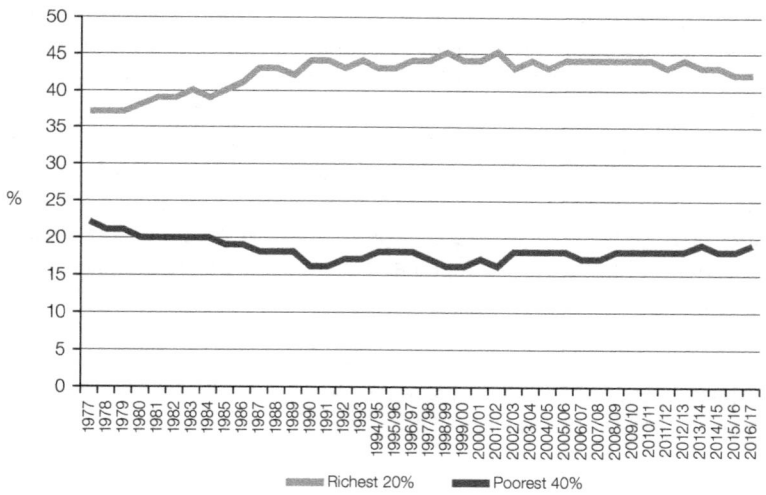

Source: Office for National Statistics, *Effects of Taxes and Benefits on Household Income: historical household-level data sets*, June 2018

The effect of taxes on the distribution of income

This is the position after allowing for cash benefits, but before allowing for taxation. What has happened to income after all taxes? This is shown in Figure 2.2 by showing how the 'Gini coefficient' (a standard measure of inequality – the higher the Gini, the higher the inequality) changes between *original income* (wages and investment income), *gross income* (original income plus cash benefits), *disposable income* (gross income less direct taxes) and *final income* (disposable income less all other taxes). Original income is the most unequally distributed. Adding cash benefits to get gross income substantially reduces the Gini (from 48.9 to 35.4 in 2016/17). Deducting direct taxes to get disposable income further reduces the Gini (from 35.4 to 32.2 in 2016/17), but taking account of indirect taxes to get post-tax income increases the Gini back to where it was before the deduction of direct taxes – in fact, to 36.4 – higher than it was after the addition of benefits.

Figure 2.2:
Gini coefficients for the distribution of income at each stage of the tax-benefits system for all households, 1977 to 2016/17

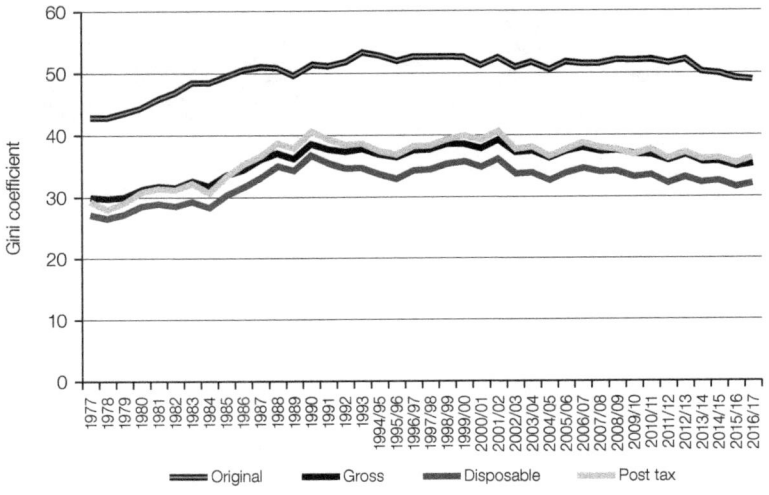

Source: Office for National Statistics, *Effects of Taxes and Benefits on Household Income: historical household-level data sets*, June 2018, Table 6

Figure 2.3 shows the share of original and post-tax income at our three time-points. The richest quintile had 46 per cent of original income in 2005/06,[4] 47 per cent in 2010/11 and 45 per cent in 2016/17. After the impact of all benefits and taxes, the richest quintile still had 44 per cent of post-tax income in 2005/06, 44 per cent in 2010/11 and 42 per cent in 2016/16. The poorest quintile had only 3 per cent, 4 per cent and 5 per cent of original income and, after all taxes and benefits, the poorest quintile had 6 per cent in each of the three years.

Figure 2.3:
Quintile shares of original and post-tax income, non-pensioner households

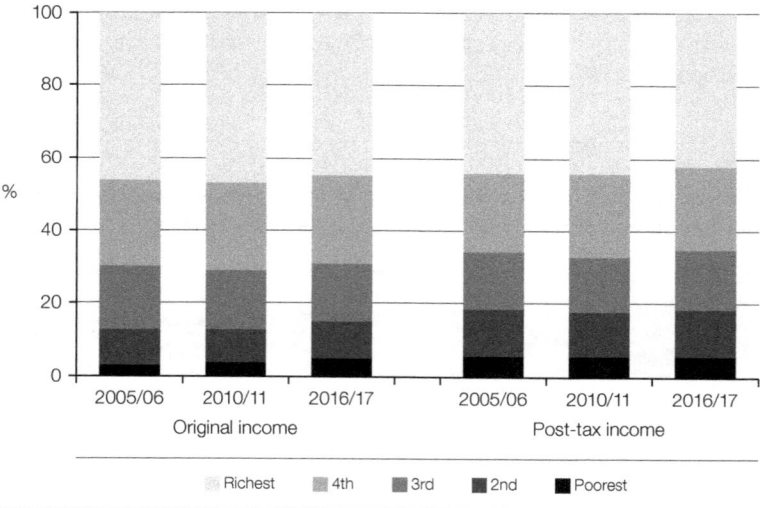

Source: Office for National Statistics, *Effects of Taxes and Benefits on Household Income: historical household-level data sets*, June 2018

The distributional process is shown in more detail in Figure 2.4. The poorest quintile starts with an original income of £7,383 in 2016/17. Cash benefits add £7,948 and services in kind (mainly health and education) are valued at £8,408. Then the poorest quintile loses £1,940 in direct taxes and £3,984 in indirect taxes and ends up with a final income of £17,815. The richest quintile starts with a much higher original income of £88,776, to this is added £3,266 in cash benefits (mainly non-means-tested benefits like the state pension), though there may be some individuals in these households receiving means-tested benefits, because we do not have a household means test. Benefits in kind are valued at £5,925. Then direct taxes deduct £21,357 and indirect taxes £10,307 and the richest quintile is left with £66,303 – nearly four times the income of the poorest quintile.

Figure 2.4:
The effects of taxes and benefits on all households, 2016/17

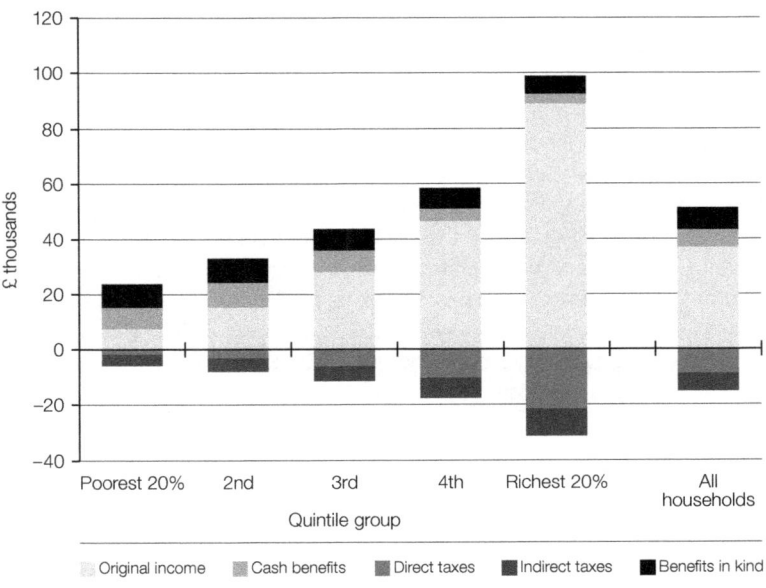

Source: Office for National Statistics, *Effects of Taxes and Benefits on Household Income: historical household-level data sets*, June 2018

Who are the rich?

The top quintile hides a huge range of income – for example, the ninth decile has mean income of £78,703 and the 10th decile has mean income of £135,421 in 2016/17. The top 1 per cent has incomes very considerably higher than that.

There is a temptation to conclude that if income is so unequally distributed, the redistribution could be accomplished simply by commandeering the fortunes of a handful of the super-rich, like the Duke of Westminster. If this were true, the interests of the middle classes could be preserved while transferring substantial resources to the poor. Only those with incomes many times the 'average' would lose out.

Figure 2.5 suggests that there is a problem with such an approach. It shows the distribution of population income after housing costs. Representative income is often taken as the mean, but mean income is £536 per week on this chart. This does not represent a typical income figure because this kind of average is dragged up by the number of very high incomes. The median is a better representation of the average and, in this case, it is £437 per week.[5] The point to recognise is that the very rich represent a very small proportion of the total. This has important implications. A household with income twice the average does not sound very privileged, and yet it is within the top 10 per cent of the income distribution and towards the top of it. The perceptions of those commenting on tax policy are often coloured by the effects on 'ordinary people' like themselves. Journalists on national newspapers and MPs do not have ordinary incomes. Nevertheless, there is scope for redistribution – there are 4.3 million people with incomes above £1,000 per week. Sixty per cent of the median – the poverty threshold – is only £262 per week and jobseeker's allowance for a single unemployed person over 25 is only £73.10 per week.

Figure 2.5:
Income distribution of the whole population after housing costs, 2017/18

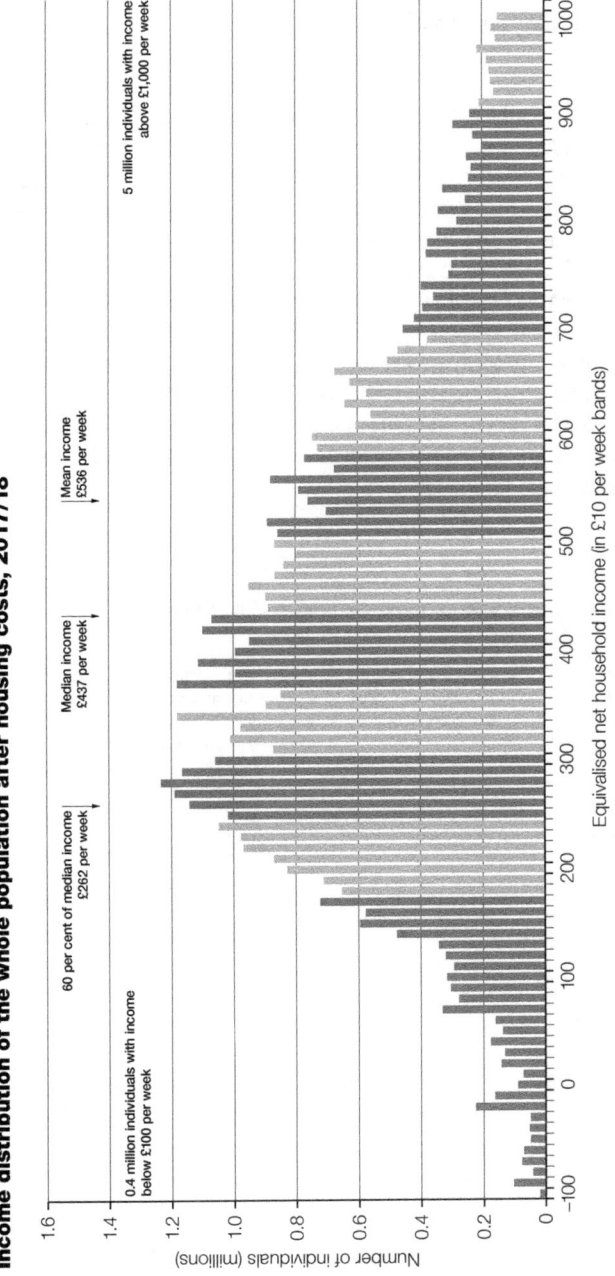

Source: Department for Work and Pensions, *Households Below Average Income 1994/95–2017/18*, 2019, Table 2.1

Where is the money?

A further problem is that the way a tax like income tax works is that the first slice of income is tax-free, the next is taxed at one rate and the top slice may be taxed at a higher rate (see Chapters 5 and 6).[6] When looking at what could be raised by increasing the higher income tax rates, it must be remembered that the bottom part of even the highest income will be below the threshold where the higher rates start; this part will not be affected by the higher rates.

What is the most which could be raised by concentrating on only the highest incomes? Table 2.1 shows the proportion of adults and families with gross income above various thresholds. £12,500 is the current tax threshold. There are a very few people with incomes above the current higher rate thresholds. The final column shows what could theoretically be raised if the top income tax rate was raised from 45 per cent to 100 per cent above each threshold.

Table 2.1:
After-tax income above various levels, 2016/17

Threshold of gross income £ per year	Percentage of adults with incomes above the threshold	Percentage of families (tax/benefit units) with gross incomes above the threshold	After-tax income[7] more than threshold £ billion
£150,000	0.7%	1.5%	£40.1
£125,000	1.0%	2.2%	£54.9
£100,000	1.6%	3.8%	£78.0
£75,000	2.9%	7.5%	£119.8
£50,000	7.1%	18.5%	£214.4
£25,000	29.7%	46.3%	£531.3
£12,500	62.3%	73.6%	£806.1

Source: Authors' analysis of Family Resources Survey and *Households Below Average Income* data

Obviously, imposing a 100 per cent tax rate on incomes above a certain level would not actually be possible without affecting behaviour. The amount raised by such a tax would be nothing like that shown – it might be nothing at all. Suppose that half of the after-tax income above each threshold could be raised in increased tax (which is still dubious – it would mean raising the top rate of tax to 72.5 per cent without provoking changes in behaviour). Then to raise £100 billion would mean putting up the rate of tax on those with gross income over £50,000 and above (as they have a total of £214 billion above that amount).

This would only affect the top 7.1 per cent of people, or 18.5 per cent of families. About half of the revenue would come from those with incomes over £75,000, but the other half would come from those with incomes between £50,000 and £75,000, and £50,000 is only just over twice the average gross income. Unless the people in such income ranges sustain some losses, the scope for raising significant revenue from those with higher incomes is much smaller, as can be worked out from the table.

Showing the effects of tax changes

The shape of the income distribution illustrated in Figure 2.5 means that it can be misleading to look at the effects of taxes by reference, say, to those with 'average' earnings and five and 10 times that amount; such earnings levels are not representative. Such calculations can also be misleading in the assumptions they make about the family structure of the examples. Often a 'typical' family is used, such as one with a man earning 'average' earnings, a woman without earnings (and 75 per cent of mothers are in paid work) and two children. Such a family is anything but typical. Even allowing for all earnings levels, such families only represent 1.9 per cent of the total. A female living alone is, in fact, more 'typical'.[8]

To avoid this type of problem, the income distribution is examined using a representative sample of all families from the Family Resources Survey. The effects are shown for successive tenths (decile groups) of the income distribution.

A further problem is that a single person with a given income is clearly better off than a couple with two children and the same income. To allow for this, families are arranged in order of their net (after income tax and national insurance contributions) 'equivalent' income. This means dividing a family's income by a certain amount to give the income for a couple who would be placed at the same point in the income distribution.

Exactly how to make this calculation is controversial: how do the costs of living for a couple living together compare with those of two single adults? What allowance should be made for children? The way this is done here is simply to give a weight of 1.00 for a single person, 0.5 for each other adult and child aged 14 and over, and 0.30 for each child under 14. So, a single person on £400 per week stays at £400 per week, a couple with two children on £400 have their income reduced to £190 (£400/2.1) and a couple without children on £400 have their income reduced to £267 (£400/1.5). This is roughly in line with the ways the social security system adjusts support for families of different types and sizes. This is not to argue that such relativities, in fact, represent the correct level (indeed, there is evidence from budget standards research that it underestimates the needs of children[9]); it is simply a convenient way of working out roughly where to allocate different families in the distribution. It does not affect the sizes and the gains and losses or the revenue implications of any tax change, just the income group into which different families are allocated. What may affect these implications are the number of earners and the share in terms of level of earnings between individuals within couples.

Figure 2.6 shows the net equivalent income levels of those placed halfway up each of the successive tenths or decile groups (the median of each group). So, a single person with a net cash income of £1,470 per week would be in the top decile group. A family of four with the same net cash income and thus an 'equivalent' income of only £700 per week would be in the eighth decile group. Table 2.2 shows where particular families would be placed in the distribution. Figure 2.6 is also a powerful reminder of the glaring inequality in living standards, even after taxes and benefits. Those in the top 10 per cent have, on average, net equivalent incomes which are eight times those of the bottom 10 per cent.

Figure 2.6:
Income distribution, 2016/17

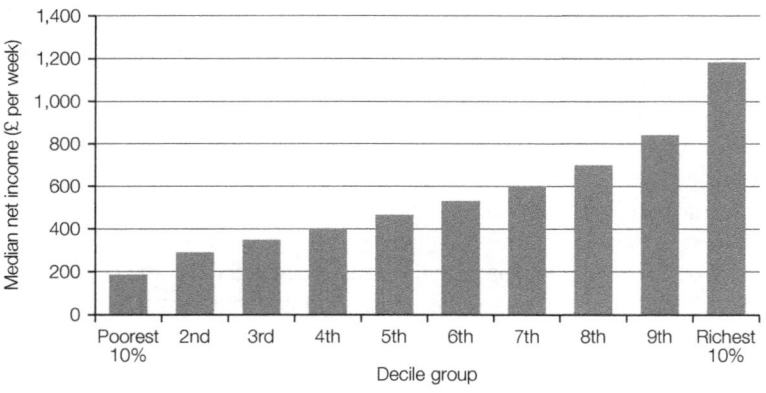

Source: Office for National Statistics, *Effects of Taxes and Benefits on Household Income: historical household-level data sets*, June 2018

Table 2.2:
Example families in each decile group of net equivalent income

Decile group	Family type	Percentage of this family type in this decile	Net mean equivalent weekly income	Net median equivalent weekly income
Poorest 10%	Single female pensioner	17.8%	£187.46	£200.00
2nd	Single, with children	21.9%	£289.07	£292.00
3rd	Single, with children	19.0%	£343.58	£344.00
4th	Pensioner couple	12.1%	£400.15	£401.00
5th	Single male pensioner	12.2%	£459.91	£455.00
6th	Single, no children	10.6%	£527.41	£526.00
7th	Couple, with children	11.0%	£604.05	£604.00
8th	Single, no children	8.8%	£699.86	£698.00
9th	Couple, no children	17.8%	£850.33	£849.00
Richest 10%	Couple, no children	18.6%	£1,553.39	£1,207.00

Source: Authors' analysis of Family Resources Survey 2017

Notes

1 See, for example, an analysis of gender and taxation at European level: www.europarl.europa.eu/RegData/etudes/STUD/2017/583138/IPOL_STU(2017)583138_EN.pdf
2 Office for National Statistics, *Effects of Taxes and Benefits on UK Household Income: financial year ending 2017*, 2018, Table 15
3 Services and benefits may also, of course, be more important for some individuals in households (in particular women, who currently often bear the major share of caring for others).
4 2007/08 data are not available.
5 The 'mean' is the total of all income divided by the number of households. The 'median' is the middle point of the distribution of households' incomes.
6 This also means that it is difficult to benefit the lowest paid by raising the tax threshold, as currently over 40 per cent earn too little to pay any income tax, with two-thirds of these being women. See www.wbg.org.uk.
7 Being survey data, this should take account of the clawback of child benefit on incomes above £50,000 and, for those above £100,000, the loss of the personal allowance between £100,000 and £123,700.
8 Ten per cent of benefit units.
9 J Bradshaw and others, *A Minimum Income Standard for Britain: what people think*, Joseph Rowntree Foundation, 2008, available at www.minimumincomestandard.org

Three
What has happened to the tax system since 2007

Jonathan Bradshaw and Tony Orhnial

The government remains committed to a low-tax economy, cutting taxes for both working people and businesses to help respond to short-term pressures.[1]

In fact, it can be seen from Figure 3.1 that there has been little change in tax revenue as a proportion of GDP since 2007. It was 33.2 per cent before the financial crisis and it was 33.2 per cent in 2016.

Figure 3.1:
Total tax revenue as a proportion of GDP

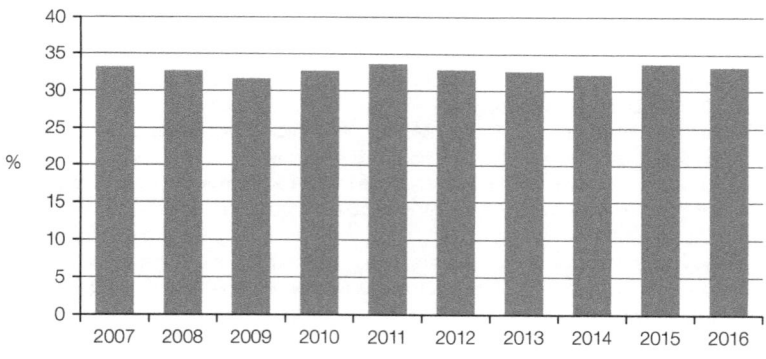

Source: OECD, Revenue Statistics: https://stats.oecd.org/index.aspx?DataSetCode=REV

The subsequent chapters contain more detailed analysis of recent changes to the different taxes. In the rest of this chapter we present a brief overview.[2]

Income tax

A starting rate of income tax of 10 per cent was introduced from 1999/00. It was abolished in 2008/09, partly to fund a reduction in the basic rate from 22 per cent to 20 per cent. In 2010/11, in response to the financial crisis, the Labour government introduced a top rate of 50 per cent. The coalition government reduced this to 45 per cent from 2013/14. It also introduced the high-income child benefit charge, which imposes additional taxation on someone with relevant income of between £50,000 and £60,000 and in whose family unit someone is claiming child benefit. This can only be avoided by the person claiming child benefit taking action to give it up.

In 2007/08, the personal allowance was £5,225 and the basic rate limit was £34,600. In 2009/10, the personal allowance rose to £6,475, partly to compensate low-income taxpayers for the loss of the 10 per cent starting rate. The basic rate limit was increased to £34,800. Since 2010/11, the personal allowance has been gradually withdrawn from those with incomes between £100,000 and (currently) £125,000, creating a band of income in which income tax liability increases by 60 pence for each additional pound of income, and incomes above £150,000 are taxed at a rate of 45 per cent. The personal allowance has been increased every year since 2010/11, from £6,475 to £11,850 in 2018/19 and the basic rate limit to £46,350. The government was committed to raising the personal allowance to £12,500 and the higher rate threshold to £50,000 by 2020 and actually did so from April 2019.

National insurance contributions

In 2007/08 the lower earnings limit was £87 per week (with a zero-rate band between this and a 'primary threshold', introduced from 2000/01, and set at £100 per week for 2007/08) and the upper earnings limit was £670 per week. The zero-rate band is particularly important for women, who are more likely to be low paid and in part-time work. The class 1 employee contribution rate was 11 per cent and 1 per cent above the upper earnings limit and the employer's contribution was 12.8 per cent on all earnings above the lower earnings limit. By 2010/11, the lower earnings limit was £97 and the upper earnings limit was £844. The contribution rates were unchanged. Under the coalition government, the lower earnings limit was increased progressively to £111 in 2014/15, but the upper earnings limit was reduced to £805. All the rates were increased – to 12 per cent and 2 per cent above the upper earnings limit – and the employer rate was increased to 13.8 per cent. In 2019/20, the lower earnings limit is £118 and the primary threshold is £166 per week, when employee national insurance contributions start to be paid, and the upper earnings limit is £962.

Self-employed people pay a flat-rate amount once their profits reach a certain level and then a percentage of profits between certain lower and upper limits. They are entitled to fewer benefits than employees. In his March 2017 Budget, the Chancellor proposed to increase the new class 4 national insurance contribution rate for the self-employed (and other non-employees) to bring it closer in line with that for employees. However, outrage from the government's own supporters resulted in these proposals being dropped,[3] though the HM Treasury line is that they are delayed 'to ensure that there is enough time to work with parliament and stakeholders on the detail of reforms'.[4]

Taxation of savings income

The taxation of income from savings has become particularly complicated.[5] A maximum of £5,000 of savings interest may be taxed at the 'starting rate for savings' (reduced from 10 per cent to 0 per cent from April 2015), provided the taxpayer's other income does not exceed the personal allowance. In addition, the personal savings allowance covers the first £1,000 of interest received by basic rate taxpayers and the first £500 received by higher rate taxpayers. The taxation of dividend income was reformed in 2016, when the tax-free dividend allowance (initially set at £5,000, but reduced to £2,000 from April 2018) replaced the previous system of 'notional' tax credits. Any dividends above the allowance are taxed at 7.5 per cent for basic rate taxpayers, 32.5 per cent for higher rate taxpayers and 38.1 per cent for additional rate taxpayers.

In addition, tax-free vehicles have been introduced for saving (individual savings accounts (ISAs)) and there have been large increases in the maximum annual amount that can be saved – from £7,000 in 2007/08 to £20,000 in 2019/20.

Capital gains tax

From 2008, following a major reform of capital gains tax announced in the 2007 *Pre-Budget Report*, capital gains were taxed at a flat rate of 18 per cent. The coalition government increased this to 28 per cent for higher rate taxpayers and the Conservative government then reduced both rates from 2016 to 10 per cent for basic rate taxpayers and 20 per cent for higher rate taxpayers. The capital gains tax-free allowance was £12,000 in 2019/20.

Inheritance tax

The threshold was £300,000 in 2007 and £325,000 in 2010. Since October 2017, the threshold (or 'nil-rate band') is increased by any unused amount of a deceased spouse or civil partner's nil rate band. This means that, in effect, married couples and civil partners can leave double the inheritance tax nil-rate band (£650,000) tax-free, even if the first to die leaves her/his entire estate to her/his surviving partner. In addition, there is a new transferable main residence allowance of £150,000 (rising to £175,000 by 2020/21). This means that by 2020/21, provided their main residence is worth at least £350,000, the effective inheritance tax threshold for a married couple or civil partners will rise to £1 million. The fact that women's estates are more likely to pay inheritance tax is not because women are more likely to be wealthy, but because they tend to live longer and so have already had estates passed on to them on their partners' deaths.

Stamp duty

The stamp duty threshold for housing transactions had been £125,000 since 2010. This has resulted in an increase in the proportion of housing transactions covered by stamp duty rising from 51 per cent to 73 per cent in 2015.[6] A series of reforms of stamp duty between 2014 and 2016 mean that the tax operates as a banded system (rather than a 'slab' system like income tax), so that the duty is charged at each rate only on the amount of the purchase price that falls within each band: 0 per cent up to

£125,000; 2 per cent between £125,000 and £250,000; 5 per cent between £250,000 and £925,000; 10 per cent between £925,000 and £1.5 million; and 12 per cent over £1.5 million. Since April 2016, an additional 3 per cent is charged if the buyer already owns a property – for example, a holiday home or a buy-to-let property. Stamp duty on share and bond transactions remains at 0.5 per cent.

Value added tax

Value added tax (VAT) is currently zero-rated on some items. It is paid at a reduced rate of 5 per cent on others, and all other goods and services are taxable at the rate of 20 per cent.

In 2008, the standard VAT rate was 15 per cent. It was increased to 17.5 per cent in January 2010 and when the coalition government came to power it was increased to 20 per cent in January 2011.

Council tax

Council tax is set locally and based on property values unchanged since 1991 (except in Wales). The main development in the tax since 2010 has been the reduction in central government funding to local authorities – now £8 billion according to the Local Government Association.[7] This has meant that local authorities have had to increase council tax to maintain services. However, they have been constrained by the Localism Act 2011, which requires a local authority to hold a referendum if it wants to increase council tax beyond what central government deems as 'excessive'.

Duties

The real level of duty on cigarettes has increased rapidly since 2008 and will be increased by 2 per cent above the Retail Price Index until 2020. However, by 2018/19 fuel duties had been frozen for eight years. The pattern of duties on alcohol has been more mixed – they were increased in the 2008 Budget but, since 2013, all alcohol duties have fallen in real terms. They were frozen in 2018/19.

Freezing duties may be electorally popular, but freezing fuel duties cost the Exchequer £830 million in 2018/19 and £225 million for the alcohol duty freeze.

Corporation tax

The present government boasts that the UK has the lowest corporate tax rate in the G20 group of countries.[8] In 2008, it was 28 per cent. After 2010, the coalition government and then the Conservative government made repeated and substantial cuts to the corporation tax rate to 19 per cent in 2018/19, and it is due to fall to 17 per cent by 2020/21.

Box 3.1:
Personal tax administration: what has changed since 1988?

The UK's pay as you earn (PAYE) system, introduced in 1944, is a 'cumulative' system of withholding, designed to collect employees' full annual liability for income tax from all their employment without the need for an end-of-year tax return (unless they have substantial income from other sources). Although it remains the main method of collecting income tax and national insurance contributions, its scope and method of operation has changed substantially over recent years. Employers are now required to use PAYE to withhold student loan repayments and child support payments, as well as to collect small tax liabilities arising from other income sources.

Furthermore, employers are now obliged, following the introduction of the 'real-time information system' in 2013, to transmit to HM Revenue and Customs (HMRC) electronically on or before each payday full details of their employees' gross pay, tax, national insurance contributions and other deductions. This has improved the accuracy of PAYE codes and enhanced the PAYE system's ability to collect the correct amount of tax due before the end of the tax year. About three-quarters of employees now settle their total tax liabilities through PAYE without completing a tax return.

For those who must submit tax returns – broadly those whose income tax liabilities are not fully collected through PAYE or other means – major changes were introduced in 1996 with the advent of self-assessment. This shifted the burden of assessing tax liabilities from HMRC to the individual taxpayer and enabled HMRC to collect tax based on the taxpayer's self-assessment, while reserving the right to audit the tax return at a later date.

Somewhere between 10 and 11 million taxpayers – just over a third of the total – are required to submit tax returns each year. Although HMRC has tried, through various means, to reduce the numbers submitting returns, the increasing complexity of the tax system has tended to thwart its efforts. For example, the introduction of the high-income child benefit charge has added around 500,000 individuals to the self-assessment population.

It is the government's ambition, announced in March 2015, to build on 'real-time information' and other digital developments to eventually remove the need to file tax returns by using information supplied during the year by third parties, such as employers, pension providers and the Department for Work and Pensions, and by taxpayers themselves to assess personal tax liabilities. As part of this development, an increasing proportion of individual tax returns received by taxpayers come 'pre-populated' with data about their employment and pension income, which they simply must check and confirm.

Notes

1. HM Treasury, *Autumn Budget 2017*, HC 587, November 2017
2. This chapter draws on T Pope and T Waters, *A Survey of the UK Tax System*, Institute for Fiscal Studies Briefing Note BN09, 2016
3. J Bradshaw and F Bennett, *National Insurance Contributions and the Self-employed in the UK*, ESPN Flash Report 2017/14, European Social Policy Network, 2017
4. HM Treasury, *Autumn Budget 2017*, HC 587, November 2017, para 3.10
5. For a briefing on the taxation of savings and gender, see J Lowe, *Savings and Investments: gender issues*, Women's Budget Group, 2018
6. A Seely and M Keep, *Stamp Duty Land Tax on Residential Property*, House of Commons Briefing SN07050, 2018
7. Local Government Association, '£8 billion funding black hole by 2025 will swallow up popular council services', 1 February 2019, www.local.gov.uk/about/news/funding-black-hole
8. HM Treasury, *Autumn Budget 2017*, HC 587, November 2017

Four
International comparisons
Jonathan Bradshaw

The tax systems in other countries are of interest for two reasons. First, their solutions to similar problems may suggest that it should be possible here. For example, several countries including Belgium, Canada, Denmark, Finland, Italy, Norway, Sweden, Spain and Switzerland already have local income tax schemes, which demonstrates that it should be administratively possible here. Other countries' tax systems may also deal with issues relevant to gender inequalities differently.[1]

Second, within an increasingly integrated world economy the tax systems of other countries constrain our own. If one country charges a much higher rate of tax on company profits than others, multinational corporations will try to ensure that their profits arise in the country with the lowest rate of tax by manipulating the prices at which the inputs and components are sold between their own divisions in different countries ('transfer pricing'). Individual countries can do little to limit this kind of activity and it may not be worthwhile if the rate differentials are small; but larger differentials will be harder to maintain.

Overall tax take

The UK is not a high tax country. Figure 4.1 shows the proportion of GDP which all taxes and social security contributions represent in OECD countries (and some non-OECD countries). The UK, at 33.2 per cent, is below the OECD average and a long way below Denmark (45.9 per cent), France (45.3 per cent) and Belgium (44.2 per cent). Also, while the tax rate has remained stable in the UK over the period 2007 to 2016, despite the financial crisis and austerity, there has been a 7 per cent rise in France, an 8 per cent rise in Germany and a whopping 24 per cent rise in Greece.

Figure 4.1:
Total tax revenue as a percentage of GDP, 2016

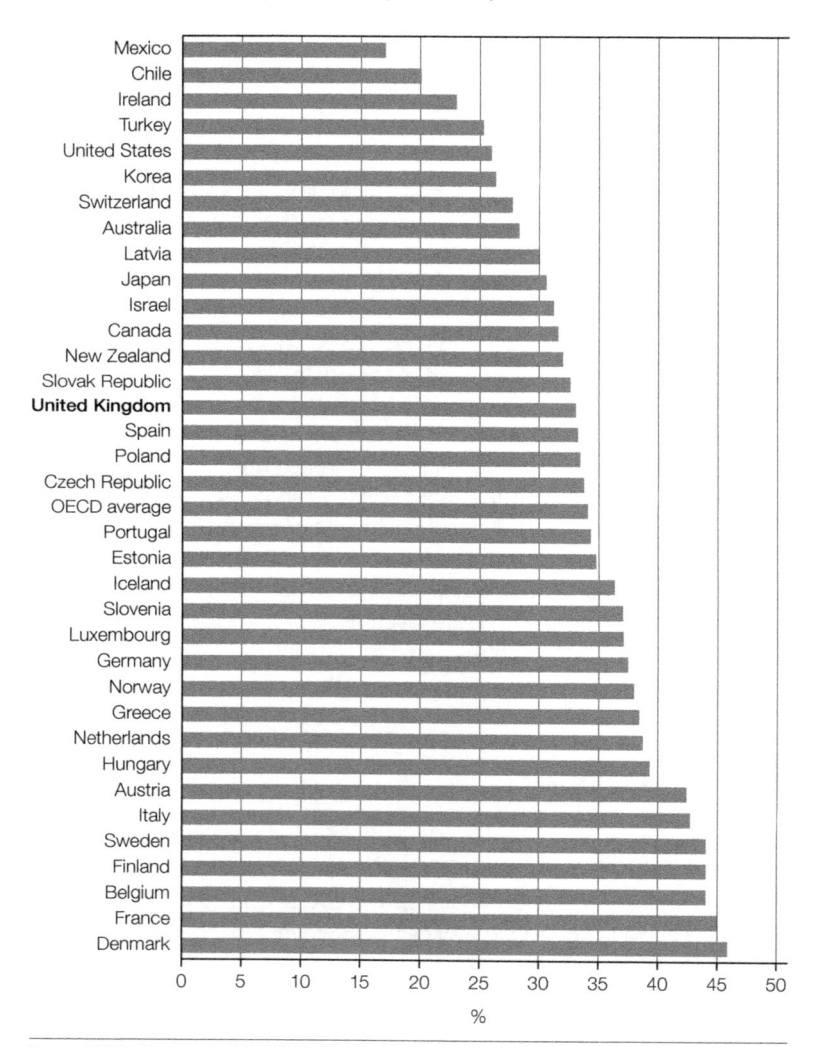

Country	%
Mexico	
Chile	
Ireland	
Turkey	
United States	
Korea	
Switzerland	
Australia	
Latvia	
Japan	
Israel	
Canada	
New Zealand	
Slovak Republic	
United Kingdom	
Spain	
Poland	
Czech Republic	
OECD average	
Portugal	
Estonia	
Iceland	
Slovenia	
Luxembourg	
Germany	
Norway	
Greece	
Netherlands	
Hungary	
Austria	
Italy	
Sweden	
Finland	
Belgium	
France	
Denmark	

Source: OECD, *Revenue Statistics 2018: tax revenue trends in the OECD*, 2018

Tax structure

Where the UK is more unusual is in its tax structure. It has a relatively low proportion of total taxes taken in direct taxes – taxes on income and social security taxes. These are, of course, the taxes which are likely to be the most progressive. Figure 4.2 shows the composition of total taxes in 2016 with selected OECD countries ranked left to right in the proportion taken in direct taxes. The UK is fourth from bottom of this league table and well below the OECD average. The UK has the highest proportion of taxes taken on property of all the countries in this comparison. As noted in Chapter 15, this is only because council tax (which is highly regressive) is included in these statistics. So although total tax on property is relatively high, this should not be interpreted as a high level of taxes on wealth – many of the people who pay council tax have minimal/zero/negative net wealth.

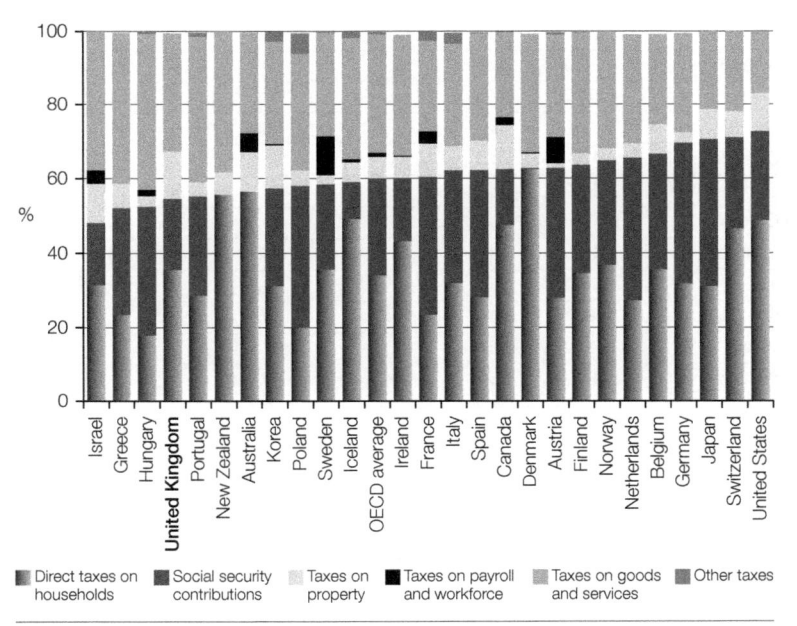

Figure 4.2:
Composition of tax revenue, 2016

■ Direct taxes on households　■ Social security contributions　▨ Taxes on property　■ Taxes on payroll and workforce　▨ Taxes on goods and services　■ Other taxes

Source: OECD, *Revenue Statistics 2018: tax revenue trends in the OECD*, 2018

Income tax rates

In comparing different countries' tax systems, almost as much depends on what is taxed – the tax base – as on the rate at which it is taxed. Differences in tax allowances, the scope of what is taxable and in the tax treatment of marriage (and civil partnerships, or other family forms) (see Chapter 8) have an important bearing on how the systems work. How the presence of children is dealt with is also important. Analysing these would, however, take more space than is available here.

Table 4.1:
Direct individual tax structures, 2017

	Bottom rate %	Top rate %	Number of bands	Maximum marginal tax rate (income tax and social security contributions) %	Maximum marginal tax rate (income tax, social security and local income tax) %
Belgium	25.0	50.0	5	60.2	110.2
Sweden	20.0	25.0	3	60.1	92.15
Finland	6.25	37.5	5	58.3	80.5
Japan	5.0	45.0	7	56.1	
Denmark	10.1	25.1	2	55.8	83.6
France	14.0	45.0	5	55.1	
Greece	22.0	45.0	5	55.0	
Canada	15.0	33.0	5	53.8	67.0
Italy	23.0	43.0	5	52.8	56.63
Netherlands	8.9	52.0	4	52.3	
Ireland	20.0	40.0	2	52.0	
Australia	19.0	45.0	5	49.0	
USA	10.0	39.6	7	48.5	
Austria	2.5	45.0	5	48.0	
Germany	*	45.0	4	47.5	
United Kingdom	20.0	45.0	3	47.0	
Norway	9.55	24.1	5	46.7	61.15
Spain	9.5	22.5	5	43.5	64.5
Switzerland	25.0	25.0	3	41.7	54.7

Source: OECD, Central government personal income tax rates and thresholds, available at https://stats.oecd.org/index.aspx?DataSetCode=TABLE_I1

So, Table 4.1 shows individual income tax structures for selected OECD countries, with countries ranked in order of the highest marginal tax rates (see Chapter 5) on those with high incomes, including local taxes and employee social security contributions where appropriate.

Three things stand out:

- Despite the UK having a middling standard rate of tax, the top tax rate (now 45 per cent) is one of the lowest. If one includes local income tax and social security contributions, our top rate is the lowest.[2]
- The UK starting rate for national income tax (20 per cent) is only exceeded in four countries.
- Most other countries have more than three bands in their income tax structure. Many of them have five or more. But the picture is different in Scotland (see Chapter 21).

This analysis only includes marginal rates due to taxation, without including the withdrawal of means-tested benefits (see later chapters in this book). In addition, it does not take account of where on the income distribution these rates come. Figures 4.3 and 4.4 attempt to fill that gap. They use the OECD tax-benefit model to analyse the tax rate – the proportion of gross income paid by two tax units (a single person and a two-earner couple with two children) as a proportion of gross income at three wage levels: 50 per cent, 100 per cent and 200 per cent of the average.[3] For the UK, these are earnings of £19,625, £39,250 and £78,501, so unfortunately the OECD model does not include cases with earnings in the highest rate band. In both Figure 4.3 and 4.4 the countries are ranked by the tax rate at 100 per cent of average earnings.

For the single person case, the UK comes just below the middle of the league table with tax rates of 14.7 per cent at 50 per cent, 23.4 per cent at 100 per cent and 45.4 per cent at 200 per cent, which are considerably lower and less progressive than, for example, Belgium, with tax rates at 17.7 per cent at 50 per cent, 40.4 per cent at 100 per cent and 56.4 per cent at 200 per cent.

The couple with children case takes account of any marriage tax allowances in the tax systems and gross income is enhanced by child benefits and allowances. The UK comes below the middle of this league table with tax rates at 1.2 per cent on gross income at 50 per cent average, 14.1 per cent at 100 per cent and 22.1 per cent at 200 per cent. These rates are considerably lower than the Netherlands, with rates of 6.8 per cent at 50 per cent, 18.2 per cent at 100 per cent and 33.3 per cent at 200 per cent.

Figure 4.3:
Income tax and social security contributions paid by a single person as a proportion of gross income at 50%, 100% and 200% national average wage, 2018

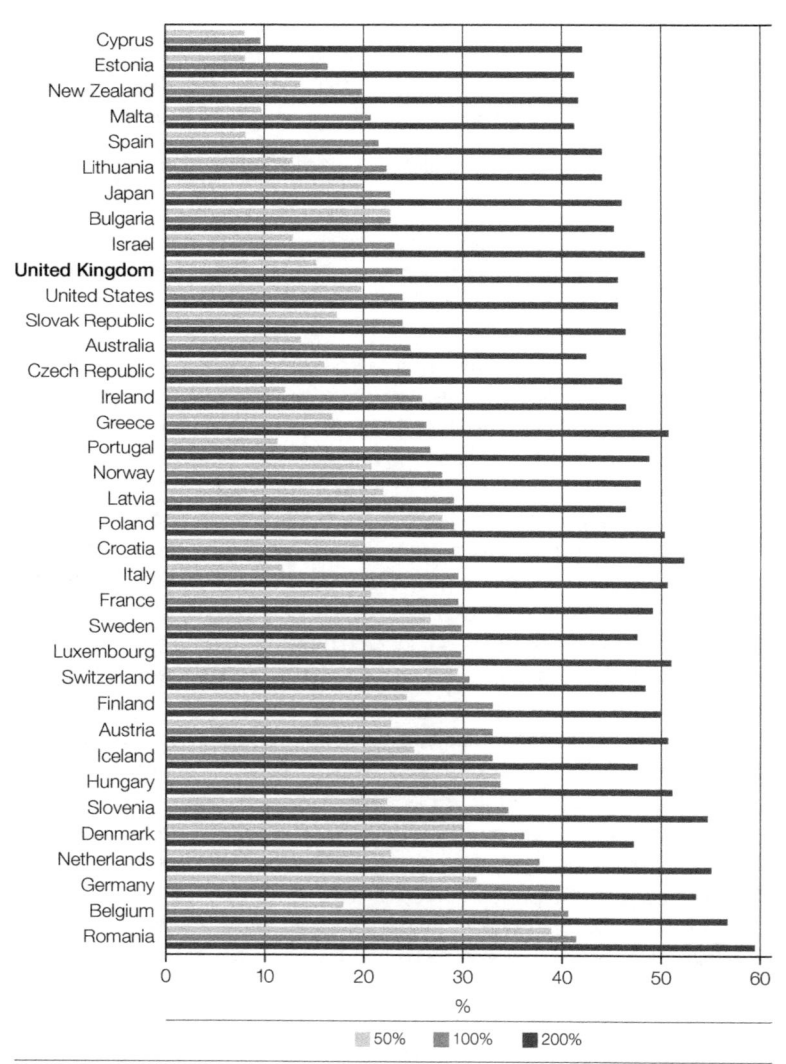

Source: Author's analysis of OECD TaxBEN model: www.oecd.org/els/soc/benefits-and-wages/tax-benefit-web-calculator

Figure 4.4:
Income tax and social security contributions paid by a two-earner couple with two children as a proportion of gross income at 50%, 100% and 200% national average wage (shared equally), 2018

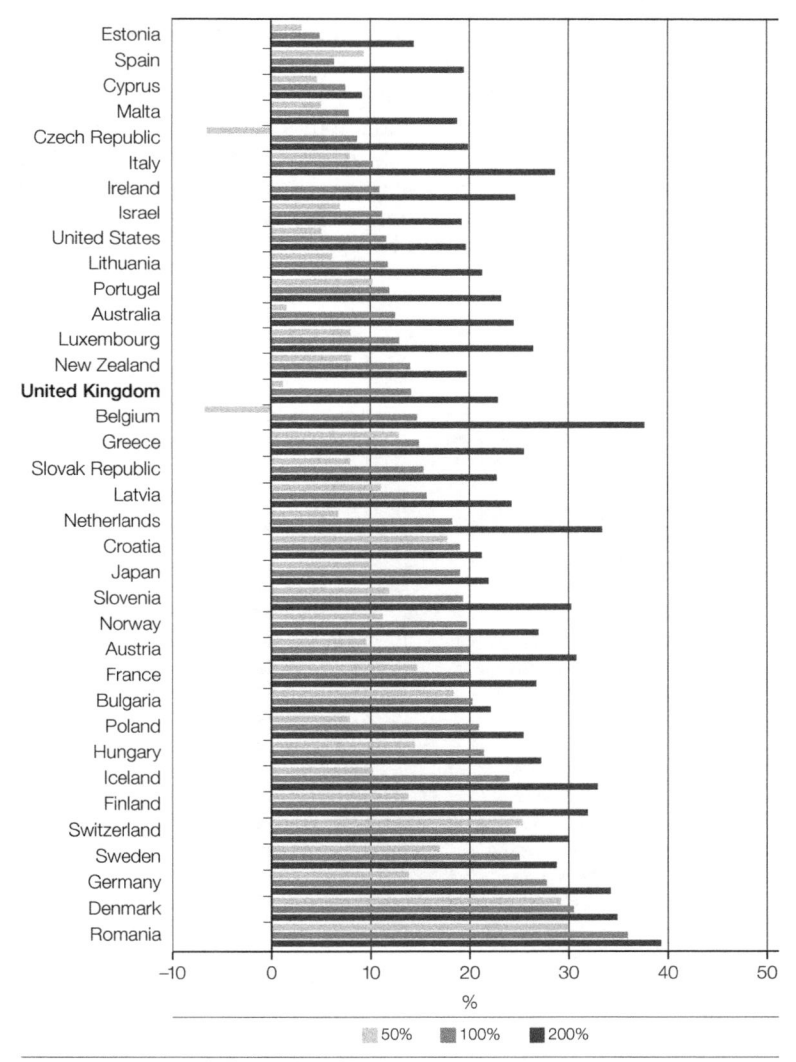

Source: Author's analysis of OECD TaxBEN model: www.oecd.org/els/soc/benefits-and-wages/tax-benefit-web-calculator

Corporation tax

The rates of corporation tax are compared for selected OECD countries in Figure 4.5. For reasons mentioned at the start of this chapter, it is hard for one country to keep a high corporation tax rate when rates in other countries are much lower. There have been reductions in corporation taxes in most countries since *Changing Tax* was published in 1988,[4] possibly because countries have been competing to attract business. It will be the owners of multinationals who benefited from this trend. Nevertheless, it can be seen that there is considerable variation in corporation tax rates, with France at the top of the league table with 34.3 per cent, and Ireland at the bottom with 12.5 per cent. The UK has the second lowest corporation tax rate of 19 per cent in 2018.

Figure 4.5:
Corporation tax rates, 2018

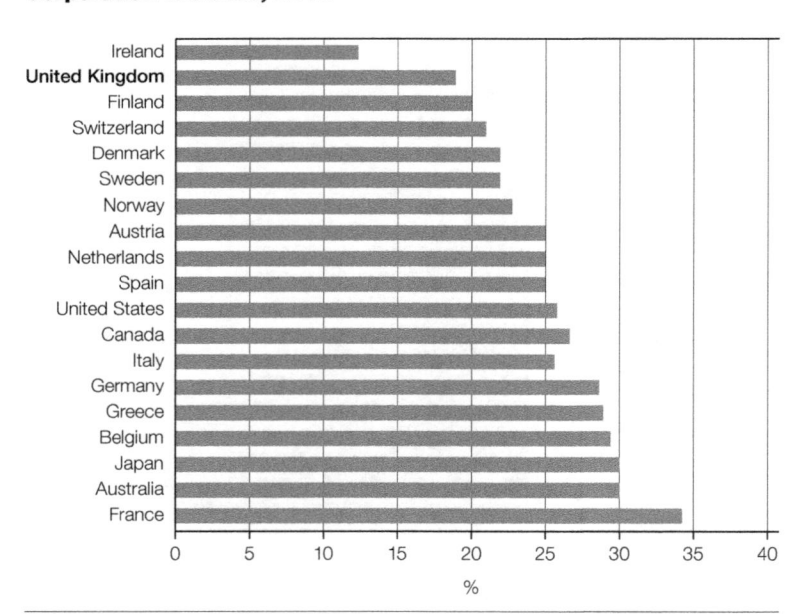

Source: Derived from OECD Tax Database: Statutory corporate income tax rates 2018

Rates of value added tax in the European Union

The European Union (EU) sets a minimum value added tax (VAT) rate at 15 per cent. But there is still a good deal of variation, with many countries having higher standard VAT rates and lower or zero rates for selected

Table 4.2:
VAT rates in the European Union, 2018

	Standard %	Reduced %	Reduced %	Reduced %	Zero %
Austria	20	13	10		0
Belgium	21	12	6		0
Bulgaria	20	9			0
Croatia	25	13	5		0
Cyprus	19	9	5		0
Czech Republic	21	15	10		0
Denmark	25				0
Estonia	20	9			0
Finland	24	14	10		0
France	20	10	5.5	2.1	0
Germany	19	7			0
Greece	24	13	6		0
Hungary	27	18	5		0
Ireland	23	13.5	9	4.8	0
Italy	22	10	5	4	0
Latvia	21	12	5		0
Lithuania	21	9	5		0
Luxembourg	17	14	8	3	0
Malta	18	7	5		0
Netherlands	21	6			0
Poland	23	8	5		0
Portugal	23	13	6		0
Romania	19	9	5		0
Slovakia	20	10			0
Slovenia	22	9.5			0
Spain	21	10	4		0
Sweden	25	12	6		0
United Kingdom	20	5			0

Source: www.vatlive.com/vat-rates/european-vat-rates

commodities – and the lower or zero rates, and the selection of commodities covered, varies from country to country. Zero rates are generally applied to intercommunity transport and, in some countries, newspapers. Reduced rates are generally applied to some foodstuffs and pharmaceuticals. Hungary has the highest standard rate in the EU (27 per cent). Denmark also has a high standard rate (25 per cent) and no reduced rates – just a zero rate for newspapers and journals (published more than once a month), and intra-community and international transport. The UK standard rate is comparatively low, and its reduced rate is the lowest in the EU (see Table 4.2).

Notes

1. See for example, G Sgueo, *Gender-responsive Budgeting*, European Parliamentary Research Service briefing, 2015, for a guide to gender-responsive budgeting, and C Coffey, MA Stephenson and S Himmelweit, *A Short Guide to Taxing for Gender Equality*, Oxfam, 2019, for a short guide to taxing for gender equality.
2. This actually hides a more complex structure for the UK. There are some very high marginal tax rates over particular income ranges. Individuals with an income above £100,000 begin to lose their personal allowance at the rate of £1 of personal allowance per £2 above £100,000 until the whole of the personal allowance is exhausted at £123,700 (for 2018/19) when the personal allowance stands at £11,850). Those whose income falls in this range face a marginal income tax rate of 60 per cent – add in national insurance contributions for those under retirement age and we have a marginal rate of 62 per cent applying to employment and self-employment income.
3. In the case of a couple, the earnings are shared: 25 per cent + 25 per cent; 50 per cent + 50 per cent; and 100 per cent + 100 per cent. The first of these cases is unlikely to exist and should probably be discounted. Given the pay gap and the common gendered division of labour within households, the other shares of earnings within the couple household may also not be typical. But the examples avoid the use of a single-earner couple with children which, as noted earlier in this book, is not 'typical' by any means (and is usually used without allocating any benefit income to the non-earning adult).
4. J Hills, *Changing Tax: how the tax system works and how to change it*, CPAG, 1988

Five
The structure of income tax rates and allowances
Tony Orhnial

In *Changing Tax*, published in 1988, John Hills covered the main personal tax issues of the day, describing, as they were being implemented, the 'Lawson reforms' of 1988 to 1990, which, among other changes, brought in independent taxation for individual women and men in married couples. This chapter outlines the main changes that the UK personal tax system has undergone since then and considers what lessons and insights they offer. It deals only with income tax rates and allowances – it does not cover the system of national insurance contributions (see Chapter 7), mainly collected through pay as you earn (PAYE) alongside income tax. Nor does it cover the taxation of savings and dividend income and of capital gains – these are in Chapter 14. As a result, it understates both the effective tax rates faced by those receiving employment or self-employment income and the full complexity of the personal income tax system.[1]

Key features of the UK income tax system

The basis of assessment

In the UK income tax is levied on an 'annual basis' – ie, on income received by the taxpayer during the whole of the tax year.[2] Most tax jurisdictions also use an annual, rather than a pay period, basis of tax assessment, but the UK is unusual in having a tax year running from 6 April in one calendar year to 5 April in the next, rather than from 1 January to 31 December in the same year.

The tax unit

Since the introduction of independent taxation in 1990, the entity assessed for income tax – the 'tax unit' – has been the individual, not the household or the couple, whether married, in a civil partnership or simply cohabiting. As a result, each individual is entitled to a personal allowance and assessed separately for income tax. That is not to say that personal tax policy does not raise gender issues (as discussed in Chapter 8), but it has meant that, at least until 2013, there has generally been no need for partners in couples or members of households to exchange information about their income to meet their income tax obligations or benefit from income tax reliefs.

Notwithstanding the changes introduced in 2013 (discussed later in this chapter and in Chapter 8), it is important to appreciate the almost totemic significance of the principle of independent taxation in the development of personal tax policy in the UK since 1990. This principle was particularly important in shaping the design of the new system of personal tax credits, introduced in 2003. The need to adhere to it prevented the new credits from being fully integrated into the income tax system because they were to be based on a household, rather than individual, income test which would clearly have been inconsistent with independent taxation.[3]

The structure of the personal tax system

Three key elements describe the structure of a personal tax system, namely:

- The definition of 'income' for income tax purposes. This can differ significantly between tax jurisdictions – for example, winnings from gambling are exempt from tax in the UK, but count as income in the USA.
- The nature and amounts of any tax-free allowances available to taxpayers.
- The schedule of income tax rates (or marginal rates of tax) applied to successive slices of income subject to tax.

Tax-free allowances can be delivered either as credits to be set against a tax bill – as they are in the USA, for example – or as deductions from gross income which, like the UK's personal allowance, determine 'taxable income' (the amount of income subject to tax). This distinction is important because if a tax-free allowance takes the form of a tax credit, it can result in a negative income tax bill, and therefore a refund for those with gross income below the level of the tax-free allowance. If it does not, those with incomes below that level do not get the full benefit of the allowance, and those on the highest incomes stand to benefit most.

Between them, the tax-free allowances to which an individual is entitled and the rates of tax applied to her/his taxable income determine that individual's total tax bill, the average rate of tax paid on her/his total taxable income and the effective marginal rate of tax to be paid if s/he earned an additional £1 of income.

The sum of all taxable income constitutes the 'base' on which income tax can be levied. So, increasing the amount of income which individuals can receive free of tax by, say, raising the personal allowance, reduces the size of the 'income tax base' to which a given tax schedule can be applied. And removing or reducing reliefs extends the size of the tax base, as does extending the scope of the definition of income to include capital gains, or bringing a wider range of benefits in kind into the tax net.

The UK personal income tax system, 1988 to 2019

At the time when *Changing Tax* was published, the UK's personal income tax system was about to adopt, because of Nigel Lawson's 1988 Budget, what was to be one of the least complex[4] structures in its history:

- The previous schedule of income tax rates – whereby successive slices of income were taxed at six different marginal rates rising from the basic rate of 27 per cent on taxable income up to £17,900 to the highest rate of 60 per cent charged on incomes above £41,200 – had just been replaced by a simple two-band structure, with taxable income up to £19,300 taxed at 25 per cent and income above that 'basic rate limit' taxed at 40 per cent.

- The complex, and arguably in part sexist, system of tax-free allowances, which depended on whether the taxpayer in question was single (and so entitled to the single person's allowance), married (the married man's allowance), a single parent (the additional personal allowance) or part of a two-earner couple (entitled to both the married man's allowance and the wife's earned income allowance), was about to be swept away by the advent in 1990 of independent taxation. This new system would determine each person's tax liability separately, whether married or single, giving each individual her/his own tax-free personal allowance.

Although some of the complexities of the old system survived for some years in a different guise – notably the married couple's allowance, the additional personal allowance, the age-related personal and married couple's allowances and tax relief for mortgage interest – taken as a whole, the 1990 system was simpler than that which had existed for most of the twentieth century and, as discussed below, than that which developed subsequently.

Main changes to income tax rates

The retreat from Lawsonian simplicity began when the (pre-election) 1992 Budget introduced a lower rate of income tax at 20 per cent charged on the first £2,000 of taxable income. This remained in place until April 1999 (by which time the lower rate band had been extended to £4,300), when the lower rate was replaced by a starting rate of income tax of 10 per cent applying to the first £1,500 of taxable income. The starting rate was abolished from April 2008, when the UK returned, briefly, to a two-rate system of income tax.

Meanwhile, the basic rate remained at 25 per cent until April 1996, when it was reduced to 24 per cent, followed by further reductions to 23 per cent in 1997, 22 per cent in April 2000 and, finally, 20 per cent in April 2008.

The higher rate has remained at 40 per cent since its introduction in 1988. It was supplemented, from April 2010, by a new additional rate of income tax, set initially at 50 per cent on taxable income exceeding £150,000, but reduced to 45 per cent from April 2013 (see Chapter 6).

Main changes to income tax allowances and thresholds

The various changes to the income tax rate schedule over the past 30 years have been accompanied by even more significant changes to the system of tax-free allowances and reliefs, which included:

- Abolishing, from April 2000, mortgage interest relief, the married couple's allowance for under-65-year-olds and the additional personal allowance, and the age-related personal allowance (from April 2016). These changes were preceded by successive reductions in the value of the tax relief they produced.

- Replacing the married couple's allowance and additional personal allowance with the children's tax credit in April 2001, only to abolish it in April 2003 to help fund the new system of integrated support for families with children through child tax credit.

- Introducing the transferable marriage allowance (from 2013),[5] and the savings, dividend, trading and property income allowances (from April 2016).

- Clawing back the personal allowance (from April 2010) from those with taxable incomes above £100,000 and (from January 2013) child benefit from those with relevant income between £50,000 and £60,000 per year (if child benefit is not given up by the person claiming it).

- Using the Scottish parliament's powers to vary income tax rates within certain limits (for the first time in 2016/17) to establish an income tax schedule with different tax bands for individuals residing in Scotland to the one applying to residents elsewhere in the UK.

A tax-raising device commonly used by governments is to 'freeze' the value of income tax allowances and thresholds, or more accurately in the case of the basic and higher rate thresholds to suspend the application of the legislation providing for them to be increased each April in line with some measure of inflation.[6] Although the personal allowance has been frozen on several occasions, on others it has risen by significantly more than the Consumer Price Index (CPI), particularly in recent years. Such increases have generally been presented as measures to benefit the lower paid, despite the fact that, as noted earlier, any gains to the lowest paid can be quite limited and many (women in particular) will already have earnings below the threshold and not benefit at all. By contrast, the taxable income threshold above which the higher rate applies has not only failed to keep up with inflation but it has been reduced[7] to restrict any benefit to higher rate taxpayers from increases in the personal allowance. Looking ahead, however, in line with the 2017 Conservative Party manifesto commitment, the Chancellor announced in his autumn 2018 Budget that the higher rate threshold would be set at £50,000 for both 2019/20 and 2020/21.

Partly because of these differences in recognising the effects of inflation in setting the thresholds, the number of individuals paying tax solely at the basic rate has only risen from 24 million in 1989/90 to 25.3 million in 2016/17, whereas the number paying tax at the higher rate has more than trebled – from 1.5 million to 4.7 million – over the same period.

Furthermore, there are no statutory provisions requiring automatic price indexation of the thresholds at which the high-income child benefit charge, the withdrawal of the personal allowance and the additional rate of income tax begin to bite. All three thresholds have remained at the level at which they were originally set. The Institute for Fiscal Studies estimates that, had it been CPI-indexed, the first of these thresholds would have been set at £55,000, rather than the current £50,000, for the tax year starting on 6 April 2019, with the effect that 270,000 fewer families would be losing some or all of their child benefit in 2019/20.[8] If the high-income child benefit charge threshold remains at £50,000, combined with an indexed higher rate threshold, the resulting outcome over time looks likely to be inconsistent with the original policy intention that benefit withdrawal should only apply where one person in the household is a higher rate taxpayer.

Similarly, had the additional rate threshold been raised by CPI inflation since its introduction in 2010, it would now stand at £180,000, with the effect that those with incomes between £150,000 and £180,000 would pay tax at the higher rather than additional rate.[9]

A final point to note in ringing the changes affecting the tax base since 1988 is that the range of employer-provided benefits in kind and expenses payments subject to tax has been extended substantially, partly to counter attempts to avoid (or defer) income tax and both employer and employee national insurance contributions by remunerating employees and directors in increasingly exotic ways.

Tax rates and allowances for 2019/20

Income tax rates for Scotland and the rest of the UK

The various changes outlined above have made the income tax system significantly more complex than it was in 1988. A taxpayer's marginal tax rate now depends on: (a) whether s/he resides in Scotland or elsewhere in the UK; (b) whether s/he or her/his partner is claiming child benefit; and (c) the composition of her/his income. Current income tax rates and thresholds for non-savings income for Scotland are set out in Table 5.2 and those for the rest of the UK in Table 5.1.

The taxation of income from savings interest and company dividends was reformed from 2016 and the current system is described in Chapter 14. However, this aspect of the personal tax system is the same in Scotland as in the rest of the UK.

Table 5.1:
UK income tax rates, 2019/20

UK tax band (except Scotland)	Gross income before tax-free allowances	UK tax rate (except Scotland)
Personal allowance	Up to £12,500	0%
Basic rate	£12,501 to £50,000	20%
Higher rate	£50,001 to £150,000	40%
Additional rate	Over £150,000	45%

Table 5.2:
Scottish income tax rates, 2019/20

Scottish tax band	Gross income before tax-free allowances	Scottish tax rate
Personal allowance	Up to £12,500	0%
Starter rate	£12,501 to £14,549	19%
Basic rate	£14,550 to £24,944	20%
Intermediate rate	£24,945 to £43,430	21%
Higher rate	£43,431 to £150,000	41%
Top rate	Over £150,000	46%

Income tax allowances

Each individual is entitled to a personal allowance (£12,500 in 2019/20[10]) and assessed separately for tax. However, that entitlement begins to be withdrawn once her/his annual income exceeds £100,000 at the rate of £1 for every £2 above the limit until it is completely exhausted at an income of £125,000. This implies an effective marginal tax rate of 60 per cent (not including national insurance contributions) over that income range.

Despite independent taxation, there is a degree of interdependence between individuals who are married or in a civil partnership in that:

- where one spouse or civil partner has no taxable income and the other pays tax only at the basic rate, s/he can transfer up to 10 per cent of her/his unused personal allowance (£1,250 in 2019/20) to her/his tax-paying partner. This is known as the 'transferable marriage allowance' (see Chapter 8); *and*
- couples with one spouse or partner who was born before 6 April 1935 are entitled to a married couple's allowance worth a tax reduction of up to £891.50, depending on the higher earner's income, in 2019/20.

A further degree of dependence between tax units arises when a partner in a couple claims child benefit. If the income of one of the partners (regardless of whether they are married, in a civil partnership or simply cohabiting) exceeds £50,000, s/he becomes liable for the high-income child benefit charge, which claws back 1 per cent of the total child benefit received for each £100 of income above £50,000 until all of it is withdrawn at £60,000. Since the total amount of child benefit received depends on both the benefit rate and the number of children and the income range for withdrawal is fixed at £10,000, the implied marginal tax rates for larger families can be well over 60 per cent.[11]

The high-income child benefit charge has also been seen by some as illustrating one of the inequities that the current system can produce when it attempts to assess the tax liabilities of one person partly based on the income of another without taking account of their joint income. So a couple in which one partner earns £50,001 and the other £0 falls within the charge, whereas another couple in which both partners earn £49,999 each does not.

Combined effects of income tax rates and allowances

The combined effects of the income tax rates and allowances which applied for the 2018/19 tax year mean that those individuals (not resident in Scotland) with gross incomes falling:

- below £11,850 – about 45 per cent of adults – paid no income tax because their income was fully covered by their personal allowance.

Although national insurance contributions are outside the scope of this chapter, it is worth noting that employees with earnings above the national insurance contribution primary threshold or the self-employed with profits above the lower profit level (both set at £8,424 in 2018/19) do pay national insurance contributions, at 12 per cent in the former case and 9 per cent in the latter, before they start paying income tax;

- between £11,851 and £46,350 paid tax at the basic rate and faced a marginal income tax rate of 20 per cent. This applies to around 24 million individuals, or just over 80 per cent of income tax payers;
- between £46, 351 and £100,000 paid tax at the higher rate – around 15 per cent of taxpayers – and had a marginal rate of 40 per cent. If they earned £50,000 or more per year[12] and they or their partner claimed child benefit, they were liable for the high-income child benefit charge (this applied to about 1,350,000 people[13]). That means that over the range of income from £50,000 to £60,000 their marginal income tax rates were:
  - 50.8 per cent if they received child benefit in respect of one child;
  - 57.9 per cent if they received child benefit in respect of two children;
  - 65 per cent if they received child benefit in respect of three children;
  - and higher rates still in line with the number of child benefit payments that needed to be 'recovered' by HM Revenue and Customs;
- between £100,000 and £123,700 – nearly one million individuals[14] – faced a marginal income tax rate of 60 per cent as their personal allowance entitlement was withdrawn; *and*
- over £150,000 were liable to tax at 45 per cent – this applied to some 430,000 individuals[15] or just over 1 per cent of taxpayers – except where their entitlement to make pension contributions out of tax-free income was tapered from £40,000 to £10,000,[16] in which case their effective marginal tax rate exceeds 45 per cent.

For Scottish residents, the system is even more complex in that it includes two additional tax bands, the starter rate and intermediate rate bands, and marginal rates above a gross income of £24,000 are one percentage point higher than in the rest of the UK.

Although the marginal tax rates cited above do not include national insurance contributions, it is important to bear in mind that including them would add 12 per cent to the effective marginal rate of tax for people with gross incomes from employment between £8,424 and £46,350 and 2 per cent for wages and salaries above that (not including employer national insurance contributions at 13.8 per cent).

Notes

1 This also means that the chapter cannot, by definition, consider the recent A Stirling, *Tapering Over the Tax: reforming taxation of income in the UK*, Institute for Public Policy Research Commission on Economic Justice, 2018, which proposes merging income tax and national insurance contributions and devising a combined 'formula-based' rate schedule.
2 This contrasts with national insurance contributions which, for employees and employers, are charged on a 'pay period' basis. This means that national insurance liability is determined by the amount of wages or salary received in a particular pay period and is independent of any amounts received before or after that period.
3 The fact that the individual is the tax unit did not, however, stop those responsible for responding to parliamentary questions putting together the amount of the award of tax credits (in effect, means-tested benefits) and any income tax payable and calculating a (negative) tax rate for a family in that situation.
4 This refers solely to the relative complexity of the structure of tax allowances and rates. Much of the complexity of the tax system – largely invisible to most taxpayers – lies in the detail of the different tax rules applying to different sources of income. So, for example, the scope for setting certain expenses against rental income for tax purposes depends on whether that income derives from an ordinary rental or a 'furnished holiday let'.
5 A Seely, *Tax, Marriage and Transferable Allowances*, House of Commons Briefing Paper SN04392, 2019
6 Since April 2011, that measure has been the previous September's value of the Consumer Price Index. Before that, the measure was the previous September's value of the Retail Price Index.
7 In 2008/09 and 2011/12 to 2014/15.
8 C Emmerson, R Joyce and T Waters, *Stealthy Changes Mean That Soon One in Five Families With Children Will Be Losing Some Child Benefit*, Institute for Fiscal Studies Observation, 7 January 2019
9 S Adam and T Waters, 'Options for raising taxes', in C Emmerson, C Farquharson and P Johnson (eds), *The IFS Green Budget: October 2018*, Institute for Fiscal Studies, 2018, p170
10 This increased to £12,500 from April 2019, and the higher rate threshold to £50,000, as announced in Budget 2018.
11 See Chapter 8. Recovery of child benefit adds 10.8 per cent to the taxpayer's marginal tax rate for one child, 17.9 per cent for two children and 25 per cent for three children. This means that an individual with three children and an income between £50,000 and £60,000 faces a marginal tax rate over that range of 65 per cent (unless the child benefit recipient gives it up).
12 More accurately, if the 'adjusted net income' (after allowing for pension contributions or other allowable items, but not the personal allowance) of one of the partners exceeds £50,000.
13 S Adam and P Johnson, *Dragging People Into Higher Rates of Tax*, Institute for Fiscal Studies Briefing Note BN247, April 2019
14 S Adam and P Johnson, *Dragging People Into Higher Rates of Tax*, Institute for Fiscal Studies Briefing Note BN247, April 2019
15 S Adam and P Johnson, *Dragging People Into Higher Rates of Tax*, Institute for Fiscal Studies Briefing Note BN247, April 2019

16 Taxpayers with taxable incomes below £150,000 (including pension contributions) are entitled to an annual pension contribution allowance of £40,000. This allowance is reduced by £1 of allowance per £2 of income above £150,000 of income until it reaches £10,000. This change was introduced in 2015/16 at the same time as the lifetime allowance was reduced from £1.25 million to £1 million.

Six
Raising income tax rates: what we knew then and what we know now

Tony Orhnial

In *Changing Tax*, published in 1988, John Hills considered various options for raising additional revenues, including restricting the tax savings afforded by various allowances and reliefs to the basic rate of income tax.[1] The main increases in the *effective* marginal rate of income tax introduced since 1988 have come about through a variety of complex changes – often referred to as 'stealth taxes' – of the sort he had in mind. As described in Chapter 5, these tax rises have involved withdrawing or limiting the benefit of tax allowances from taxpayers on higher incomes, using the tax system to claw back child benefit and reducing the amount of tax-free income that can be contributed to an individual's pension fund. The reason why successive governments have adopted these opaque and complex approaches to raising taxes is wholly political: both Conservative and Labour election manifestos have generally ruled out increases in income tax rates.[2]

The top rate of income tax has only been overtly increased once since the higher rate of 40 per cent was introduced in 1988. The new additional rate of income tax, applying to incomes above £150,000 was first announced in the November 2008 *Pre-Budget Report*: it was to be set at 45 per cent and would take effect from April 2011. A few months later, in his 2009 Budget, Alistair Darling, the then Chancellor, decided that the additional rate would be set at 50 per cent – the highest personal income tax rate in the G20[3] – and would be introduced from April 2010, a year earlier than he envisaged. The measure was expected to affect around 1 per cent of taxpayers (300,000 individuals) who paid about 30 per cent of the income tax revenue raised in 2009/10 and to raise £1.3 billion in 2010/11, followed by £3.1 billion and £2.7 billion in subsequent years.

It was made clear at the time that these estimates were subject to considerable uncertainty because the size of the 2010/11 tax base had been estimated from 2007/08 tax data and, although the Treasury had attempted to take account of it as far as possible, the estimates remained very sensitive to the behavioural response of taxpayers affected by the rate rise.

The issue of how taxpayers affected by a tax rise respond to it, and the extent to which they attempt to mitigate its effects on their post-tax income, is a critical factor determining its Exchequer yield and therefore whether it is worth doing from a budgetary perspective. (That does not necessarily mean that it is not worth doing from a political or 'optical' perspective.)

The question of behavioural responses to tax rises was considered in *Changing Tax*:[4]

> There are, however, genuine arguments about the economic effects of taxation which should not be ignored... The main accusation is that high taxes on the rich act as a 'disincentive' and reduce economic growth, eventually lowering everyone's living standards.

John Hills considered that the available contemporary research provided little evidence of significant effects on men's work incentives (although there might be some effect on the propensity of married women to take up paid employment, which is an important way in which child poverty in couples can be reduced, and also make it more likely that if the couple splits up the woman continues to earn as a lone parent). This relative lack of response by men might have been because, at the time, few employees had the flexibility to vary their working hours or to retire earlier than they otherwise would.[5]

However, he went on to argue that:[6]

> ... there are two constraints which really do seem important in setting economic limits to taxation. The first is that people with particular skills may have the option of going abroad if they could improve their standard of living by doing so... The second is tax avoidance and evasion... If individuals' regular income is taxed very heavily, it will be worth their while to engage in the most complicated (and economically wasteful) exercises to transform it into another form.

A great deal of research has been undertaken since 1988 to understand and estimate the overall responsiveness of total taxable incomes to changes in marginal tax rates – the 'taxable income elasticity' – a critical factor in costing changes in tax policy for budgetary and other purposes. However, that elasticity can vary at different points on the income distribution and according to the type of income involved, and also depends on the tax planning opportunities offered by the tax system in question. In any case, there is no consensus on the size of any response, least of all for the UK.

Most studies have been based on data from the USA and overseas because the UK's highest rate had remained unchanged since 1988. The most relevant UK study of the taxable income elasticity for high-income individuals is therefore based on data from the 1970s and 1980s, and the authors note that this could overstate the current elasticity, perhaps because there are fewer opportunities for avoidance because of changes to the tax system since the 1980s.[7] On the other hand, it could equally well understate the potential response for a variety of reasons, including the availability of more flexible employment terms and a higher propensity to engage in tax planning, because there are fewer opportunities for avoidance as a result of changes to the tax system since the 1980s.

Another factor is the steady rise in company formation in the UK in the past 15 or more years. Incorporation offers, among other advantages, greater opportunities than employment or self-employment to defer or advance the receipt of income in the form of dividends or to convert it into a capital gain. And there is strong evidence to suggest that, given these opportunities, the incomes of owner-managers are more responsive to tax incentives than those of employees.[8]

The first study of the Exchequer effects of the introduction of the additional rate, based on an analysis of 2010/11 tax returns, was carried out by HM Revenue and Customs (HMRC) in 2012 in conjunction with the then Chancellor's decision to cut the top rate to 45 per cent.[9] It concluded that the behavioural response had been substantially greater than assumed in the Budget 2010 estimates and that 'between £16 billion and £18 billion of income is estimated to have been brought forward to 2009/10 to avoid the additional rate of tax'.[10] The potential for such forestalling was inevitably enhanced by the fact that the planned rate rise was announced well in advance of its implementation and was described as 'temporary'.

Conveniently for the then Chancellor, George Osborne, HMRC also concluded that:

- 'the estimated revenue-maximising rate of tax for those with incomes over £150,000 is between 45 per cent and 50 per cent, and that the Exchequer impact of varying the rate close to this level is relatively low';[11] *and*
- behavioural responses were likely to cut the £3 billion or so Exchequer cost of reducing the additional rate of income tax to 45 per cent to some £100 million per year.[12]

Both the Office for Budget Responsibility and the Institute for Fiscal Studies were in broad agreement with HMRC's analysis at the time it was published, stressing the uncertainty attached to all such estimates of the likely yield from raising income taxes, particularly for those on higher incomes.[13] Later studies by Institute for Fiscal Studies economists suggest that:

- 'although our central estimates of the taxable income elasticity are higher than those of HMRC (2012), the significant uncertainty around our estimates mean that one cannot be sure that the 50 per cent tax rate did not raise or indeed cost substantial revenues';[14]
- 'it is also plausible that the re-introduction of the 50 per cent rate could reduce revenues somewhat';[15] *and*
- 'policymakers will therefore need to reconcile themselves to uncertainty about the revenue effects of changing the top rates of income tax'.[16]

The analysis also found evidence that 'the overall high degree of responsiveness of high earners to the former 50 per cent rate was driven by those with the very highest incomes: those with incomes between £150,000 and £200,000 appear to be only a third to a half as responsive to tax rates as [the] £150,000 plus group as a whole'.[17] It went on to suggest that, as a result, any additional revenue from the 2017 Labour Party manifesto proposals to tax incomes between £80,000 and £150,000 at 45 per cent and incomes exceeding that at 50 per cent would 'come predominantly from those with incomes between £80,000 and £200,000, rather than those with the very highest incomes'.[18] The UK evidence is inevitably coloured, as mentioned earlier, by the nature of the announcement of the introduction of the 50p rate.

Finally, it is important to note that, alongside these studies of recent UK experience, the theoretical debate among public finance economists has shifted dramatically in the last decade. The generally accepted view until then was that the 'optimal' (revenue-maximising) top marginal rate of income tax was to be found somewhere at or below 50 per cent is being questioned by some prominent economists, who suggest that substantially higher rates might be sustainable in appropriate circumstances.[19]

Some conclusions

Several conclusions might be drawn from the tax-raising experience of the past 30 years:

- The income tax base has been significantly eroded by recent above-inflation increases in the personal allowance, a policy that generally benefits those on the lowest incomes least[20] – in particular, women (two out of three of those with annual taxable incomes are now below the level of the allowance[21]).

- All too often governments have relied on *fiscal drag* – raising tax allowances and thresholds more slowly than prices or earnings – to raise revenue without raising tax rates, or even while reducing headline rates.

- Worse still, the failure to index the thresholds for a variety of personal tax measures introduced since 2010, including, but not exclusively, those discussed in Chapter 5, are clearly:[22]

  > ... making a nonsense of any pretence of sensible design: the government is not even attempting to take a principled view of exactly which families should be keeping all of their child benefit, who should be paying higher rates of tax, and so on. Instead it is simply allowing these choices to be buffeted around each year by inflation.

- These and other elaborate wheezes to raise income tax revenue without raising headline rates of income tax have created an unnecessarily opaque personal tax system with a variety of very high (localised) effective marginal rates of tax, mostly at relatively high levels of income.

- Perhaps partly because of this complexity, the degree to which the income tax system is progressive (and has become more progressive since 2007/08) is not well understood. In this context it is worth noting that the Survey of Personal Incomes data (for 2015/16) reports that the bottom 50 per cent of taxpayers accounted for only 9.4 per cent of total income tax liabilities, that 60 per cent of income tax is paid by the top 10 per cent of taxpayers and that just under 29 per cent (up from 24.4 per cent in 2007/08) by the top 1 per cent.[23] And that the average rate of tax rises from 7.3 per cent of total income for those with incomes in the range £15,000–£20,000, to 10.3 per cent for £20,000–£30,000, 21.6 per cent for £50,000–£100,000, 33.4 per cent for £150,000–£200,000 and 39.1 per cent for those with incomes above £200,000.[24]

- Because of the particular circumstances surrounding its introduction, analysis of the UK experience of raising the top rate of income tax to 50 per cent offers little evidence for or against the proposition that reinstating that rate or introducing higher nominal rates of tax for incomes in excess of £150,000 would raise significant amounts of additional revenue.

All of this suggests that we should proceed with caution in advocating higher rates of income tax as an effective way of raising substantial additional revenue. We should focus first on making any proposed rises stick by reducing the scope for those on the highest incomes to mitigate the changes by the perfectly legitimate means of shifting income between tax years or by receiving it in the form of a capital gain. And we should avoid further eroding the tax base by continuing to extend the personal allowance (beyond statutory indexation) or by adding further complexity to a system that is already incomprehensible to many. But none of this is straightforward or easy, either technically or politically.

Finally, looking at income tax policy in the 30 years since the publication of *Changing Tax*, it is difficult to escape the conclusion that successive governments have promoted, in their manifestos and their policy decisions, the myth that low levels of income taxation are fully compatible with good-quality public services, a well-functioning welfare state and falling levels of poverty. This has led them to raise tax revenues in increasingly opaque ways – resulting not only in the unnecessary complexities described above, but also in an apparent rupture (in the general public's mind at least) of the link between taxation and the funding of public services and other social objectives, including the eradication of child poverty. The experience of the past few years – with ailing public services and rising levels of child poverty – provides ample evidence that this approach is not sustainable in the longer term, particularly in the light of the demographic challenges that lie ahead. As Martin Wolf concludes, in his recent *Financial Times* article, there is no easy way forward but 'the starting point must be with a debate on what the country wants and how to fund it. The pressures will not vanish. Politics has to find an answer.'[25]

Recommendations

In the short term

- Abolish the high-income child benefit charge in order to reinstate child benefit as a universal benefit for families with children, reduce complexity and unfairness in the personal tax system and reverse a breach of the principle of independent taxation.
- Introduce statutory Consumer Price Index indexation of all tax thresholds, including those for withdrawing the personal allowance and for the additional rate of income tax, in order to establish a fair and coherent approach to determining the real-terms tax liability of individual taxpayers.
- Avoid above-inflation increases in the personal allowance or introducing new tax reliefs – to stop further erosion of the income tax base.
- Launch a public information campaign to promulgate the messages that: tax revenues fund public services and expenditure on measures to combat poverty and other social ills; it is the duty of every citizen to pay her/his fair share of taxes; and high-quality public services are not compatible with low levels of personal taxation.
- Reinforce those messages by adding 1p to each of the basic, higher and additional rates of income tax. The Institute for Fiscal Studies estimates that this could raise some £6 billion per year.
- Announce a consultation on the options to equalise the marginal rates of tax paid on income received from employment, self-employment and a personal service company.

In the longer term

- Introduce a package of measures (following the consultation) to reduce or eliminate tax advantages attached to providing services through self-employment or personal service companies. This would help secure the personal income tax base.
- Consider turning the current personal allowance into a refundable tax credit against an individual's tax bill. Such a change to a system of 'negative income tax' would require very careful investigation: it would involve major re-engineering of HMRC and employer computer sys-

tems and software and very substantial disruption for both. It is unlikely to be deliverable within the lifetime of a single parliament.[27]

- Establish an independent commission to examine the theoretical and empirical evidence on the revenue-raising potential of different income tax schedules and their distributional consequences (including for women and men, and those with and without children) and to make recommendations on the schedule most appropriate to the UK. This would require a significant increase in HMRC's analytical resources to provide the data necessary to support this work. (More widely, such a commission would also need to take account of the effects on the income tax base of any redefinitions of the income tax base arising from the adoption of measures recommended in Chapters 12–15.) This approach would not de-politicise the design of the personal tax system, but it would at least provide a platform for a national debate and a coherent baseline to guide and evaluate future reforms.

Notes
1. J Hills, *Changing Tax: how the tax system works and how to change it*, CPAG, 1988, pp18–19
2. These manifesto commitments have generally been crafted to exclude national insurance contributions, so employee rates have risen from 9 per cent in 1988/89 to the current 12 per cent, and employer rates from 10.45 per cent to 13.8 per cent.
3. This was the case only for headline income tax rates, excluding social security deductions like national insurance contributions, where in the UK the rate falls from 12 per cent to 2 per cent on incomes above the upper earnings limit (£50,000 in 2019/20).
4. J Hills, *Changing Tax: how the tax system works and how to change it*, CPAG, 1988, p17
5. J Hills, *Changing Tax: how the tax system works and how to change it*, CPAG, 1988, p17
6. J Hills, *Changing Tax: how the tax system works and how to change it*, CPAG, 1988, p17
7. M Brewer, E Saez and A Shephard, 'Means-testing and tax rates on earnings', in Institute for Fiscal Studies (ed), *Dimensions of Tax Design: the Mirrlees Review*, Oxford University Press, 2010
8. S Adam, H Miller and T Pope, 'Tax, legal form and the gig economy', in C Emmerson, P Johnson and R Joyce (eds), *The IFS Green Budget: February 2017*, Institute for Fiscal Studies, 2017; and S Adam and others, *Frictions and Taxpayer Responses: evidence from bunching at personal tax thresholds*, Institute for Fiscal Studies Working Paper W17/14, 2017
9. HM Revenue and Customs, *The Exchequer Effect of the 50 per cent Additional Rate of Income Tax*, March 2012
10. HM Revenue and Customs, *The Exchequer Effect of the 50 per cent Additional Rate of Income Tax*, March 2012, para 6.3
11. HM Revenue and Customs, *The Exchequer Effect of the 50 per cent Additional Rate of Income Tax*, March 2012, para A.23
12. HM Revenue and Customs, *The Exchequer Effect of the 50 per cent Additional Rate of Income Tax*, March 2012, para A.21 and Table A2

13 J Browne, *The 50p Income Tax Rate*, Institute for Fiscal Studies, 2012
14 J Browne and D Phillips, *Updating and Critiquing HMRC's Analysis of the UK's Top Rate of Tax*, Institute for Fiscal Studies Working Paper W17/12, 2017, p3
15 J Browne and D Phillips, *Estimating the Size and Nature of Responses to Changes in Income Tax Rates on Top Incomes in the UK: a panel analysis*, Institute for Fiscal Studies Working Paper W17/13, August 2017, p1
16 J Browne and D Phillips, *How Do the Rich Respond to Higher Income Tax Rates?*, Institute for Fiscal Studies Observation, 22 August 2017, p5
17 J Browne and D Phillips, *How Do the Rich Respond to Higher Income Tax Rates?*, Institute for Fiscal Studies Observation, 22 August 2017, p2
18 J Browne and D Phillips, *How Do the Rich Respond to Higher Income Tax Rates?*, Institute for Fiscal Studies Observation, 22 August 2017, p3
19 For example, P Diamond and E Saez, 'The case for a progressive tax: from basic research to policy recommendations', *Journal of Economic Perspectives*, 25(4), 2011, pp165–90; and T Piketty, E Saez and S Stantcheva, 'Optimal taxation of top labor incomes: a tale of three elasticities', *American Economic Journal: Economic Policy*, 6(1), 2014, pp230–71
20 M Brewer and R Kanabar, *The Role of the UK Tax System in an Anti-poverty Strategy: economic principles and practical reforms*, Institute for Social and Economic Research, 2016, p14
21 House of Commons, *Hansard*, answer to parliamentary question, 23 March 2015, cited in S Himmelweit, *Tax and Gender: briefing from the UK Women's Budget Group on the impact of changes in taxation policy on women*, 2018, p2
22 C Emmerson, R Joyce and T Waters, *Stealthy Changes Mean That Soon One in Five Families With Children Will Be Losing Some Child Benefit*, Institute for Fiscal Studies Observation, 7 January 2019, p4
23 Some of this arises, of course, from the very unequal distribution of pre-tax incomes in the UK.
24 HM Revenue and Customs, *UK Income Tax Liabilities Statistics*, May 2018
25 M Wolf, 'How the UK can finance the rising burden of public spending', *Financial Times*, 10 January 2019
26 S Adams and T Waters, 'Options for raising taxes', in C Emmerson, C Farquharson and P Johnson (eds), *The IFS Green Budget: October 2018*, Institute for Fiscal Studies, 2018, pp158–59. Although the distributional consequences of such an approach may not be ideal, it could serve as a vehicle for promulgating the message that paying tax, at all but the lowest levels of income, is an important aspect of citizenship and the only sustainable means to fund the social conditions we all aspire to, including eradicating child poverty. But that should not disguise the need for a more fundamental review of the income tax base and how it might be extended and secured.
27 See A Harrop, *For Us All: redesigning social security, for the 2020s*, Fabian Society, 2016 for a similar proposal. Described as an 'individual credit', it could also be described as a 'partial basic income'. Harrop proposes it could form a universal 'tier' as a foundation for other forms of support. A partial basic income is discussed in more detail in Chapter 10.

Seven
National insurance
Stephen McKay

Origins of national insurance

The current system of national insurance in the UK reflects its origins as a form of insurance that is run at the state level and which insures against several negative life events, in return for financial contributions paid into the system. Some of those events could potentially be the subject of private insurance, but that may be either impracticable (for example, insuring against the need to go into a care home[1]) or expensive (such as health insurance in the USA). National insurance offers the prospect of pooling risks across people, using compulsory membership to avoid some of the problems that may, and on some occasions have, befallen schemes of private insurance. Conversely, car insurance is compulsory but privately provided; home contents insurance is voluntary and privately provided.

Receipts from national insurance payments are paid into the national insurance fund, which is kept separate from tax revenues. This fund is used to pay contributory benefits, largely on a 'pay-as-you-go' basis – current receipts cover current benefits. A small proportion of the national insurance fund is also used to fund the NHS.[2]

The introduction of national insurance under the National Insurance Act 1911[3] was one of the first steps towards creating the system of cash benefits in the UK.[4] Initially, there were two schemes running in parallel: one for health and pension insurance benefits (administered by 'approved societies', including friendly societies and some trade unions) and the other for unemployment benefit (directly administered by the government). However, coverage was restricted to particular occupations (about 2.5 million workers), with many left uncovered. The *Beveridge Report* in 1942 proposed the expansion and unification of the welfare state under a scheme of what is also called social insurance. The architect of the post-war system put it as follows, that the scheme would be:[5]

> ... first and foremost a plan of insurance – of giving in return for contributions benefits up to subsistence levels, as of right and without means test, so that individuals may build freely upon it.

The National Insurance Act 1946 (and National Assistance Act 1948, for means-tested support) established the cash benefit elements of the modern welfare state that persists, at least in some components, today. The underlying idea is that people face several risks that have particularly harmful consequences for their incomes – unemployment, sickness and disability. In time, people may also expect to cease work and to have a period of retirement. National insurance contributions are collected while people are working (or credited in circumstances in which they are unable to contribute – particularly useful not just for those who are unemployed or who cannot work through illness or disability, but also for people caring for children or disabled/older people, often women). The system then pays out when they experience any of the risks identified.

In many countries, the system of social insurance is designed to provide earnings-related benefits rather than the flat-rate benefits common in the UK. A few UK benefits have previously had links to the level of contributions – such as the 'additional pension' that has variously been funded under the graduated retirement benefit (covering contributions made between 1961 and 1975), the state earnings-related pension scheme (SERPS, 1978–2002), the state second pension (S2P, 2002–2016) – but UK benefits are now almost all flat rate. Contributions were also initially set at the same level for all people, until 1975 when these contributions finally ceased to be flat rate and became earnings related.

Some elements of the system reflect the assumptions of the 1940s. Until 2016, those joining non-state pension schemes could elect to have part of their national insurance contributions rebated to such schemes ('contracting-out'), partly incentivising private provision (and creating a scandal of mis-selling of personal pensions). Until 1977, it was possible for married women to pay a much lower rate of contributions (through the 'married women's option') in return for not accumulating rights to the basic state pension and most other contributory benefits. Instead, they had an entitlement (equivalent to 60 per cent of the basic rate), based on their husband's contributions, when they both reached state pension age.[6]

The current system of national insurance

Workers and their employers pay national insurance under several schemes, principally class 1 for employees and class 2 for the self-employed. Class 1 contributions are for employees earning more than £166 a week who are under pension age. They are paid at 12 per cent of earnings above this minimum level, dropping to 2 per cent of earnings above £962 a week. Employer national insurance contributions are a 13.8 per cent tax levied on salaries (above a threshold) paid to employees. Self-employed people contribute on earnings of £6,365 a year or more. Work done through self-employment faces no equivalent of employer national insurance contributions and the main rate is lower than the main rate for employees (9 per cent, rather than 12 per cent).

It is also possible to make voluntary class 3 contributions, to help fill gaps in a national insurance record. Credits towards national insurance are made for those unable to work because of illness, unemployment or caring responsibilities.

A key feature is that national insurance is charged only on *earnings*, not on all sources of income. So, there are no national insurance contributions to pay on income from savings and investments, nor on pension income, nor on earnings after retirement – although all are subject to income tax. Nor does a capital gain on previously held assets attract national insurance contributions, even if these provide the main source of income for some people (capital gains tax applies). Moreover, there are no allowances against national insurance; and it is not levied on all fringe benefits from work (though some of these benefits are captured under a separate class 1A or 1B). To some extent, this may be justified by the nature of the risks insured – the benefits to which there is entitlement relate to loss of *earnings*, and not (for instance) loss of capital income or inadequate capital gains.

These main classes of national insurance act as contributions towards the state pension (all classes), contribution-based jobseeker's allowance (class 1 only), contributory employment and support allowance, and bereavement support payment (classes 1 and 2).

In recent decades, many average workers will have seen more of their earnings taken up with national insurance contributions and less with income tax:[7]

- 1978/79: basic rate of income tax was 33 per cent; national insurance contributions levied at 6.5 per cent above the lower threshold;

- 1989/90: basic rate of income tax was 25 per cent; national insurance contributions levied at 9 per cent above the lower threshold;
- 1999/2000: basic rate of income tax was 23 per cent; national insurance contributions levied at 10 per cent above the lower threshold;
- 2009/10: basic rate of income tax was 20 per cent; national insurance contributions levied at 11 per cent above the lower threshold;
- 2019/20: basic rate of income tax was 20 per cent; national insurance contributions levied at 12 per cent above the lower threshold.

Issues with national insurance

There are several issues with the system of national insurance, both as implemented in the 1940s and subsequently.

Contributions regressive on higher earnings

A built-in aspect is that national insurance contributions are regressive on higher earnings. This reflects the formerly flat-rate system of contributions for flat-rate benefits and, more recently, the fact that, because of ceilings on the amount of benefit paid out, the national insurance system only ever insured a particular segment of earnings.[8] However, national insurance contributions are now firmly earnings related, even if the benefits paid are almost always flat rate, with previous earnings-related benefits now largely abandoned (and, even then, only on a slice of earnings).

The cash payments made do rise as earnings increase (see Figure 7.1). However, while the *proportion* of earnings that goes to national insurance contributions rises with income (progressive) up to the higher limit, it then falls rapidly for those on higher earnings (see Figure 7.2). National insurance contributions are progressive across a wide band of middle and upper earnings, but regressive once earnings exceed around £50,000 a year. Applying the same rate throughout all earnings levels, as happens for the employer contribution, would be progressive while also generating some very large losses of income for those better-off people affected. An increase in the additional rate of 1 percentage point (from the current 2 per cent) would raise about £1 billion.[9]

National insurance 63

Figure 7.1:
National insurance contributions, cash amount by weekly earnings

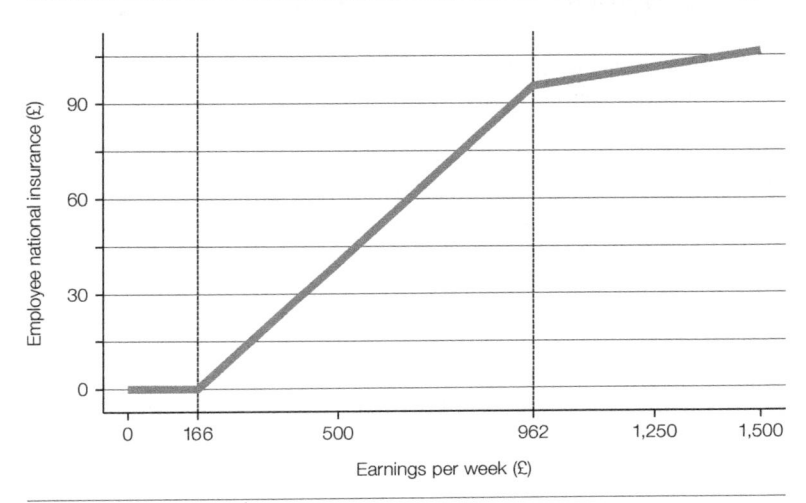

Source: Calculations by author from 2019/20 rates and thresholds.

Figure 7.2:
National insurance contributions, percentage of weekly earnings

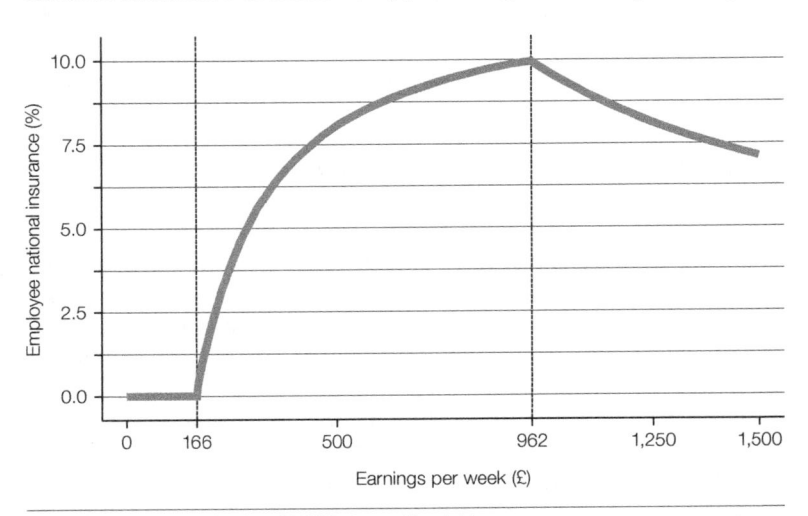

Source: Calculations by author from 2019/20 rates and thresholds.

To the benefit only of workers

National insurance provides cover against well-defined eventualities – such as unemployment and retirement – for those who have made the requisite contributions. It is not a general protection against being on a low income. If people do not have enough contributions, they are ineligible, which includes those just leaving school, perhaps disabled from an early age, or not having had recent contact with the labour market, or those who have exhausted a level of entitlement through long-term receipt of benefits. Many women, who are more likely to work part time, be absent from the labour market for caring responsibilities, and/or receive low pay, may not be able to meet the contribution conditions for benefits, which have been tightened. It used to be possible for a part-time worker to receive part-time unemployment benefit if s/he qualified, and for someone to receive a lower benefit rate if s/he did not meet the full contribution conditions; but neither of these possibilities has existed for some time. It can therefore be argued that in an increasingly flexible labour market the national insurance system has become less flexible.

Risks not covered: 'new social risks'

There are also 'new social risks' that are not covered, such as the risk of family breakdown and the creation of lone-parent families with rather high risks of poverty. Beveridge was aware of this possibility but could not devise a system of separation allowances capable of winning wider approval.

Assumptions about the roles of men and women

National insurance and some related provisions often assumed (and to a lesser extent still do) a particular division of labour within the family and ideas about the protection offered through marriage. Some of the clearer inequities (like the married women's option) have been removed; only recently were benefits equalised for widows and widowers (and mostly levelled down). Some provisions, though challenged in 2018, differ according to marital status. Until civil partnerships (2005) and same-sex marriage (2014), rights did not extend beyond heterosexual unions. Even so, entitlements still flow through formal unions rather than other kinds of relationships. However, at the time of writing the Supreme Court has ruled that unmarried widows might gain benefits designed for married couples.[10]

Subject to state changes

It is, perhaps, easier for the state to make changes to its insurance scheme than it is for private insurers who have legally binding arrangements with their members. So, for example, the Social Security Act 1986 halved the amount of additional pension that could be inherited, from all to 50 per cent. The (then) Department of Social Security (DSS) did not update the information available to the public, and staff gave wrong information when people asked about SERPS – despite the 14-year lead time for the legislation to take effect. The Parliamentary Ombudsman:[11]

> ... finds the Department guilty of maladministration. I strongly criticise DSS for failing to make their leaflets on retirement pensions and surviving spouses' benefits sufficiently comprehensive and up to date in this important respect following the enactment of the 1986 Act, and for their repeated failure to do so until spring 1996.

A long-term policy to equalise men's and women's state pension ages between 2010 and 2020 was sped up for women, with an influential campaign arguing that insufficient notice and information was provided, particularly for women born during the 1950s.[12] When state pensions were introduced in 1908, the state pension age was established at 70; this was then reduced to 65 in 1925, but then in 1940 was further dropped to 60 for women, but not men.

The self-employed

Self-employed workers enjoy an advantage in paying lower national insurance contributions than employees, and now receive more comparable benefits following the removal of earnings-related pension provision in the new state pension. A recent move to increase their level of contributions in the 2017 Budget had to be quickly reversed in the teeth of strong opposition to moves that affected this diverse group, often on lower earnings.[13] The self-employed are a growing part of the UK labour force: rising from 3.3 million people in 2001 to 4.8 million (15 per cent of the labour force) in 2017.[14]

Employers

Employers make separate national insurance contributions. Splitting the formal incidence of national insurance between employee and employer may change the headline rate paid by workers, but that does not mean that people are somehow exempt from the effects of higher employer contributions – whether as workers, customers or shareholders. However, there is some evidence that the effective incidence of employer payments is not fully on the workforce,[15] meaning that increases in employer national insurance contributions do not simply lead to reduced wages – the legal structure being of significance, rather than irrelevant, to the question of who ultimately pays.

Options for reforming national insurance

Integration with income tax

The above history was partly to clarify that national insurance is distinct from tax and, in particular, from the system of income taxation. For many observers, and particularly some economists, the distinctions between these two are relatively unimportant, regarded as some kind of historic anomalies that are best swept aside in favour of a single system of direct taxation that was more 'rational'. For them, there is little reason not to merge the national insurance system with the income tax system. According to the *Mirrlees Review*:[16]

> National insurance is not a true social insurance scheme; it is just another tax on earnings, and the current system invites politicians to play games with [national insurance contributions].

However, clearly there are strong institutional differences between the schemes, in terms of the kinds of income on which the different charges are levied, and the periods over which assessments are currently made (annual for income tax; relating to pay period for national insurance). Others have instead noted the 'market failures' within private insurance that prevent companies providing adequate support against the relevant risks.

Convergence with income tax

Although there are clear problems with a complete merger with income tax, there are ways in which the systems could be brought closer together. In particular, the exclusion of many forms of income from the remit of national insurance could be considered – ie, income from pensions, savings and capital gains. This would potentially generate sizeable revenues, and not require full integration.[17] Others have argued in favour of raising the threshold at which employees' contributions start to be paid, reaching that of income tax.[18]

'Back to Beveridge': revitalising national insurance

Discussions about integration overlook the potential importance of the 'insurance principle' inherent in national insurance, and its potentially greater support as a form of social security. Social insurance is different from private insurance: there is no expectation of higher contributions from those facing the most risks, avoiding 'adverse selection'. As a payment in return for rights, it is generally thought to be more widely supported than other types of fiscal transfer (ie, taxes) levied by the central government. It also includes all workers, not simply redistributing from higher to lower income (even if particular elements are redistributive). There are enough issues with the Beveridgean vision to be sceptical about a wholesale return to that system, but other approaches may be considered. The Commission on Social Justice proposed such ideas during the mid-1990s, but even in such fertile times for policy development it did not win much support, and it quickly 'faded into obscurity'.[19]

Conclusions

Beveridge reminded us that social insurance was only one part of the necessary elements for social progress – capable of slaying only one of his five giants ('want') on the road to reconstruction. It would therefore be wrong to consider tax finance in isolation from other factors. Nevertheless, the direction of national insurance in the UK seems clear. As with social security more generally, the recent emphasis has been on securing the living standards of older people, particularly those receiving the state pension. Those of working age have seen their contributory entitlements slowly chipped away, with now rather fewer contributory benefits for those of working age. The introduction of universal credit confirms the move towards a form of negative income tax, introduced at the same time as entitlement to some contributory benefits was shortened. At the same time, the amounts levied through national insurance contributions have been rising compared to income tax, at least on the earnings of the average worker.

Many countries – from the neoliberal USA to the social democratic Nordics – have contributory entitlements of a more secure and more generous basis compared with the UK. However, Australia and New Zealand have never embraced such an approach. It seems difficult to envisage a move to high contributory benefits, which have not really been part of the UK system – although in terms of the extension of social insurance, both the areas of potential reforms, that is parental leave and social care (both particularly beneficial for women), can be envisaged as being dealt with in this way. Nor does the full integration of tax and national insurance appear feasible and would in any case create lots of winners and losers. Where reforms could gain traction is in a wider base for national insurance than at present. Earnings are affected by both national insurance contributions and income tax, in a way not levied on other forms of incomes.

Recommendations

- From time to time, analysts and others consider the scope for integrating income tax with national insurance contributions. We reject such wholesale reform as likely to be unworkable, particularly in the short term. Such a reform would create large numbers of winners and losers.

- Despite rejecting complete integration of income tax and national insurance contributions, further moves to have consistency in their application are sensible. In particular, the rises in the point at which income tax is paid have far outstripped where national insurance contributions begin to be payable is in need of review.

- The relative regressivity of national insurance contributions arises from the upper earnings limit. Lifting this limit could generate relatively large amounts of revenue – which, under current rules, however, would need to be spent on contributory benefits or possibly the NHS. The national insurance system could be made more inclusive, in relation to people in the 'flexible labour market' and those on low pay, with particularly beneficial effects for women. It would be important to do this while at the same time ensuring that the advantage of people feeling they have a stake in the national insurance system was maintained.

Notes

1 A Dilnot, *Fairer Care Funding: the report of the Commission on Funding of Care and Support*, 2011
2 For fuller details see A Seely, *National Insurance Contributions (NICs): an introduction*, House of Commons Briefing Paper SN04517, 2017
3 See *Journal of Poverty and Social Justice*, 19(3), 2011, a special edition on 'The centenary of the 1911 National Insurance Act in Britain', for more details.
4 N Whiteside, 'Social protection in Britain 1900–1950 and welfare state development: the case of health insurance', in S Castillo and R Ruztafa (eds), *La Previsión Social en la Historia*, Siglo XXI, pp519–531, 2009 mentions antecedents too.
5 W Beveridge, *Social Insurance and Allied Services*, HM Stationery Office, 1942; Institute for Public Policy Research, *Social Justice: strategies for national renewal – the report of the Commission on Social Justice*, Vintage, 1994, para 10
6 D Thurley and R Keen, *State Pension Age Increases for Women Born in the 1950s*, House of Commons Briefing Paper CBP-7405, 2017
7 Institute for Fiscal Studies, 'Fiscal facts: tax and benefits', www.ifs.org.uk/tools_and_resources/fiscal_facts
8 Statutory maternity pay does pay 90 per cent of earnings, but for only six weeks, and although this is part of the social protection system, it is not usually seen as a social insurance benefit, because the employer pays it out.
9 HM Revenue and Customs, *Direct Effects of Illustrative Tax Changes*, KAI Indirect Taxes, Customs and Coordination, April 2019
10 *In the matter of an application by McLaughlin for Judicial Review (Northern Ireland)* [2018] UKSC 48, www.supremecourt.uk/cases/docs/uksc-2017-0035-judgment.pdf
11 Parliamentary Ombudsman, *State Earnings-related Pension Scheme (SERPS) Inheritance Provisions* (3rd Report for Session 1999–2000), HC 305, The Stationery Office, 2000
12 But see H Pemberton, 'WASPI's is (mostly) a campaign for inequality', *The Political Quarterly*, 88(3), 2017, pp510–16
13 F Bennett, 'Social protection for the self-employed in the UK: the disappearing contributions increase', *Journal of Poverty and Social Justice*, Policy Press, 2019
14 Office for National Statistics, *Trends in Self-employment in the UK*, February 2018
15 See S Adam, B Roantree and D Phillips, 'The incidence of social security contributions in the United Kingdom: evidence from discontinuities at contribution ceilings', *De Economist*, 165(2), 2017, pp181–203
16 Institute for Fiscal Studies and J Mirrlees (eds), *Tax by Design: the Mirrlees Review*, Oxford University Press, 2011
17 Office of Tax Simplification, *Closer Alignment of Income Tax and National Insurance: a further review*, Cm9354, 2016
18 Quite recently, T Clougherty, *Make Work Pay: a new agenda for fairer taxes*, Centre for Policy Studies, 2018
19 C Haddon, *Making Policy in Opposition: the Commission on Social Justice, 1992–1994*, Institute for Government, 2012, p11

Eight
Taxation, couples and children
Fran Bennett

Introduction

In *Changing Tax*, there were two sections on what was then called 'the taxation of husband and wife'.[1] This was because the report was published in 1988, on the cusp of significant changes to the taxation of married couples (and lone parents). One chapter dealt with the situation prior to the changes in 1990, and one with alternatives to the proposed changes to be introduced at that time. Today, the taxation of couples also involves same-sex partners in marriages and civil partnerships.

This chapter also includes a discussion of child benefit. This is in part because it replaced not just family allowances, a cash benefit, but also the child tax allowance, and is equivalent to an allowance for children within the income tax system. In addition, currently it may also affect couples' income tax bills, as we saw in Chapter 5, because of a recent policy change. But we do not go beyond this here to discuss other elements of the taxation of couples.[2]

It might be thought that the taxation of couples in the UK was settled in 1990, when the independent taxation of husband and wife was introduced. However, debate about the issue continues. First, some interpreted the joint means testing of couples' resources for tax credits, introduced in 1999 and reformed in 2003, as contradicting the principle of independent taxation.[3] The then government denied this – though it may ideally have wanted to bring in tax credits by incorporating a means test based on household incomes in the income tax system. In reality, tax credits were just another variety of means-tested benefits – even if some were initially paid through the pay packet by employers, and thus offset against income tax due. However, answers to parliamentary questions insisted that the important issue was the combined effect of income tax, national insurance contributions and tax credits, leading to somewhat surreal calculations of apparently negative 'tax rates' for households.

In addition, some actual policy changes since 1990 have, to some degree, turned the clock back, in that someone may find the income of her/his married/civil partner taken into account as well as her/his own in the income tax system. This is due to two recent policy measures: the transferable tax allowance and the high-income child benefit tax charge (the latter also including cohabitees, and lone parents). So we need to examine the reasons for these policies and their implications.

The ongoing debate is significant for two additional reasons. First, it involves a key, more general, issue – the appropriate unit of taxation. While tax is levied in practice on incomes (or assets), not people, a decision must be made in relation to income tax about whether to amalgamate the incomes or assets of people living together, and when that may be appropriate. And the consequences of doing so need to be considered, including the impact on individuals' incentives and the likelihood of affecting the degree of (in)equality of income between partners.[4]

So the taxation of couples is just as relevant now as it was nearly 30 years ago. In addition, given current equality concerns, we should arguably be interested in principle in the resources available to individual men and women over their life course, regardless of their decisions about their marital/civil partnership status, not just the position of households at a point in time.

Secondly, although 'taxation is often represented as operating within a distinct realm of economic policy in which gender considerations are extraneous',[5] Susan Himmelweit of the Women's Budget Group[6] argues that the fiscal system as a whole does have a gendered impact.[7] This is in part because the public expenditure financed by taxation is often of particular benefit to women, due to their greater likelihood of having lower incomes and of caring for dependants (which are often interrelated). Tax cuts, on the other hand, disproportionately benefit men, as they tend to have higher incomes; and this has increasingly been the case in the UK recently, as repeated increases in the personal tax allowance benefit fewer and fewer women on low earnings, since many have already been taken out of the range of income tax by previous cuts.

History

Prior to 1990, husbands' and wives' incomes were amalgamated for income tax purposes. This was because at that time husbands were legally responsible for the payment of tax on their wives' incomes, which were treated as though they belonged to them as well, and taxation was joint for married couples. In recognition of his wife's presumed dependence, a husband received the married man's tax allowance. From 1942, wives could get the same level of allowance as a single person – the wife's earned income allowance – if they were in employment.[8] Lone parents got the same as married men, through an additional personal allowance; female breadwinner couples received as much in allowances as two-earner couples.

One of the key campaigns of the women's movement in the UK in the late 1970s and early 1980s was for 'legal and financial independence' for women.[9] A specific demand was for the independent treatment of women in the income tax system. A wider group of women was also increasingly protesting about letters on their tax affairs being sent to their husbands, and wanted privacy and control. Pressure on the Conservative government led to a Green Paper in 1986.[10]

The issue preoccupying the government seemed to be not so much the tax treatment of men versus women, or even people with children versus those without, but instead the balance between single- and dual-earner couples, and especially the desire not to disadvantage traditional single-earner (usually 'male breadwinner') families. The Labour government that took office in 1997 seemed to have a similar focus when discussing the need for a 'family-friendly tax system'.[11] Policy makers arguing in favour of supporting one-earner families often do not ask why one adult may be out of the labour market, or whether it may make more sense to direct any additional resources to them rather than to their partner; and they tend not to focus on gender inequality, or challenge a traditional division of labour. In addition, they often examine the resources available to the household as a whole at one point in time, rather than the incomes of the individuals making up that household in a more dynamic perspective.

One option put forward from this perspective in the 1986 Green Paper was a tax allowance that would be transferable between spouses. But such an arrangement would have supported the partner in work (usually the man) and resulted in disincentives for a potential 'second earner'. It would also have used up resources that could instead be used for social priorities, including support for all those with children regardless of marital or employment status. It was rejected.

As noted, independent taxation was introduced in 1990, and married women started dealing with their own tax affairs. The married man's allowance (later the married couple's allowance) was retained, however, to avoid creating losers. This was, as John Hills notes in *Changing Tax*, very poorly targeted.[12] In later years, it was first reduced (by a Conservative government) and then phased out (by a Labour government), except for couples aged 65 or over.[13] The argument of the women's lobby and poverty groups was that support for marriage (or assumed adult dependence within marriage) should be replaced by support for indisputable cases of dependence, such as children, and other care relationships. But the resources saved were not used for increasing child benefit and helping carers, as these groups and others had suggested. Labour briefly introduced a 'children's tax credit' as part of the income tax system in 2001, but this was abolished in 2003, with the new tax credits.[14] And even today, married couples and civil partners are still treated differently from unregistered cohabiting couples in some other parts of the tax system – for example, for capital gains tax and inheritance tax.[15] Indeed, Gordon Brown as Prime Minister in effect doubled the inheritance tax allowance for married couples.[16] But these areas of the tax system are not examined here in relation to taxing couples.

The introduction of independent taxation has often been characterised as benefiting better-off women in particular. Those on lower incomes do not pay income tax; and women with more savings benefited more from the separation of their income from their husbands', as investment income as well as earnings was treated separately as a result.[17] However, measures could have been taken simultaneously to increase taxation on better-off individuals, but were not; and the investment income surcharge was abolished in 1985, before independent taxation was introduced.

Recent changes

It is often argued that we have independent assessment for taxation and joint assessment for benefits. Neither of these statements is wholly correct. In relation to tax, under the coalition government (2010 to 2015) pressure from traditionalist groups such as Christian Action Research and Education (CARE)[18] resulted in the introduction of a partially transferable tax allowance for married couples and civil partners in 2015. As Chapters 5 and 6 explain, when one spouse or civil partner has no taxable income and the other pays tax only at the basic rate, up to 10 per cent of their unused personal tax allowance (£1,250 in 2019/20) can be transferred to the tax-paying partner. As the personal tax allowance is raised in real terms, this partial transfer becomes increasingly valuable.

However, there have been many criticisms of this move,[19] in part because the transferable allowance breaches the principles of independent taxation and increases the incentive to be a traditional one-earner family. Neither does it go to the partner at home with no income, or an income too low to pay tax, but instead to the higher earner in the couple – 85 per cent of whom are men – on the assumption that support will be provided. As the then Prime Minister said with great clarity: 'if... your partner doesn't use all of their personal tax allowance, you'll be able to have some of it'.[20]

In addition, it was estimated that only one in three married couples would be entitled, many of them pensioners, and only 18 per cent of families with children would benefit. The take-up in practice, however, has been much lower, with HM Revenue and Customs warning in 2017 that two million couples were losing out,[21] although take-up is now some 60 per cent.[22] While the government argued that this move was only a 'signal' about the importance of marriage and civil partnership, and while the payment is too small to have much impact on incentives not to earn an independent income (at under £4 per week on its introduction), some commentators have argued that it could be the thin end of a wedge to be expanded in future. Instead, it is argued, if partners with no or little income should be supported, this should be done directly, for example through well-paid parental leave and carers' leave, rather than increasing the income of their partners and widening the differential within the couple.

In addition, in 2013 the coalition government introduced the high-income child benefit charge (more accurately on the government website called the 'high income child benefit tax charge').[23] The justification was that those on higher incomes should contribute to reducing the deficit at a time of austerity. However, this charge only applies to better-off people who are raising children at the time. In addition, tax cuts implemented then and since have benefited those on higher incomes, but child benefit is being frozen for four years. Thus, the balance in the fiscal system between those with and without children has been skewed in favour of the childless.

The way the charge works is that when someone in a couple is claiming child benefit, if her/his income and/or that of her/his partner is higher than £50,000 per year, this person must pay the high-income child benefit charge. This imposes additional income tax worth 1 per cent of the child benefit for each £100 of income above this, until this is equal to the amount of child benefit at £60,000 per year.[24] (The marginal tax rate imposed therefore rises with each additional child.) This also applies to lone parents. It has been argued that this may create a disincentive to asking for promotion or a pay rise, because of the high marginal tax rate created. The Institute for Fiscal Studies has estimated that one in five families may lose some child benefit because of this in the near future.[25]

The only way to avoid this outcome is for the claimant (usually the mother) to give up child benefit. Over half a million people chose to do this in 2016/17.[26] This has caused concern, as a claim is necessary for state pension rights to be maintained while someone is at home caring for a child, and many mothers are reportedly failing to claim at all because of the charge.[27] There is a way to preserve the right to pension in this situation. But this requires additional knowledge and action.

So, while universal credit was introduced to simplify the benefits system, the income tax system was simultaneously through these two moves being made much more complicated. It is also difficult to see a coherent and justifiable rationale for either move.

Issues at stake

In *Changing Tax*, John Hills argued that taxing married couples (now civil partners too) raises problems which cannot be resolved in a wholly satisfactory way.[28] He saw the issues as being about the objectives of an income tax system, which could include being progressive, with people on higher incomes paying a higher proportion of their income in tax; being neutral towards marriage; and being independent of the distribution of income between the members of the couple, in terms of how much tax is levied. Stuart Adam makes similar points.[29] The decision on whether to have independent or joint taxation may therefore depend on how important each of these principles is thought to be; whether progressivity is measured on the basis of the individual or couple; and whether other principles are also thought to be important, and amenable to being achieved at least in part through the arrangements for taxing couples.

Giving some weight to the idea that everyone should be encouraged to have autonomy, that this is more likely if they have their own independent income, and that there should be greater equality between women and men suggests that independent taxation is preferable. Having two earners in a couple is also an important way to tackle in-work poverty, particularly among families with children.[30] If this is so, it is important to recognise the impact of joint taxation on the work incentives of the potential 'second earner' in a couple – and the fact that 'second earners' are usually shown to be more sensitive to the operation of work incentives.

In addition, Fran Bennett and Susan Himmelweit argued in favour of additional principles for a tax system, including taking into account family costs (taxable capacity), to ensure that those with similar incomes but different costs have a similar standard of living.[31] This is sometimes called 'horizontal equity' in tax jargon. In the UK, this has been achieved through child benefit since the late 1970s, when it replaced both family allowances and child tax allowances. We also suggested principles of fairness within households, as above, in terms of a more equitable division of income between partners; and autonomy for all, by enabling everyone to have an independent income and the chance to earn. We supported the idea that the tax someone pays should not be influenced by the presence or actions of a partner (equivalent to tax neutrality towards marriage – or partnership). We recognised, as did Hills and Adam, that some of these principles are in tension. But none of them suggests a case for subsidising marriage or civil partnership, which create no needs in and of themselves.

Indeed, assuming and incorporating one partner's dependence on the other into the tax system seems even less well suited to today's families, which are increasingly fluid and flexible; so the case for independent taxation could be seen as being stronger today than when introduced in 1990, especially with increasing numbers of complex families and growing individualisation of savings, investments and debts.[32] The case for 'horizontal equity' in taxation – in relation to actual fiscal dependence, meaning in particular the presence of children – is also strong, and justifies child benefit for all those with children at whatever income level, with additional tax paid by all who are better off if that is thought desirable.[33] Our concern should be with the balance of resources within households as well as between them, and the implications of policy measures for roles and relationships, opportunities and income trajectories for individuals both now and over the whole life-course.[34] But we must also recognise that taxation can only ever be one part of a much broader strategy to achieve a more equitable distribution of resources.

Recommendations

In the short term

- Abolish the transferable tax allowance for married couples and civil partnerships.
- Abolish the high-income child benefit charge and restore the real value of child benefit following the four-year freeze and earlier failures to uprate it in line with inflation.

In the longer term

- Introduce improvements to parental leave payments and other non-means-tested benefits to replace earnings in order to provide (more generous) resources directly to non-earning individuals, including those in couples.
- Increase child benefit at least in line with inflation, and by more than this if personal tax allowances are increased by more.
- Consider other reforms to the tax system as a whole to make it more gender sensitive. Suggestions are made in the relevant chapters in this report.

Notes
1. J Hills, *Changing Tax: how the tax system works and how to change it*, CPAG, 1988, pp23–27
2. For an overview of gender and taxation, see S Himmelweit, *Gender Impact of Taxation*, Women's Budget Group, 2017.
3. For example, discussed in F Bennett, 'Gender issues in tax reform: the example of the UK', unpublished paper for 'Gender, tax policies and tax reform in comparative perspective' conference organised by Levy Economics Institute, Bard College, USA, 17–18 May 2006
4. This is considered for nine European countries using the microsimulation model EUROMOD in F Figari and others, 'Inequalities within couples: market incomes and the role of taxes and benefits within Europe', *Eastern Economic Journal*, 37(3), 2011, pp344–66.
5. B Cass and D Brennan, 'Taxing women: the politics of gender in the tax/transfer system', *eJournal of Tax Research*, 1(1), 2003, pp37–63
6. The Women's Budget Group is an independent network of leading academic researchers, policy experts and campaigners analysing public spending and Budgets: www.wbg.org.uk.
7. S Himmelweit, *Gender Impact of Taxation*, Women's Budget Group, 2017
8. The situation was rather more complex for married couples whose income took them into the higher rate band. See J Hills, *Changing Tax: how the tax system works and how to change it*, CPAG, 1988, p23
9. R Lister, 'Being feminist', *Government and Opposition*, 40(3), 2005, pp442–63
10. HM Treasury, *The Reform of Personal Taxation*, Green Paper, Cmnd 9756, 1986
11. G Brown, Budget speech, 17 April 2002
12. J Hills, *Changing Tax: how the tax system works and how to change it*, CPAG, 1988, p24
13. The same process took place in relation to the linked additional personal allowance for lone parents.
14. F Bennett, 'Myths about the tax and benefit system', *Benefits*, 11(3), 2003, pp199–200(2)
15. Low Incomes Tax Reform Group, *Couples in the Tax and Related Welfare Systems: a call for greater clarity*, Chartered Institute of Taxation, 2015, especially Chapter 4
16. 'Inheritance taxes cut for couples', BBC News, 9 October 2007, http://news.bbc.co.uk/1/hi/7034399.stm
17. See J Hills, *Changing Tax: how the tax system works and how to change it*, CPAG, 1988, p24, for more detail on this.

18 Christian Action Research and Education, 'Family and tax', www.care.org.uk/our-causes/marriage-and-family/family-and-tax. Some of the same people are also involved in an offshoot called Tax and the Family: www.taxandthefamily.org.
19 For example, F Bennett and S Himmelweit, *Recognising Marriage in the Tax System will not Benefit Women*, Women's Budget Group, 2013
20 In 'Marriage is good for Britain – and that's why I'm backing it with a tax break, says David Cameron', *Daily Mail*, 27 September 2013; and see 'Marriage transferable tax allowance announced by government', HM Treasury press release, 30 September 2013
21 B Milligan, 'Two million couples missing out on tax break, says HMRC', BBC News, 22 September 2017, www.bbc.co.uk/news/business-41365084
22 S Adam, 'Taxing families', presentation for joint Institute for Fiscal Studies and Chartered Institute of Taxation meeting, 26 June 2018
23 www.gov.uk/child-benefit-tax-charge
24 Income is calculated in a specific way for this purpose, as 'adjusted net income' – for example, disregarding pension payments and charitable donations. See www.gov.uk/child-benefit-tax-charge for more information.
25 C Emmerson, R Joyce and T Waters, *Stealthy Changes Mean That Soon One in Five Families With Children Will Be Losing Some Child Benefit*, Institute for Fiscal Studies Observation, 7 January 2019
26 S Adam, 'Taxing families', presentation for joint Institute for Fiscal Studies and Chartered Institute of Taxation meeting, 26 June 2018
27 'Stay-at-home parents risk losing out on pensions', Treasury Committee press release, 26 July 2018
28 J Hills, *Changing Tax: how the tax system works and how to change it*, CPAG, 1988, Chapters 8 and 9
29 S Adam, 'Taxing families', presentation for joint Institute for Fiscal Studies and Chartered Institute of Taxation meeting, 26 June 2018
30 K Lawton and S Thompson, *Tackling In-work Poverty by Supporting Dual-earning Families*, Joseph Rowntree Foundation, 2013
31 F Bennett and S Himmelweit, *Recognising Marriage in the Tax System will not Benefit Women*, Women's Budget Group, 2013
32 H Laurie and MY Kan, 'Changing patterns in the allocation of savings, investments and debts', *Sociological Review*, 62(2), 2014, pp335–58
33 See, for example, F Bennett with P Dornan, *Child Benefit: fit for the future*, CPAG, 2006
34 Principles cited in J Veitch with F Bennett, *A Gender Perspective on 21st Century Welfare Reform*, Oxfam, 2010, adapted from M Daly and K Rake, *Gender and the Welfare State: care, work and welfare in Europe and the USA*, Polity Press, 2003

Nine
Tackling tax reliefs
Adrian Sinfield

Chapters 5 and 6 describe the basic tax structure. This chapter further explores tax reliefs and related subsidies, their costs and how little we know about who gets what from them. Governments affect people's and organisations' activities and resources by directly financing services and benefits. They can also decide not to tax income, capital and other resources to support and encourage certain objectives, such as saving for private pensions, making use of childcare and promoting home ownership.

Using tax reliefs is not tax avoidance: that is examined in Chapter 20. Effectively, government policies are being run through the tax system. They are not part of the 'tax gap', but can be seen as what Richard Murphy has called 'the tax policy gap'. This is:[1]

> ... the value of the tax reliefs, allowances and exemptions given by a government for offset against a source of income that might otherwise be taxable. So tax is not paid, but no one avoided it: the government had no intention that it should be paid.

However, as Chapter 20 makes clear, these reliefs can, and have been, exploited in 'fiscally exciting ways' to reduce tax bills.

The main form of tax relief in the UK is a tax allowance set against the individual's marginal rate of income tax. The marginal rate is the highest rate that would be paid were it not for the allowance. A tax allowance of £1,000 provides someone with an income below the personal tax allowance of £12,500 a year with no benefit at all. Someone paying only the basic rate of 20 per cent saves £200 a year on a tax allowance of £1,000, but anyone also liable to the higher rate of 40 per cent saves £400. Liability to the additional rate of 45 per cent saves £450 (slightly different rates apply in Scotland).

So the higher the income, the greater the absolute benefit from a tax allowance with one important exception since 2010: the personal allowances of those with taxable incomes over £100,000 a year are phased out, so they receive no benefit at all from these allowances above £125,000. ('Taxable income' is after deducting, for example, pension contributions and charitable donations.) In addition, a few tax reliefs are not available above an income of £100,000, or are restricted in other ways.

Most reliefs are 'upside-down' benefits because they provide more to those with higher incomes who would generally be regarded as having fewer needs.[2] 'Means-enhancing', they reinforce inequalities, in marked contrast to the very many public spending benefits which are means tested and so limited to those on lower incomes. They tend to benefit men more than women and those without children more than those with children because of the relative position of these groups in the income distribution.

The known scale and distribution of tax and related reliefs

Many income tax reliefs have a very long history, but accounting for them is still not well developed. Estimates only began to be released annually in the late 1970s. In 2011, it became evident that HM Revenue and Customs (HMRC) only listed 400 of the 1,042 that the Office of Tax Simplification identified.[3] Some have since been abolished, but more have been introduced. The Office of Tax Simplification classified virtually half as special cases for special interest groups, targeted to influence behaviour and/or establishing thresholds for exemptions. The National Audit Office and the Public Accounts Committee have been very critical:[4]

> Despite our repeated recommendations, HMRC still does not make tax reliefs sufficiently visible to support parliamentary scrutiny and public debate about areas where the UK chooses not to collect tax.

Some more detail, scrutiny and research have resulted, but still costs are only estimated for under 200 reliefs.

An independent report concluded: 'No one in either the Treasury or HMRC is accountable for either the value for money or the cost of tax measures.'[5] On the most expensive income tax relief, for pensions, there has been no value for money assessment but 'widespread acknowledgement that tax relief is not an effective or well-targeted way of incentivising saving into pensions'.[6]

The HMRC list of what it now calls 'estimated costs of principal tax reliefs' is divided into three categories. Tax expenditures 'help or encourage particular types of individuals, activities or products for economic or social objectives'. Structural reliefs 'can reasonably be regarded (or partly regarded) as an integral part of the tax structure' and, finally, some reliefs have both tax expenditure and structural components.[7] What is, or is not, a tax expenditure is much debated nationally and internationally. The near doubling of the cost of the basic personal allowance in eight years raises questions as to whether it is only structural, especially while basic working-age benefits have been frozen. Some examples of costed reliefs from the HMRC list are shown in Table 9.1.

Most of the main income tax reliefs over and above the personal allowances with any welfare function subsidise some form of private social policy provision – for example, private pensions, childcare, exemption of the first £30,000 paid on termination of employment. In 2018/19, their cost came to some £27 billion, equivalent to some 15 per cent of the income tax actually collected.

Significant insulation from austerity

These reliefs have not been subject to the same 'austerity' regime that, we are told, has required considerable cuts to public spending and, in particular, reductions or freezes of the social security benefits needed by those on very low incomes. Very few tax reliefs have been reduced, except those for private and occupational pensions. Yet pension tax relief still costs £25.6 billion net (ie, after deducting tax on pensions currently in payment). National insurance contribution exemptions on payments into these private pensions cost another £18.1 billion. Despite substantial limits on the higher paid, those on what HMRC terms 'adjusted' incomes above £210,000 a year are still entitled to claim income tax relief up to £4,500 on pension contributions. This works out at £86.50 a week, £13.40 more a week than the basic, and currently frozen, contributory and income-based benefits of £73.10.

Contributory benefits are financed by the national insurance fund. Were some of the £18 billion of national insurance exemptions effectively supporting private pensions reduced, this public benefit would not have to be frozen. National insurance is a basic pillar of the welfare state intended to meet need, not to benefit indirectly those with incomes even above £210,000 while most working-age national insurance recipients are on very much lower incomes.

Table 9.1:
Some tax and related reliefs, 2018/19 forecasts

	£ million
Income tax	
Relief for non-state pensions (net)	25,600
Marriage allowance (mixed)	910
Employer-supported childcare	430
Exemption of first £30,000 paid on termination of employment	900
Income tax exemptions of benefits (mixed)	
Child benefit	1,165
Long-term disability benefits	1,635
Income tax personal allowances (structural)	108,150
National insurance contribution exemptions	
Employer contributions to approved pensions	18,100
Employer-supported childcare	370
Capital gains tax	
Gains arising on disposal of only or main residence	27,200
Inheritance tax (mixed)	
Nil rate band for chargeable transfer below threshold for estates left on death	17,000
Exemption of transfers on death to surviving spouse	2,530
VAT	
Zero-rating food	18,600
Zero-rating domestic and international transport	5,450
Domestic fuel and power, reduced rate	4,850
Climate change levies relief (structural)	730

Notes:
1 Estimates in £ millions on basis of revenue foregone.
2 Tax expenditures, except where indicated.
3 Mixed = both tax expenditure and structural components.
4 Child benefit now omitted from HMRC list, latest previous year included.

Source: HM Revenue and Customs, *Estimated Costs of Tax Reliefs*, Bulletin, KAI Indirect Taxes, Customs and Coordination, 31 January 2019

There is no regular distributional analysis for tax reliefs. Occasional estimates are released for pensions tax relief alone. In 2015/16, about half of pensions tax relief went to the top 10 per cent of income tax payers while the bottom half got just over 10 per cent.[8] In fact, this may underestimate the imbalance, as it is doubtful that this includes the relief on investment funds. Then, nearly £8 billion, it made up one-fifth of the total cost of income tax reliefs for pensions (no estimate for capital gains tax relief).[9]

The scale of tax reliefs going to the better off helps to explain the lack of progressivity in total taxes (see also Chapter 1). Contrary to widespread belief, the official annual survey reveals that the total tax system has long been, at best, basically proportionate, not progressive, with a continuing higher incidence of total taxes on the bottom fifth of households, those with the least money. By 2016/17, the bottom fifth's total taxes had risen to 38.6 per cent of their gross income from 35 per cent the previous year, not only clearly above the average (34.2 per cent), but also above the top fifth (34.4 per cent).[10] The reduction in the total tax take due to reliefs means that less money has been made available to public services and social security payments (from which low-income families, and women in particular, benefit). The effect is doubly problematic.

The need for policy action

Tax reliefs and tax expenditures have received increasing attention from bodies such as the Institute for Fiscal Studies, the Resolution Foundation, the Fabian Society, the Institute for Public Policy Research and Tax Justice UK. International agencies are taking more account, with the World Bank asserting that tax expenditure 'violates' both vertical and horizontal equity.[11] Since 2014, the European Commission has required member states to provide tax expenditure reports. A 2016 OECD working paper, *Tax Design for Inclusive Economic Growth*, argued that:[12]

> Scaling back tax expenditures that are not well-targeted at redistributive objectives may help achieve both greater efficiency and a narrower distribution of disposable income.

Fuller analysis of benefits and value for money

To obtain a fairer and more efficient system, we need, first of all, much more published evidence and open discussion about the aims and achievements of the great range of tax reliefs and related subsidies. What are the costs? How equitable are they? What value for money do they provide? Which should we keep or modify to reduce inequalities? These need to be regularly evaluated by the National Audit Office and Public Accounts Committee.

A particular shortcoming is the lack of regular and comprehensive data on the distribution of the resulting benefit to recipients. In the largely hidden world of means-enhancing tax reliefs 'subterranean politics… allow policies to pass that would not survive if subjected to the bright light of political scrutiny or the cold calculations of accurate budgeting'.[13]

In the official household survey, the bottom half of households has been shown to receive more from the government than it pays into it, while the top half pays in more than it receives.[14] This encourages the claim that the better off are having to bear the 'burden of the welfare state' as part of the 'burden' of taxation. But that argument does not take account of the benefits from tax and related reliefs. A special independent analysis for 2004/05 showed that the top 10 per cent of taxpayers gained 70 per cent of the benefits from tax reliefs over and above the personal allowances.[15] Regularly including the impact of tax reliefs in the effect of taxes and benefits on incomes could lead to better-informed debate and policy making on how far taxation affects the distribution of resources across society.

Allocate tax spending and public spending together

Fairer allocation between tax reliefs and social security benefits would be easier to achieve if spending through the tax system were regularly considered alongside public spending. Used in budgetary decision making in Canada and the USA for some years, this arrangement was stopped after changes in government.

In Table 9.2 well over one-quarter of the total public and tax spending of some £150 billion for retirement is directed to private pensions and mostly benefits the better off, but this is very little known.[16]

Table 9.2:
Comparison of main public and fiscal spending on social security in retirement, 2017/18

	Total £ billion	Percentage
Pension credit	£5.37	3.6%
State pension	£93.8	62.6%
Housing benefit (older only)	£5.9	3.9%
Winter fuel payments	£2.02	1.4%
Other public benefits	£1.06	0.7%
Total public spending	**£108.13**	**72.2%**
Income tax reliefs net	£24.3	16.2%
National insurance exemptions	£17.4	11.6%
Total fiscal welfare	**£41.7**	**27.8%**
Total 'public' and 'tax' spending	**£149.83**	**100%**

Source: Department for Work and Pensions, *Annual Report and Accounts 2017/18*, HC 1108, June 2018; HM Revenue and Customs, *Estimated Costs of Tax Reliefs*, Bulletin, KAI Indirect Taxes, Customs and Coordination, 31 January 2019

Reduce inconsistencies in treatment between tax and benefits

There should be more consistent treatment of tax reliefs and social security benefits. For example, the ceiling for the new tax-free childcare system is an income of £100,000 per year, while the point for starting to reduce child benefit is only £50,000.

Another example is provided by above-inflation increases in personal tax allowances, while most working-age benefits in public spending (including child benefit) are being frozen for four years till 2020, after being held to 1 per cent for some earlier years. Since April 2012, the main working-age benefits have risen by 3 per cent while the tax threshold has been lifted by 46 per cent. The saving to government of the four-year 'benefit freeze' alone deprives beneficiaries of some £3.5 billion a year[17] – another reason why poverty is forecast to increase. By contrast, the rise in the basic income tax allowance in the 2018 Budget alone cost nearly £4 billion. Those on lower incomes will receive much less, if any, benefit from this. Many social security beneficiaries are not employed, so they do not gain: many in work do not earn enough to get much, if any, benefit from it, and two-thirds of those earning under the tax threshold are women.

Switch as many tax allowances as possible to tax credits

A tax credit is not set against income, but against the tax due. A tax credit of £200 benefits everyone equally by £200, provided at least £200 income tax is due. It is also possible for those with less income to receive a payment so that they obtain the full value of the tax credit, as with child and working tax credits. This is much fairer.

Refund national insurance exemptions to public expenditure

The Treasury could refund the national insurance fund for all, or some, of the contribution exemptions on non-state pensions and/or impose reduced contributions on those employed post state retirement age.[18] National insurance is intended to support contributory benefits, but a significant amount is effectively subsidising the private pensions industry. Such reliefs are not included in the national insurance fund accounts and we have found no occasion where any part of the government has considered the pension national insurance exemptions, currently £18.1 billion. (See also Chapter 7 for other measures, such as increasing the lower national insurance contribution rate for higher incomes.)

More radical options

The total tax reliefs for any one person could be limited to a few thousand pounds above the personal allowance. Requirements to disclose income received and taxes paid could be introduced, as in some Scandinavian countries, given the long failure to tackle the issues of fiscal inequalities more vigorously. More moderate institutional changes could include an Office for Tax Responsibility and a Ministry of Taxation to ensure greater accountability.[19]

Conclusion

Some changes that would lead to a scaling back of largely upside-down, regressive tax reliefs have been outlined – very sweepingly to keep this chapter short. Others relating to wealth are discussed in Chapters 12 to 15.[20] Savings in one relief can lead to little change or even increased losses through the use of another, especially with so little evidence and analysis on which to base policies. Changes can be very difficult to make because the losers tend to be numerous, and generally better and louder at complaining when most changes are affecting the better off more.[21] However, both the expensive mortgage interest relief and the married man's/married couple's tax allowance, once regarded as untouchable, were eventually abolished with support from all parties – and with reductions in inequality.

Tax reliefs may require more sustained public and policy-making attention if wider, powerful support is to be obtained for carefully planned changes that lead to significant and lasting reductions in poverty and inequality. But there are many opportunities to make a start and these can encourage further changes.

Notes

1 R Murphy, 'Tax avoidance is not theft', Tax Research UK blog post, 13 December 2018, available at www.taxresearch.org.uk/Blog/2018/12/13/tax-avoidance-is-not-theft
2 SS Surrey, *Pathways to Tax Reform: the concept of tax expenditure*, Harvard University Press, 1973, p37
3 Office of Tax Simplification, *Review of Tax Reliefs: final report*, 2011
4 National Audit Office, *Tax Reliefs*, HC 1256, April 2014, and *The Effective Management of Tax Reliefs*, HC 785, November 2014; M Hodge, *Called to Account*, Little, Brown, 2016, Chapter 9. Quote is from Public Accounts Committee, *HMRC's Performance in 2015/16*, HC 712, December 2016, second main conclusion, emphasised in original.
5 J Rutter and others, *Better Budgets: making tax policy better*, Chartered Institute of Taxation, Institute for Fiscal Studies and Institute for Government, 2017, p31
6 Treasury Committee, *Household Finances: income, saving and debt*, HC 565, July 2018, paragraph 117
7 HM Revenue and Customs, *Estimated Costs of Tax Reliefs*, KAI Indirect Taxes, Customs and Co-ordination, January 2019, Table on 'estimated costs of principal tax reliefs'
8 Treasury Committee, *Household Finances: income, saving and debt*, HC 565, July 2018, Chart 5.1
9 HM Revenue and Customs, *Cost of Registered Pension Scheme Tax Relief*, PEN 6, 2018
10 Office for National Statistics, *The Effects of Taxes and Benefits on Household Income: financial year ending 2017*, June 2018, Table 8 in the accompanying dataset
11 World Bank, 'Why worry about tax expenditures?', *PREMnotes*, No. 77, 2003, p2
12 B Brys and others, *Tax Design for Inclusive Economic Growth*, OECD Taxation Working

Papers No. 26, 2016, p51
13 JS Hacker, *The Divided Welfare State: the battle over public and private social benefits in the United States*, Cambridge University Press, 2002, pp43–44 – but the conclusion applies to the UK too.
14 For example, Office for National Statistics, *The Effects of Taxes and Benefits on Household Income: financial year ending 2016*, April 2017, Chapter 4
15 Own calculations based on M Brewer, L Sibieta and L Wren-Lewis, *Racing Away? Income inequality and the evolution of high incomes*, Institute for Fiscal Studies, Briefing No. 76, 2008, Table 1
16 See Resolution Foundation, *A New Generational Contract: the final report of the Intergenerational Commission*, 2018
17 C Beatty and S Fothergill, *The Impact on Scotland of the new Welfare Reforms*, Centre for Regional Economic and Social Research, Sheffield Hallam University, 2016, p9, Table 2
18 Institute for Fiscal Studies and J Mirrlees (eds), *Tax by Design: the Mirrlees Review*, Oxford University Press, 2011, Chapter 11; C Emmerson, C Farquharson and P Johnson (eds), *The IFS Green Budget: October 2018*, Institute for Fiscal Studies, 2018, Chapter 5.4; Resolution Foundation, *A New Generational Contract: the final report of the Intergenerational Commission*, 2018
19 R Murphy, 'The Tax Gap and what to do about it', in W Snell (ed), *Tax Takes: perspectives on building a better tax system to benefit everyone is the UK*, Tax Justice UK, 2017, p20
20 See also T Bell and A Corlett, 'How wealth taxes can raise billions more without scaring any horses', Resolution Foundation blog post, 3 January 2019
21 T Kelsey, *An Unexpected Cut: revisiting the Diamond Commission and assessing inequality in post-war Britain*, Resolution Foundation, 2018

Ten
Tax and social security
David Finch

This chapter considers the interaction of the tax system and social security. The UK's social security system for working-age families is largely targeted and, as a result, means tested. Entitlements that are means tested tend to be gradually withdrawn as incomes, largely from earnings, rise. The rate of withdrawal effectively creates a tax rate at the margin, and the shape and scale of financial incentives that are a consequence can have important behavioural impacts on patterns of work and ultimately incomes, in particular for those groups who are most sensitive to such incentives – especially mothers.

The social security system

Social security is a system of financial support paid to individuals or families by the government. In the UK, that system of support is heavily focused on provision for low-income families, people in most need who tend to be out of work, disabled, or who have children and relatively low household earnings. Whereas some countries have significant contributory provision, the UK system for working-age families is largely means tested – although there is a range of individual contributory and contingent benefits, including for those of working age and not just pensioners, which are particularly important in giving women access to an independent income in their own right.

For pensioners, the contributory state pension accounts for the bulk of government provision and indeed 44 per cent of all social security spend, as shown in Table 10.1. The government also provides £23.6 billion of support for disabled people, largely through personal independence payment and, in the case of pensioners, attendance allowance, to help to meet the additional costs caused by disability. For context, it is helpful to understand the overall social security budget, but the focus of this chapter is provision for working-age families.

Table 10.1:
Benefits expenditure by type, 2017/18

Benefit	£ billion
State pension	93.8
Tax credits	25.0
Disability benefits	23.6
Housing benefit	22.3
Incapacity benefit	14.5
Other	14.2
Child benefit	11.3
Pension credit	5.4
Income support	2.1
Jobseeker's allowance	1.7
Total	**213.9**

Source: Department for Work and Pensions, *Autumn Budget 2018: expenditure and caseload forecasts*, November 2018

The main elements of support for working-age families are in the midst of reform into a combined system called universal credit. But whether considering the legacy system the new scheme replaces, or the reformed system, provision consists of six key income-related elements for households with different characteristics:

- unemployment (jobseeker's allowance);
- long-term sickness/disability (employment and support allowance);
- primary carers of children (income support);
- children (child tax credit);
- working families (working tax credit);
- housing costs (housing benefit).

All these elements are being combined into the single benefit universal credit, along with support for childcare costs for working families (which can also be claimed in the legacy system via working tax credit). However, universal credit is not a single working-age benefit. Contributory forms of jobseeker's allowance and employment and support allowance continue to exist alongside universal credit, and provide resources which do not depend on the presence, actions or resources of a partner; but they are both time-limited (though for employment and support allowance, only for those in the work-related activity, rather than the support, group) and are also deducted pound for pound against any universal credit entitlement. The time-limiting of employment and support allowance for the work-related activity group has deprived many individuals in couples, in particular, of a source of independent income. Some provision, such as council tax support and forms of in-kind benefits like free school meals and local welfare provision, remain outside universal credit and are delivered by agencies other than the Department for Work and Pensions. Child benefit also continues to be paid completely separately from universal credit, and though not means tested the eligibility threshold is relatively high – entitlement starts to be reduced if a family contains at least one person earning more than £50,000. It can also provide a key source of independent income for a mother (or main carer), especially if the universal credit payment is being made to the other partner's account.

In both the legacy system and universal credit, entitlement is reduced, or withdrawn, as income from other sources – primarily earnings – increase. The rate at which those benefits are reduced for a given increase in earnings can be thought of as a marginal effective tax rate. For example, for every additional pound of net earnings (after income tax and national insurance contributions) universal credit entitlement is reduced by 63p – a marginal effective tax rate of 63 per cent. If that person is also paying income tax and national insurance, the overall marginal effective tax rate increases to 75 per cent.

One important difference between the structure of universal credit and tax credits is that the latter calculates entitlement based on gross pay. Any changes to income tax or national insurance will not affect income from tax credits (though it does affect income from housing benefit). In universal credit, the opposite is true. This means that changes to income from the tax system will have less of an impact on overall net income for a recipient of universal credit. That can help where taxes rise, but will also reduce the income gain of any income tax cuts aimed at lower paid workers.

Figure 10.1 plots the potential marginal effective tax rate faced by an individual/individuals in a stylised household at different hours worked at the minimum wage under both the legacy system and universal credit. In both systems, different rates apply depending on which elements of support the household is entitled to, their earnings and whether they are paying income tax or national insurance. Below we set out these interactions and the corresponding marginal effective tax rate in more detail for a specific type of household – ie, following a lone parent as s/he moves into work and increases her/his hours of working:

- In the legacy system:
  - Initially there is a marginal effective tax rate of 0 per cent because the first £20 a week of earnings is ignored in calculations.
  - The marginal effective tax rate rises to 100 per cent because for each pound of earnings above that small disregard, a pound of benefit is withdrawn.
  - The marginal effective tax rate then increases to 83 per cent because above a certain income threshold tax credits are withdrawn at a rate of 41 per cent of gross earnings and housing benefit is withdrawn at a rate of 65 per cent of what income remains. (This combination is particularly likely for lone parents and one-earner couple families.)
  - There is a further increase in the marginal effective tax rate – reaching 91 per cent – when income tax and national insurance are also paid. Tax credits do not account for income tax, and national insurance. Housing benefit is calculated accounting for earnings, income tax, national insurance and tax credit income.
  - When entitlement to housing benefit has been completely withdrawn, the marginal effective tax rate drops to 73 per cent.
  - Large drops in the marginal effective tax rate occur at 16 and 30 hours when an income boost is provided by working tax credit when working at least those hours.
- In universal credit:
  - The marginal effective tax rate remains at 0 per cent until a certain level of net earnings are reached – this is the 'work allowance', essentially a higher earnings disregard.
  - Beyond the work allowance, there is initially a marginal effective tax rate of 63 per cent from the single universal credit taper rate, reducing entitlement by 63p for every pound of additional earnings.
  - The marginal effective tax rate increases to 67.5 per cent when paying national insurance only and then 75 per cent when also earning enough to pay income tax. The 63 per cent taper is applied to the earnings that remain after tax and national insurance are paid, or in other words to net earnings.

For simplicity, these examples exclude council tax support and are limited to the basic rate of income tax. Council tax support can typically place an

Figure 10.1:
Example marginal effective tax rates in tax credits and universal credit, lone parent renter earning the national living wage, 2019/20

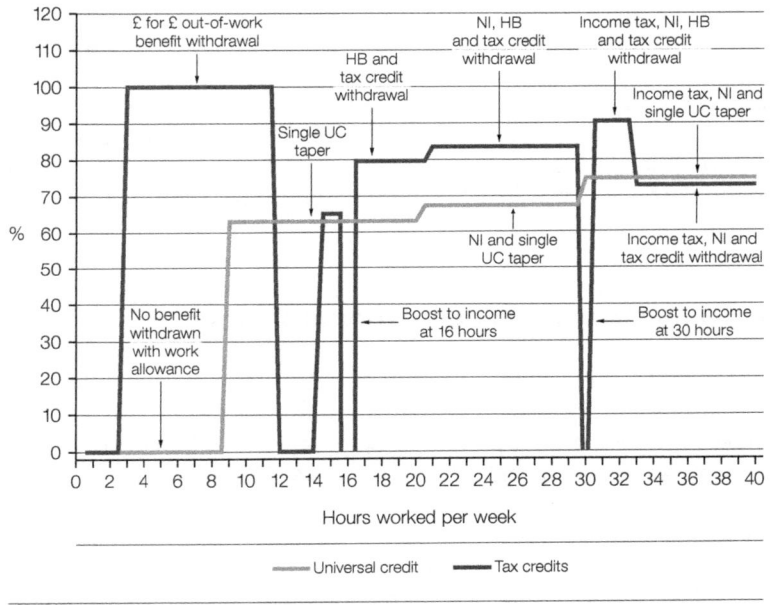

[Figure: Line chart showing marginal effective tax rates (%) on y-axis (0-120) against hours worked per week (0-40) on x-axis, comparing Universal credit and Tax credits. Annotations include:
- £ for £ out-of-work benefit withdrawal
- No benefit withdrawn with work allowance
- Single UC taper
- HB and tax credit withdrawal
- NI, HB and tax credit withdrawal
- Income tax, NI, HB and tax credit withdrawal
- Income tax, NI and single UC taper
- NI and single UC taper
- Income tax, NI and tax credit withdrawal
- Boost to income at 16 hours
- Boost to income at 30 hours]

Note: UC = universal credit NI = national insurance HB = housing benefit
Source: Resolution Foundation analysis using its microsimulation model

additional withdrawal rate of 20 per cent applied to income after other taxes and benefits have been accounted for. For those outside the benefits system, their marginal effective tax rate would be 12 per cent when paying national insurance only, 32 per cent when also paying income tax at the basic rate, increasing to 42 per cent when earning above the higher rate threshold.

A further distinction to make is that the above considers the marginal effective tax rate of an individual as s/he moves into work. Such rates will nearly always be determined on an individual basis with regard to the UK tax system, but benefit entitlement is calculated on a household (in fact, a benefit unit – a nuclear family) basis. Ultimately, for a given set of circumstances, the marginal effective tax rate from the benefits system for either the 'primary' or 'second' earner will be similar. The main exception is the case of a couple with one existing earner. In universal credit, the work allowance will have applied to the first earner, so the universal credit taper applies to all earnings of the second earner. Otherwise it is interactions with the tax system in combination with the benefits system that tend to create a significant difference – for instance, if one earner already pays income tax at the basic rate while the other earns below the personal tax allowance. This also means that for lower income households the effect of the benefit taper rate on income at low levels of earnings differs significantly from higher income households where a low-earning individual is only subject to the tax system – in particular, for lone parents and 'second earners' who are more likely to be earning at this level.

Financial incentives and patterns of work

As with any other part of the tax system, the structure of the benefits system, its generosity and the rate at which it is withdrawn can have an impact on how people behave. For example, faced with a return of only 25p in the marginal pound earned, we may anticipate that people would only take an increase in their earnings (either through a new job or working more hours) for a significant increase in gross pay, unless there are non-monetary preferences for working more.

The design of a benefits system will usually aim to take account of such financial incentives, but doing so is difficult given that governments operate within fiscal constraints. This conundrum is captured by the 'iron triangle' of welfare reform – unavoidable tension between the level of support paid, the strength of financial incentives and the overall cost of the system. Fixing any one of those factors will require a trade-off between the remaining two. And, of course, there are trade-offs within each – for example, support may be more focused on one group of the population, such as children, than another.

The speed at which these marginal effective tax rates take effect in practice are important to consider, particularly if we want to understand how people may respond to them. In universal credit, entitlement is paid each month based on the circumstances of the household in the preceding month. That means the marginal effective tax rates discussed above will take effect relatively quickly. In the tax credits system, if annual earnings change by less than a given amount (currently £2,500), there would be no change in entitlement at that time. If there is a significant change in earnings, the recipient must notify HM Revenue and Customs, and then her/his local authority if s/he receives housing benefit. Each agency will then process the change, meaning that it is likely to take some time before changes in income actually feed through to the household's income.

At the same time, the extent to which people may respond to financial incentives will also depend on whether they understand what the effect might be. That is difficult, given the complexity of both benefit systems, especially the legacy scheme which involves multiple benefits being withdrawn at various rates. Indeed, one aim of introducing universal credit was to make financial incentives clearer. Historically, some people were put off from moving into work because they mistakenly thought they may lose entitlement to housing benefit and be worse off, when in reality they would have been financially better off.

Past research suggests that lone parents and the lower earner in a couple with children (usually the mother) tend to be the most responsive to financial incentives. This makes sense, given they are more likely to make choices to trade off caring responsibilities with paid employment. Given the gender pay gap and the common gendered division of responsibilities within households, these 'choices' may be more apparent than real. Clearly, not all decisions made are governed purely by the financial – for example, cultural norms may mean greater weight is given to family responsibilities over formal work. Other, primarily non-financial, barriers may exist that strong financial incentives simply cannot overcome, such as having caring responsibilities or lacking the skills required to find employment.

Reforms to social security

Policy makers have been concerned about the effect of such interactions in the design of the benefits system even as far back as the Poor Laws developed in the sixteenth century. In more modern times, the introduction of family credit in the 1980s built on the introduction of family income supplement, seeking to ensure that people found themselves financially better off in work than out of it in an attempt to solve the unemployment trap created by out-of-work benefits.

Since the late 1990s, the tax credits system (initially working families' tax credit in 1999, then working tax credit and child tax credit from 2003) sought to improve financial incentives to enter work and, at the same time, help reduce child poverty.[1]

It was a significant increase in scale on its predecessor, among other reasons because child tax credit absorbed the short-lived children's tax credit and because the government was determined to act on child poverty, and aimed to balance incentives and poverty reduction by increasing levels of support for families who were in and out of work. Tax credits were also structured in a way that targeted support to reward specific work outcomes, especially among lone parents.

Figure 10.2 plots how a lone parent's net income changes as s/he works more hours in the legacy system. When out of work, her/his income consists of income support, child tax credit and housing benefit. At a small number of hours of work, her/his income support is withdrawn pound for pound. S/he receives a significant boost to income once working exactly 16 hours – through the payment of working tax credit – which ensures a clear financial return to starting work.

Beyond this point, working more hours or earning more leads to a gradual increase in income because tax credits and housing benefit are withdrawn at a combined rate of at least 80 per cent. This design has helped increase the employment rate for lone parents,[2] while the 'sweet

Figure 10.2:

Net weekly income after housing costs for a renting lone parent with one child earning the national living wage, tax credits, 2019/20

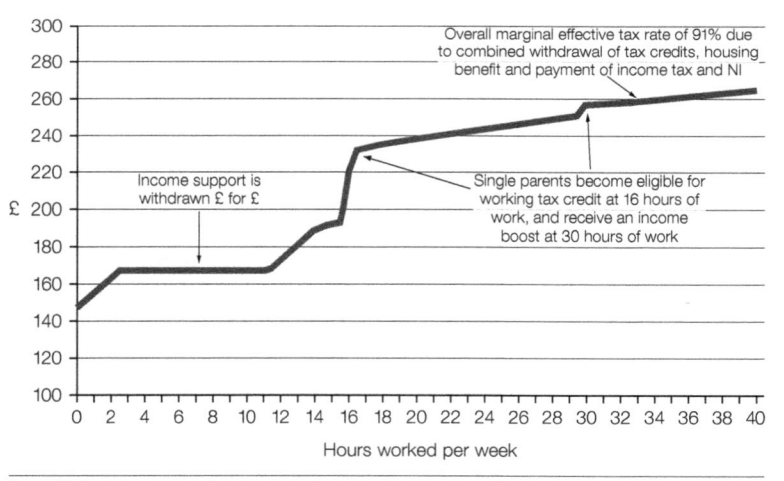

Note: this analysis assumes that the family element has been removed. For simplicity, we ignore council tax and the system of support towards paying council tax bills. Tax and national insurance thresholds are those announced in Budget 2018. Rent is assumed to be £135 a week, and all adults are assumed to be aged 25 or over.

Source: Resolution Foundation analysis using its microsimulation model

spot' at 16 hours has led to a bunching of lone parents who rent their homes working exactly those hours.[3]

The design of universal credit builds on the legacy system, with the aim of simplifying support by not only combining six benefits into one but also withdrawing entitlement at a single rate through the 63 per cent 'taper'. Figure 10.3 shows how net income plays out for the same hypothetical example used in Figure 10.2, but this time under universal credit.

When working a low number of hours, no universal credit entitlement is withdrawn, creating a strong financial incentive to move into work. Once earnings reach the level of the 'work allowance' (equivalent to £65 a week in this example), the taper applies with universal credit withdrawn at a rate of 63 per cent, rising to 75 per cent once paying tax. This forms a potential 'sweet spot' at the point the taper kicks in beyond which the rewards of working additional hours or earning more are limited. A further comparison of the two systems, as part of a discussion of the advantages and disadvantages of a means-tested system, is in Chapter 11.

Figure 10.3:
Net weekly income after housing costs for a renting lone parent with one child earning the national living wage, universal credit, 2019/20

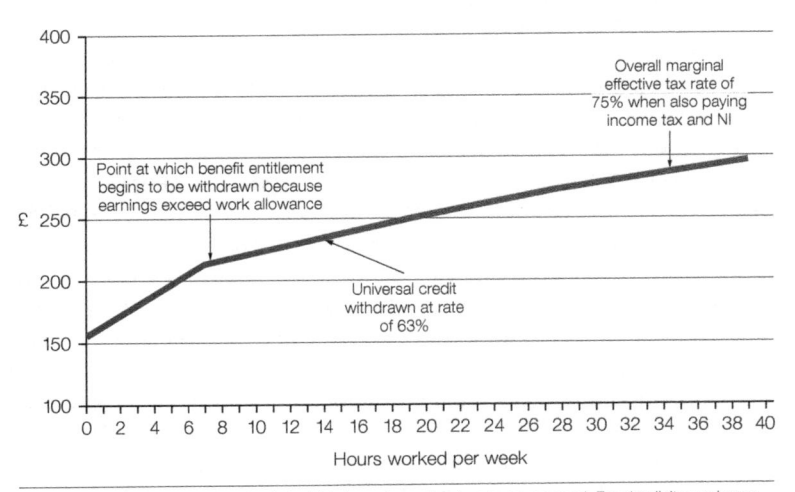

Note: this analysis assumes that the first child element premium has been removed. For simplicity, we ignore council tax and the system of support towards paying council tax bills. Tax and national insurance thresholds are those announced in Budget 2018. Rent is assumed to be £135 a week, and all adults are assumed to be aged 25 or over.

Source: Resolution Foundation analysis using its microsimulation model

It is perhaps worth noting that child benefit is paid whether or not the adult is in employment and so does not exacerbate either the unemployment or the poverty trap. It also 'follows the child', continuing to be paid regularly as employment or family situations change, giving at least a modicum of security to low-income families with children.[4]

It is too early to assess whether universal credit will lead to an alteration in working patterns, but based on past behaviour we might expect a concentration of people at the level of earnings which matches the level of the work allowance. We could also expect some renters working additional hours because the very highest marginal effective tax rates that are a feature of the legacy system have been removed. However, the opposite may be true for homeowners who would now have a higher overall marginal effective tax rate. The key risk of concern is that these new structures trap lone parents at low earnings levels, and therefore low income.

A further group which is likely to see a significant shift in the strength of financial incentive structures, and which we know tends to be responsive to financial incentives, is the lower earning partners, or 'second earners' in couples with children. Historically, this has tended to be the mother although shifts in work patterns, especially in lower income families, means an increasing tendency for the father to be the lower earner.[5] They may face similar constraints to lone parents in that they may need to balance work with caring responsibilities.

Financial incentives for this group were a concern in the tax credits regime, where their earnings would be immediately subject to a withdrawal rate of at least 41 per cent. That concern is greater in universal credit where the marginal effective tax rate rises to 63 per cent. Once again, this highlights a clear trade-off in the design of a means-tested system: a given level of spend is targeted at primary earners through the work allowance, leaving a weaker financial incentive for second earners.

The payment of childcare costs is a final factor that can also be considered as part of the marginal effective tax rate and tends to be an additional concern for the main carer of children. In universal credit, up to 85 per cent of childcare costs paid by parents are covered (as opposed to 80 per cent, and then 70 per cent, in tax credits). Despite this level of generosity, and the separate 30 free childcare hours a week provided to working parents of three- and four-year-olds through a different policy, childcare costs are still limited in terms of the number of children covered and the ceilings on costs (that have not been increased since 2005); and they can increase the marginal effective tax rate further. A person earning the minimum wage, paying childcare costs for two children out of her/his remaining additional income once tax and national insurance are paid and universal credit withdrawn, can be left with as little as 5p of the additional pound earned. If childcare costs are above the average, s/he could even be worse off from working more. This is a particular problem for parents seeking to work more than the part-time hours covered by the free childcare offer, or with children under the age of three.

Future of social security in tackling poverty

Large questions about the successful delivery of universal credit remain and many of these relate to the extent to which the system can respond to, and fit with, the complexity of people's lives. It is not until the early part of the 2020s that all entitled families are expected to be on the new system, so there is still time to improve its design. In the context of financial incentives this is important, because they depend not only on the size of the financial return, but also on people being able to rely on and trust the system.

From a poverty perspective, the right financial incentives, mixed with financial and practical support, can make a real difference to household incomes. The increased employment rate for lone parents over the last decade is just one sign of policy success in this area. However, the current context presents two key challenges for social security, and universal credit in particular.

First, it will be important to make sure that benefit reform keeps pace with changes in the structure of the labour market. The UK labour market has been remarkably successful at maintaining high employment rates, which have also translated to low levels of worklessness, but the share of the population in low pay remains high. Whereas in the 1990s and early 2000s work was seen as the key route out of poverty, now around two-thirds of children in poverty live in households in which someone works.[6] To be truly fit for the future, the design of universal credit will need to shift to provide better support for low-paid workers to progress and boost their pay.

Second, wider cuts to working-age benefits are likely to undermine much of any improvement to incomes that responses to the new financial incentives created by universal credit could bring. During the four-year cash freeze in the rates of most working-age benefits, which started in April 2016, if net incomes were to keep pace with inflation, the earnings would need to rise by around four times the rate of inflation. Perhaps posing the greatest risk to increasing not just the number of families in poverty but the depth of poverty is the limiting of support from the child element to two children. For a family to replace the £2,800 a year the child element can provide, it would have to increase its earnings by over £11,000 a year.

Ultimately, financial incentives are only one policy tool that can be brought to bear to tackle poverty. Optimising financial incentive structures to increase participation rates and encourage people to increase their earnings will be undermined if the generosity of the system fails to provide an effective safety net.

Notes

1 A Corlett and others, *The Living Standards Audit 2018*, Resolution Foundation, 2018
2 M Brewer and others, *Did Working Families' Tax Credit Work? The impact of in-work support on labour supply in Great Britain*, Institute for Fiscal Studies for Inland Revenue, 2003
3 D Finch and L Gardiner, *Back in Credit? Universal credit after Budget 2018*, Resolution Foundation, 2018
4 F Bennett with P Dornan, *Child Benefit: fit for the future*, CPAG, 2006
5 S Harkness, *Second Earner to Primary Breadwinner? Women's wages and employment*, Resolution Foundation, 2015
6 Department for Work and Pensions, *Households Below Average Income 1994/95 to 2017/18*, 2019

Eleven
Direct taxes and cash benefits: effects and reforms

Alan Marsh

This chapter concerns the business of national and local government in taking money from households' incomes in direct taxes and paying them social security benefits in cash. Often, they do both for the same households, which makes more sense than it seems because, for example, taxes are not assessed on how many children depend on your income, but your entitlement to some benefits is. Disabled people pay taxes on the same basis as everyone else, but receive benefits to help them with their additional needs. It is also important to note (see Chapter 10) that income tax is levied on individual incomes, while many (though by no means all) benefits are given, or withheld, on the basis of household incomes,[1] which makes aligning their respective fiscal functions more difficult than it might be.

The effect of direct taxes and cash benefits

Before housing costs are deducted or any adjustment made for household size, UK households received an average of £37,270 from earnings, private pensions, rents and investments in the financial year 2016/17 – called their *original income* (see Figure 11.1).

To this, the government added £6,374 in cash benefits, giving them an average *gross income* of £43,645. From this, direct taxes (income tax, national insurance contributions, taxes on rents and dividends, and so on) took £8,397, leaving them with an average *disposable income* of £35,247, or £678 per week. Adjusted for household size, this figure is £32,676 per year, or £628 per week.

It is important to remember that households on average incomes are quite well off because the vast incomes of the richest drag the average up to about the 67th percentile – only a third receive more. More typically, those on the 50th percentile – half have more income, half less – have the *median* equalised disposable income of £27,300 a year, or £525 per week. After housing costs are deducted, the average is £517 and the median is £425.

The amounts given and taken vary across the income distribution. The richest fifth have an original income 12 times greater than the poorest fifth, a gross income six times greater and a disposable income still more than five times greater (see Figure 11.1). This is how much the net effect of direct taxes and benefits reduces income inequality. This calculation can be taken further to include the effect of indirect taxes (such as VAT, and fuel, alcohol and tobacco duties) and even the value of benefits in kind (education, health provision and so on)[2] (see Chapter 2). But in this chapter we are concerned only with the policy choices that govern how this direct giving and taking by government is done: essentially the first three elements of Figure 11.1.

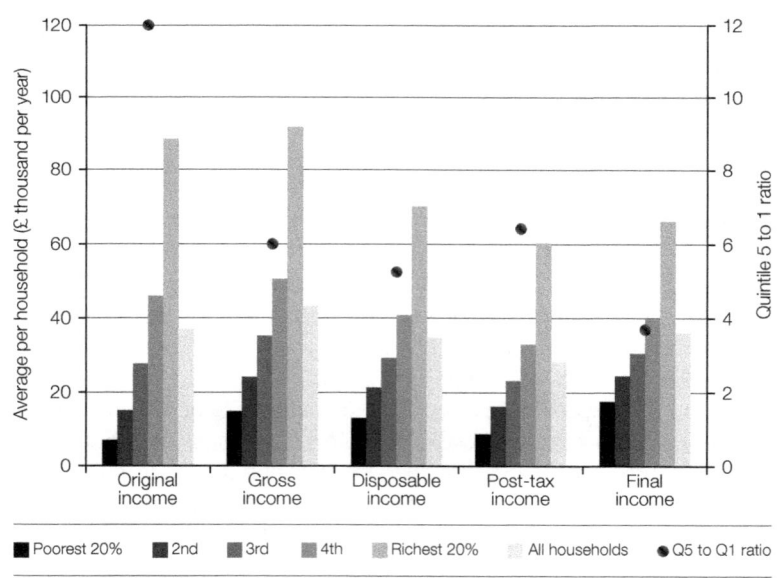

Figure 11.1:
The effect of taxes and benefits, all households, 2016/17

Source: Office for National Statistics, *Effects of Taxes and Benefits on UK Household Income: financial year ending 2017*, June 2018, Figure 3

The important thing to notice about Figure 11.1 is that almost everyone gets benefits. Even the richest fifth have their original incomes topped up by more than £3,000 a year, on average. Those not receiving any at present will almost certainly receive benefits at some point in their lives, when they have children, for example, and when their state pension arrives. And almost everyone pays direct taxes too, reducing the average gross income of the poorest fifth by about £3,700 per year, though the benefits they receive leave them ahead of their original income by £5,400.

Indirect taxes increase inequality, while benefits in kind reduce it to a final ratio of about four to one in favour of the richest compared with the poorest fifth.

Taxing benefits

The full story of the way taxes and benefits interlock is beyond the scope of this chapter, except to note that some benefits are taxable, and some are not. Some benefits that replace income, such as the state pension, carer's allowance, and contribution-based (but not income-based) jobseeker's allowance, are taxable. Those claiming contribution-based jobseeker's allowance for a month or two, for example, who then go on to resume paid work, will have the benefit they received added to their annual income for tax assessment. This is thought fairer to their fellow workers who remained in work for the same 12 months. 'Contingent' benefits – such as those given because claimants have dependent children, a disability, or housing costs they would not otherwise be able to afford – tend not to be taxable. The issue of equity does not apply in the same way.

The introduction of tax credits further complicated the relationship between taxes and benefits. Working tax credit adds to the wages of low-paid workers who, typically those with dependent children, would otherwise be better off out of work and claiming benefits. (Child tax credit is paid to families with adults both in and out of paid work.) As a form of negative income tax based on net earnings and other income, it would defeat its own purpose to try to tax tax credits.

There are, however, two ways to tax benefits.

- **By HM Revenue and Customs (HMRC).** If taxable benefits (such as state pension and contribution-based jobseeker's allowance) take recipients' annual incomes beyond the (2019/20) tax-free personal allowance of £12,500, tax is paid through HMRC adjusting codes or sending a bill.

- **By Department for Work and Pensions (DWP) withdrawal rates.** Entitlement to cash benefits may be reduced, or actually denied, because claimants have other income, typically from a partner living with them, or large amounts of savings.[3] As the incomes of recipients increase, so a fraction of each new pound is withdrawn from the benefits paid – typically between 60p and 70p – until entitlement is extinguished (see Chapter 10). As explained in Chapter 10, these withdrawal rates are known as 'marginal effective tax rates', though it might be fair to add that it is a strange 'tax' whereby those who 'pay' the most end up with the better incomes.

Benefits treated in this way are means tested while those given without counting other income are universal benefits – either available tax-free to everyone or, more typically, to everyone whose extra needs (children, disability, high rents and so on) merit them. It is this choice between means testing and universalism that governs policy towards the administration of tax and benefits.

Means testing

The main argument in favour of means testing social security benefits is that it is held to be indefensible to give public money to people who do not need it. It is far better, and plain common sense, to concentrate benefits on the poorest households who need them most. This way, the most help can be given to those who need it most, at the least expense to public funds. Yet 'targeting', as it is called, attracts a long list of criticisms:

- **It is a 'tax' on the better off.** A policy reform that moves existing entitlement to benefits down the income range is effectively a tax increase for middle-income households, whose benefits are taken away. Their dismay at such a move would strengthen public opposition to any further tax increases and may reduce future tax revenues that might have been better used to increase the incomes of households in poverty. It is not a zero-sum game that allocates a fixed amount of benefits from a fixed amount of government income.

- **It stigmatises low-income households.** When benefits are solely for 'them' at the expense of 'us' it becomes too easy for those with an unsympathetic view of poverty to increase public resentment and oppose benefit increases and welfare support. Those of a pro-welfare persuasion find it harder to defend and promote cash transfers to people living in income poverty.

- **It creates a 'poverty trap'.** As explained in Chapter 10, those making the journey from unemployment to working self-sufficiency can face a steep upward slope as their tax credits and other benefits are withdrawn as they earn more. The difficulty for policy is that small reductions in the withdrawal rate, lessening the 'poverty trap', can bring huge increases in the population entitled to help. It is particularly paradoxical that 'second earners' in a couple can potentially take their family out of poverty, but face disincentives due to a combination of means-tested benefits and taxation to which they have been shown to be particularly sensitive. This works against one of the best ways to tackle child poverty.

- **Its administration is costly.** The DWP employs 75,000 staff and spends £6 billion in administration, much of it determining claimants' eligibility to means-tested benefits and policing their behaviour.[4]

- **It can damage claimants.** UK benefits leave many families below the poverty line, with all the discouragement and hardship that brings. More than that, the process of claiming and maintaining a claim can be dismal and discouraging. A high level of proof is required of claimants' efforts to find work and those who fail to satisfy officials are sanctioned by reduced or withheld payments. Introducing his report on the UK, the UN Special Rapporteur on Extreme Poverty said that the introduction of universal credit in the UK had 'plunged people into misery and despair'.[5] Also, the unmerited humiliations visited upon many disabled claimants for income-related employment and support allowance are well documented: in 2016 alone, there were 92,000 tribunal rulings against DWP decisions, which included those against the denial of non-means-tested disability benefits too.[6]

- **It is prone to costly errors.** In 2016/17, £3.5 billion was overpaid to claimants, which had to be recovered, while £1.6 billion was underpaid.

- **It can suffer low take-up rates.** There can be error on both sides. Claimants can be unaware of their eligibility for benefits, especially in the case of in-work tax credits, which 35 per cent of eligible workers fail to claim. Forty per cent of eligible pensioners fail to claim pension credit, as do 20 per cent of people entitled to housing benefit and, perhaps deterred by its denial to others, income support/employment and support allowance. The money foregone by eligible non-claimants from these three benefits alone amounted to over £10 billion in 2016/17. In contrast, annual take-up of the near-universal child benefit averages 96 per cent.[7]

- **It makes the income of partners subject to the presence, actions and resources of another person.** This can potentially affect partnering decisions[8] and/or create friction within couples, and makes it more difficult to give financial independence and autonomy to individuals.

Universal benefits

UK social security benefits given without checking on a claimant's other income are called 'universal' benefits. This is somewhat misleading because they are not available to everyone; they remain *contingent* benefits and are available mainly to families with dependent children (child benefit), to disabled people (disability living allowance and personal independence payment), and (for a limited period) to newly unemployed people who have a sufficient record of national insurance contributions (contribution-based jobseeker's allowance and contributory employment and support allowance).

Such benefits have many advantages. They are simple and inexpensive to administer. Almost everyone entitled to them will receive them and their relative simplicity suppresses error and discourages fraud. Recipients are less likely to feel stigmatised or harshly dealt with, whereas middle-income people who qualify feel they have a legitimate stake in the benefits system. Such benefits can give some autonomy, especially to those who may have no other source of income, or who may be living in an unequal relationship.[9] And they value their stake more than may be supposed, as was seen in 2016 when families having either parent or guardian earning more than £50,000 per year had to pay additional income tax or give up their child benefit under new legislation.

Combining many of the advantages both of targeting and universality, these contingent benefits are easier to defend:

- Child benefit assists families bringing up dependent children, traditionally paid directly to mothers, who reliably spend the money on their children, promoting the welfare of the growing generation.

- Contribution-based jobseeker's allowance preserves the principle introduced by the 1942 *Beveridge Report* that workers would pay contributions when in work and receive help when they are unemployed. For six months, their entitlement is unchallengeable. (The same is true for entitlement to contributory employment and support allowance, although for those in the work related activity group this is also now time-limited, to a year.)

- Disability living allowance and its replacement for adults, personal independence payment, both recognise that people with physical or mental disabilities have mobility and self-management needs that should be supported from public funds, whatever their other income, especially as those subsidies often assist them to maintain themselves in paid work.

However, some criticisms remain:

- They are expensive. Child benefit alone costs about £12 billion a year.

- Some people who never have children complain of discrimination, though they are reminded that having a new generation at all is as essential to their future welfare as it is to the parents'.

- Contribution-based unemployment benefits are not means tested, but recipients must fulfil all the conditions requiring proof of their efforts to find new paid work, however unfavourable may be the local labour market, thus experiencing many of the damaging pressures of means-tested benefits.

- Many disabled people have difficulty getting their condition acknowledged as eligible. They can experience a sceptical hearing from officials, often leading to periods without support, pending appeals.

A basic income?

For many, maintaining an adequate original income, reliably year on year, is becoming more difficult, even in the richest countries. Machines are now replacing workers at an ever-accelerating rate; up to a third of all current jobs may vanish in the next few years.[10] This has been said before, of course, and new jobs arose for people to take up. But the present trend towards low-paid, insecure work in the service sector is strongly established and is seriously undermining the government's faith that work is the best way out of poverty. The present system does not achieve this. Now, more than two-thirds of children living in poverty have at least one working parent, sometimes two. Means testing will find too few means and the cost to social security of supporting poor wages and spells of unemployment will rise.

Nevertheless, having replaced workers, machines make wealth. Five machine-rich global companies[11] currently hold £560 billion in cash alone, which is more than twice the amount the UK government spends each year on social security benefits. Equally, though, poor workers are poor customers. They are poor voters too, who may seek politically radical ways of improving redistribution in their favour. All this has revived interest in an old question: should the complex, inadequate and sometimes demeaning system of means-tested and contingent benefits and tax allowances all be swept away and replaced by a single payment, regardless of the recipient's income or circumstances? Should there be a 'basic income', paid monthly to everyone, solely on the basis of citizenship?[12]

Support for a basic income is heard from the political Left and Right, which suggests it may be an idea whose time has come. Left and Right, though, have very different ambitions. The Left wants to enhance the welfare state, the Right wants to abolish it – the state discharging most of its duties to citizens with a single monthly cheque.[13] Nevertheless, arguments in favour of a basic income are attractive to many:[14]

- Perhaps more than anything, the lack of a work requirement means a basic income may promise greater individual freedom, dignity and opportunities for creative and fulfilling participation in a twenty-first century society of uncertain work.

- It may reduce the take-up of poorly paid, insecure and disagreeable service work, thereby perhaps increasing the wages and improving the conditions of those who continue to provide such work.[15]

- It attaches to citizenship an element of entitlement and fairness that promotes social solidarity.

- It would increase women's independent income, though there is also concern that a low state benefit without links to the labour market or the right to return to employment could – like some 'cash for care' schemes in other countries – lead to a prolonged labour market exit by women in particular.

- Since a large proportion of the extra revenues needed would come from taxes on higher earners, it would reduce income inequality.
- The administration costs would be small, saving perhaps £4–5 billion a year.

It may as well be said now that a naive form of basic income that was substituted for all the present means-tested and contingent benefits and provided an adequate income for everyone, would not work. It would certainly not work if most, or all, the extra taxes required were raised from personal incomes. Having, as they must, surrendered their tax allowances for a basic income, still the extra marginal taxation on earned and other income would be prohibitive.[16] Whereas current UK spending on benefits and direct social care totals £283 billion a year, a basic income providing even a modest £10,000 a year to every adult would require almost twice that (£520 billion). Keeping every individual above the poverty line would require £848 billion – 83 per cent of government spending and a third of GDP.[17] If other areas of government spending were to be maintained, marginal tax rates would exceed 65 per cent, plus national insurance contributions for those in work, both payable on all income.

None of this is impossible, of course, but we would live in a very different political economy. In the view of the Right, for example, much of other government expenditure would not be maintained. Individual welfare would have to be purchased. As several critics have written, an affordable basic income would not be adequate – particularly for those with greater needs – and an adequate basic income would not be affordable.[18]

Could the money be raised elsewhere? From 2011, citizens of Kuwait, for example, each received about $4,000 a month and free basic food (to prevent inflation), all supported from oil revenues.[19] Alaskans have long enjoyed annual tax-free residents' payments from theirs – $1,600 in 2018. UK oil revenues would not stretch that far, but greater access to accumulated private and corporate wealth might make up a significant fraction of the difference (see Chapter 19). A more serious carbon tax would raise more and have the added benefit of slowing global warming. All these proposals, though, would require a large shift in public support for government powers of taxation and a change in corporate tolerance.

Whereas it is true that almost any form of basic income would reduce income inequality (though not necessarily rates of income poverty) it would do so unfairly. It fails to recognise both the variation in people's needs and the economies of scale available to people who share households. Couples would gain, single people would lose. On the other hand, it could be argued that to give each individual their own benefit, and couples twice the amount that single people get, means that partnership decisions are not going to be influenced by benefits. It is difficult to imagine a UK benefits system that did not acknowledge that rents in Greater London are three times those in the North East,[20] that families with children ought to receive extra support, and that disabled people should receive support for their additional mobility and care needs. A basic income that was in any way adequate would still have to provide this additional contingent support and thereby forfeit much of its claim to simplicity.

Fiscal considerations aside, the sharp political rock upon which a full basic income scheme would likely founder is popular resistance to the prospect of high rates of taxation supporting some citizens who choose not to work or do very much at all. This is why Tony Atkinson formulated his 'participation income', whereby a subsidy to support inadequate means-tested benefits ought to depend on work or other participation of a useful kind: study, parenting, caring, volunteering, and so on.[21]

A partial basic income?

As David Piachaud observes, in the end, a basic income is no more than an administrative procedure to transfer money.[22] It says little about what policy is being pursued. It can be used to get the state out of people's lives, promoting rugged individualism and independent communities. Or it can be the way to reduce poverty and secure greater social solidarity and equality. If the aim is to reduce poverty, then the outcomes for a basic income are surprisingly uncertain. As Luke Martinelli says:[23]

> Demonstrating that UBI [universal basic income] could have positive distributional consequences does not mean that it would be the best or most effective way to reduce poverty, or that the required tax rises would be politically acceptable.

Might it be possible, though, to introduce a *partial* basic income that would provide a minimum income guarantee to everyone and so reduce reliance on means-tested benefits? UK taxpayers are not strangers to this idea since that is what, essentially, child benefit and the state pension are. A partial basic income would simply replace these and then extend payments to everyone else.

Stewart Lansley and Howard Reed at Compass have put forward a painstaking proposal to at least begin a transition away from means testing towards greater universality.[24] The first key step would require everyone to exchange their tax allowances for cash and pay a low tax rate (15 per cent) on the newly-exposed income (the first £12,500). Higher up, three pence is added to each tax rate (23p, 43p, and 48p) and the national insurance contribution thresholds are abolished. That is a lot more tax (about 15 per cent more), but not the truly painful rates associated with a full basic income scheme. The proposal also favours increased taxes on property, wealth and carbon use. But the *net* cost of the scheme is not trivial: about £28 billion per year.

These tax increases would allow £60 a week to be paid to each adult, £40 for each child and the state pension to rise to £175 a week. Housing benefit, employment and support allowance and universal credit would remain available, disregarding £25 a week of basic income when calculating entitlement, as would non-means-tested benefits to disabled people. This at least would be a start. Better terms could be introduced if the future turns out to be the machine-wealthy, post-work world many promise.

These changes would have a beneficial impact on poverty rates, reducing both child poverty and the remaining pensioner poverty by a third and in-work poverty by a fifth. Almost no one in the bottom 20 per cent of the income distribution will lose, and women among them would gain most. This advantage to women is one of the stronger arguments in its favour (though note the concern about potential labour market exit by women in particular as a result of receiving a small income from the state). The index of overall income inequality (the 'Gini coefficient') will fall a little: from 0.377 to 0.337.

These outcomes would be welcome, but perhaps the better word for partial basic income is that it is an *anti-destitution* measure, more than an *anti-poverty* measure. Most tellingly, that non-trivial £28 billion of extra cost would simply restore public spending on social security as a proportion of national income back to its 2010 levels, such has been the extent of austerity-driven cuts. And these cuts have hurt. Whereas the UK system has never been very good at keeping people out of poverty, it has hitherto been quite good at keeping people, especially families, out of *dire* poverty. This is no longer true.

As Ruth Lister points out in her introduction to the Compass scheme, the manifest failures of universal credit, leaving claimants without support for weeks or unjustly sanctioned, the 'shredding' of the support once available from the social fund, now vanishing into local authority discretion, and the insecurity of low-paid work, all mean that:

> Shockingly words such as 'hunger' and 'destitution' are now part of the vocabulary used to describe what is happening; their most visible expression are the growing incidence of rough sleeping and reliance on food banks.

A partial basic income would close food banks, shelter the homeless and allow young people especially a less anxious path through the sparser times of their lives, getting through education, entering work, starting families.

If the focus is to be on an anti-destitution measure, then a simpler method is proposed by the New Economics Foundation, which estimates that simply turning tax allowances for those with earned or other income into a weekly payment to everyone, including those with no taxable income, would be almost as effective.[25]

Arguments against a partial basic income remain:

- It would add to complexity, not abolish it. Even the apparently simple idea of redistributing tax allowances would incur heavy new administration costs.
- It would be hard to convince middle-income taxpayers that their £60 a week was adequate compensation for their increased taxes, even if they welcomed the social improvements claimed for a partial basic income. The incentive for ever more ingenious tax avoiding would be much greater, reducing promised revenues.
- Single people would lose more than couples, who get twice as much for fewer outgoings, per head.
- Sixty pounds a week will not keep anyone. While this reduces the objection to 'money-for-nothing scrounging', without paid work they would still have to claim means-tested benefits, which would still enforce a work-requirement.

Thus, the retreat to a partial scheme breaches all the principles held to recommend basic income: a liveable income, simplicity, fairness, the avoidance of stigma, and universality regardless of circumstances. Overall, the choice may come down to opportunity cost. Extra taxes might well be better spent on improved public services (health, education, housing), which might address longer-term reductions in poverty. Here and now, given £28 billion a year or the high net cost of any basic income scheme, restoring the cuts to benefits, increasing child benefit, and abolishing the 'two-child limit', the benefit cap and the 'bedroom tax', would all quickly reduce income poverty and set us back on the promising path to abolishing poverty followed up to 2010.

Notes

1. Strictly speaking, benefits are given to a 'benefit unit' since there might be more than one unit in a single household, typically an older couple and a grown-up child.
2. See Office for National Statistics, *Effects of Taxes and Benefits on UK Household Income: financial year ending 2017*, June 2018, Figure 2
3. Savings begin to affect benefits if claimants have more than £6,000 in savings, while £16,000 will end their entitlement to means-tested help.
4. National Audit Office, *A Short Guide to the Department for Work and Pensions*, 2017
5. Office of the High Commissioner (UN Human Rights), *Statement on Visit to the United Kingdom, by Professor Philip Alston, United Nations Special Rapporteur on Extreme Poverty and Human Rights*, London, 16 November 2018
6. National Audit Office, *A Short Guide to the Department for Work and Pensions*, 2017. The DWP spent £39 million defending its decisions at tribunals and courts.
7. HM Revenue and Customs, Child Benefit, *Child Tax Credit and Working Tax Credit: take-up rates 2015/16*, 2017, p13, Table 1
8. See for example, R Griffiths, 'No love on the dole: the influence of the UK means-tested welfare system on partnering and family structure', *Journal of Social Policy*, 46(3), 2017, pp543–61
9. F Bennett and S Sung, 'Dimensions of financial autonomy in low-/moderate-income couples from a gender perspective and implications for welfare reform', *Journal of Social Policy*, 42(4), 2003, pp701–19
10. See for example, J Manyika and others, *Jobs Lost, Jobs Gained: what the future of work will mean for jobs, skills, and wages*, McKinsey Global Institute, 2017
11. Google, Apple, Microsoft, Cisco and Oracle. The wealthiest 16 companies have $1.2 trillion salted away.
12. Given that currently many non-citizens are left without recourse to public funds, leaving even those with children destitute, this would be a contentious qualification for a 'universal' basic income.
13. See, from the Left, P Van Parijs, 'Why surfers should be fed: the liberal case for an unconditional basic income', in *Philosophy and Public Affairs*, 20(2), 1991, pp101–31. And from the Right, C Murray, *Guaranteed Income as a Replacement for the Welfare State*, The Foundation for Law, Justice and Society, 2006
14. See for example, D Hirsch, *Could a 'Citizen's Income' Work?*, Joseph Rowntree Foundation, 2015
15. There is a complex counter-argument that, instead, employers would be discouraged from providing better terms and conditions, knowing that workers have back-up income and will offer themselves for work at lower wages. However, statistical modelling of the distributional effects of a basic income provide no real insight into the likely labour market effects. The evaluation of recent examples, in Alaska and the recently abandoned Finnish pilot scheme, suggests they may be slight.
16. Eliminating tax allowances and national insurance lower and upper thresholds would raise £118 billion.
17. Centre for Social Justice, *Universal Basic Income: an effective policy for poverty reduction?*, 2018
18. See for example, L Martinelli, *Assessing the Case for a Universal Basic Income in the UK*, Institute for Policy Research, University of Bath, 2017
19. Only a third of Kuwait's four million population are citizens.
20. About £1,500 per month compared to £500.

21 AB Atkinson, 'The case for a participation income', *The Political Quarterly*, 67(1), 1996, pp67–70
22 He continues: 'Starting from or believing in a mechanism is misguided. It is surely more productive to start from the goals of policy and then consider the best means of achieving them.' See D Piachaud, 'Basic income: confusion, claims and choices', *Journal of Poverty and Social Justice*, 26(3), 2018, pp299–314.
23 L Martinelli, *The Fiscal and Distributional Implications of Alternative Universal Basic Income Schemes in the UK*, Institute for Policy Research, University of Bath, 2017
24 S Lansley and H Reed, *Basic Income For All: from desirability to feasibility*, Compass, 2019. See also M Torry, *An Evaluation of a Strictly Revenue Neutral Citizen's Income Scheme*, EUROMOD Working Paper EM 5/16, Institute for Social and Economic Research, University of Essex, 2016, and M Torry, *An Update, a Correction, and an Extension, of an Evaluation of an Illustrative Citizen's Basic Income Scheme: addendum to EUROMOD working paper EM12/17*, EUROMOD Working Paper EM 12/17a, 2018
25 A Stirling and S Arnold, *Nothing Personal: replacing the personal tax allowance with a weekly national allowance*, New Economics Foundation, 2019

Twelve
Taxing wealth: an overview
Andrew Summers

Proposals for taxing wealth have recently reappeared on the political agenda after several decades in which existing taxes on inheritances, capital gains and capital income have faced gradual erosion. Since the mid-1970s, total private wealth in the UK has more than doubled from around 250 per cent to over 600 per cent of GDP,[1] and yet over the same period, revenues from taxes on wealth have remained at around only 2 per cent of GDP (see Figure 12.1).[2]

Wealth has always been, and remains, much more unequally distributed than income; wealth inequality in the UK has also been increasing (at least on some measures) in recent years (see Figure 12.2). The top 1 per cent currently own around 20 per cent of private wealth, and the top 10 per cent own more than half.[3] Meanwhile, the bottom 1 per cent have net debts, and the bottom 10 per cent have no net wealth.[4] This picture is further complicated by changing patterns of ownership of savings and investments within the household.[5]

Public concern about wealth inequality has begun to generate mainstream political traction. There is now remarkably broad-based political support for the idea that taxes on wealth should take an increasing share of overall tax revenues, upending the conventional preoccupation with taxes on labour income and consumption. This marks an important shift. However, there is much less agreement about precisely what form these measures should take, or about how much revenue they could realistically raise.

Current taxes on wealth

Taxes on wealth can be divided into three main types: taxes on *transfers* of wealth; taxes on *returns* on wealth; and taxes on *holdings* of wealth.

Here and in the following chapters, **'taxes on transfers'** refers to policies for taxing *net* transfers of wealth, which occur where there has been a gift or bequest from donor to recipient. The only UK tax that fits this definition is inheritance tax, which applies to gratuitous transfers arising on death, as well as some lifetime gifts made within seven years of death. In some sense, transaction taxes such as the UK's stamp duty land tax might also be regarded as a tax on transfers of wealth. However, here there is typically no *net* transfer (where assets are exchanged at market value), so they are not included within this category.[6]

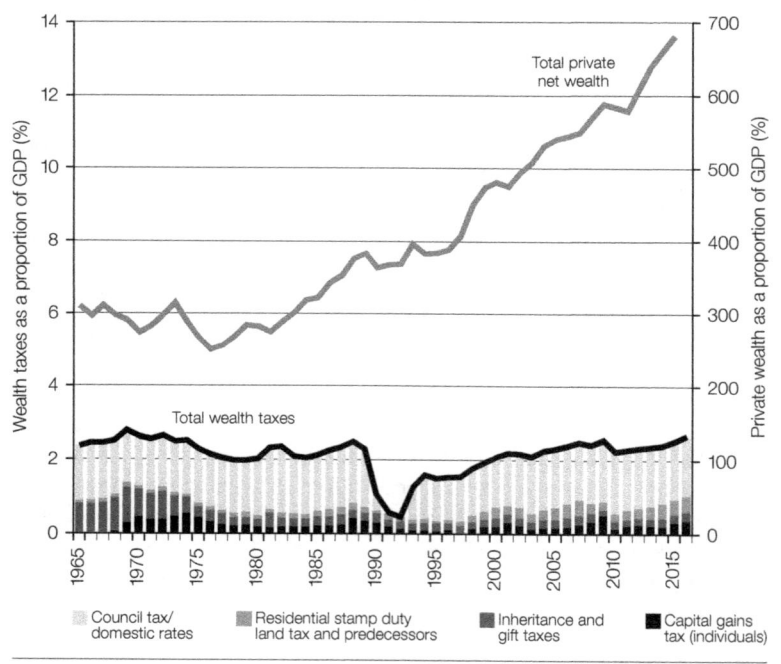

Figure 12.1:
Wealth, and taxes on wealth, as a share of GDP

Note: Resolution Foundation analysis using the Wealth and Assets Survey, British Household Panel Survey, National Accounts data, and data from D Blake and M Orszag, 'Annual estimates of personal wealth holdings in the United Kingdom since 1948', *Applied Financial Economics*, 9(4), 1999, pp397–421

Source: A Corlett and L Gardiner, *Home Affairs: options for reforming property taxation*, Resolution Foundation, 2018, p15, Figure 1

Figure 12.2:
Top wealth and income shares

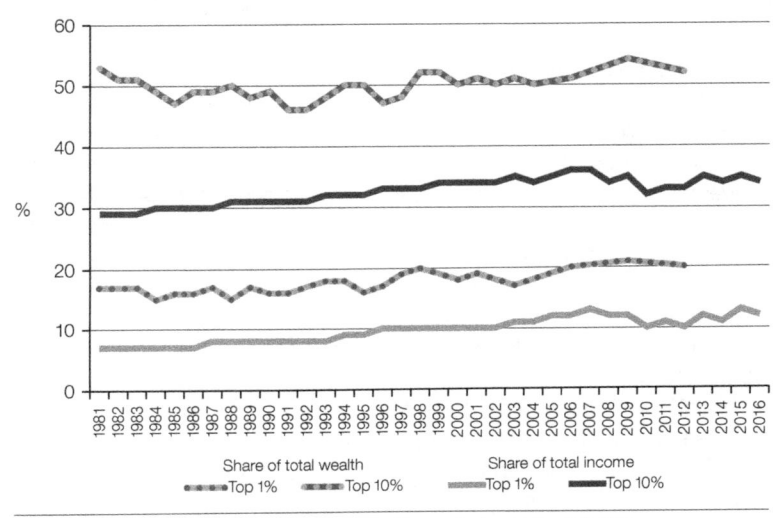

[Chart showing top wealth and income shares from 1981 to 2016, with four lines: Share of total wealth Top 1% and Top 10%, and Share of total income Top 1% and Top 10%. Y-axis shows percentage from 0 to 60.]

Note: 'Wealth' is net private wealth. 'Income' is personal income for income tax, before tax.
Source: World Inequality Database: https//wid.world/country/united-kingdom

'Taxes on returns' refers to policies for taxing the income or gains that accrue to owners of wealth. There are two main UK taxes that fit this definition: income tax (applied to income from investments) and capital gains tax. Under income tax, different tax rates and allowances apply to different types of investment income. In the UK, capital gains are charged under a separate tax; this differs from the position in many other countries, where at least some types of capital gain are taxable as income. The UK's capital gains tax has been subject to a rollercoaster of reforms since its introduction in 1965.

'Taxes on holdings' refers to policies for taxing the ownership of wealth. There are currently no taxes in the UK that directly fit this description. Perhaps the two closest are council tax, which applies to residential property, and the various stamp duties that are charged on transactions involving land and shares. The archetypal tax on holdings is a net wealth tax. The UK has never had this type of tax; an annual wealth tax was proposed by the Labour government in 1974, but it was never enacted.

Why tax wealth (more)?

Why might we want to increase taxes on wealth? Two types of justification can be given (these are not mutually exclusive).

First, there is the aim of achieving fairer *outcomes* in the distribution of wealth. On this approach, we can assess whether the UK's current distribution is 'fair', essentially just by looking at a snapshot of it. If we find that some people have too little, or others have too much, or the gap between rich and poor is too large, we may conclude that the current distribution is unfair; we may then seek to use the tax system to redistribute wealth from those who have most to those who have less.[7]

Second, there may also be a concern to achieve fairer *processes* for the distribution of wealth. Here we need to know not just what the current distribution of wealth looks like, but also how it came about. If some people do not 'deserve' the full extent of their wealth, or wealth is determined by brute luck, then we may think that the distribution is unfair. We may then seek to use the tax system to redistribute wealth from those who do not fully deserve it, or who have been lucky, to those who deserve more than they currently have.

Aside from these two types of justification, policy makers often raise a third issue, which economists refer to as 'efficiency' or the elimination of distortions. In general terms, efficiency involves maximising the total of something, irrespective of its distribution. Economists usually aim at maximising 'utility' or 'preference satisfaction', summed across the whole population. Tax policies are sometimes evaluated as though efficiency is obviously the primary goal that policy makers should be aiming for. Of course, it is an important consideration, but not the only one.

What do each of these concerns imply for reforms to taxes on wealth? If the aim is to improve fairness of outcomes, the strongest justification for taxing wealth more is that the revenue could be used to help the worst off, particularly those currently living in poverty. A further reason for taxing wealth specifically, is that this would contribute *directly* to reducing the gap between rich and poor. This gap has become a matter of increasing public concern, not least due the threat that it poses to social cohesion and the entire political system.

If the concern is with fairness of processes, one compelling reason for taxing wealth is that many of the ways in which wealth is currently accumulated are plainly unfair. 'Desert' is hard to define in the abstract, but real-life examples of undeservingness are not difficult to find. Can anyone really claim that they 'deserve' their inheritance, or their stock market gains, or their rental income, more than someone else deserves their income from work? If one thinks that desert matters, then having higher rates of tax on work than wealth is surely topsy-turvy.

Finally, there may be a concern that taxing wealth would not work in practice. Proposals for redistributing wealth must be evaluated not only from a static perspective, but also taking into account how people are likely to respond: policies that superficially look progressive may turn out not to be. However, there are no grounds whatsoever for supposing that our current system of taxes on wealth is optimally efficient. On the contrary, there seem to be plenty of opportunities here to improve both distributive justice *and* efficiency.

Prospects for reform

The extreme inequality of wealth in the UK provides motivation to reform taxes on wealth, but it also presents a policy challenge. Precisely because wealth is so unequally distributed, it would be difficult to raise significant revenue from taxing wealth without considerably increasing effective rates at the top of the distribution. This challenge is quite different from the one often raised in the context of taxes on income from work – there, the difficulty is instead that generating significant revenue requires tax increases to extend quite far down the distribution. Both options raise political difficulties, but for different reasons.

The risks involved with tax reforms that specifically target the rich (as taxes on wealth inevitably would), are twofold. The first concerns the political process. Many rich people are not implacably opposed to taxes on wealth. However, those who are often wield significant political power, both in shaping public opinion and through direct engagement in the policy-making process. The second risk concerns behavioural responses (see Box 12.1): perhaps the rich are so especially responsive to the tax system that targeting this group is futile, or even counterproductive?

These two risks are related. The main obstacle to taxing wealth may not be that large behavioural responses *will* occur, but rather that the reforms stall from the outset because policy makers become convinced that they *would* occur. Politicians are vulnerable to sources proclaiming that if taxes on wealth were increased then the rich would leave the country, or would invest less, or would cease their entrepreneurial activity. Superficially, many of these proclamations look credible because it is true that many well-intentioned reforms of the past have turned out to raise much less revenue than expected.

In response to these anxieties, it is crucial that politicians are educated about the difference between real and artificial responses to the tax system (see Box 12.2). These are often conveniently conflated by critics of taxing wealth. Opposition to taxes on the rich often trades on the impression that this group is especially responsive in their *real* economic activity. By contrast, most available evidence shows that policies tend to fail instead because the rich are especially good at devising *artificial* responses. Policy makers need to understand this, and (re)design the tax system accordingly.

The UK's tax system is currently an accretion of improvised tinkering that is impossible to defend on any principled basis;[8] our existing taxes on wealth reflect the worst elements of this system. There is growing political will to look again at the taxation of wealth, and in this respect prospects for reform are good. Major reforms of the taxation of wealth have been proposed by the Institute for Fiscal Studies, Resolution Foundation and the Institute for Public Policy Research.[9] All these reform packages involve difficult choices and compromises; any would be a vast improvement on our current system.

Box 12.1:
The Laffer curve

The Laffer curve was famously sketched on a napkin by American economist Arthur Laffer to depict the idea that, for any tax, the revenue-maximising rate will be somewhere between 0 and 100 per cent. Raising tax rates will increase revenue up to a point (the apex of the curve), but any further increases will then have the perverse effect of *decreasing* revenue. However, on its own this insight does not tell us what the revenue-maximising rate is; identifying that point is subject to two important difficulties.

First, the shape of the curve is almost always subject to significant evidential uncertainty because it requires a *causal* analysis of the tax's effect on behaviours, raising numerous empirical challenges. Opponents of tax rises often point to previous occasions where tax rates went down, and revenue subsequently went up. But this merely demonstrates correlation, not causation, and fails to distinguish the impact of changes in tax rates from the numerous other economic factors that affect tax revenues over time.

Second, the shape of the curve is not fixed, but rather is itself a function of public policy. Changes to the design of the tax, its enforcement, other economic and social policies, all affect the revenue-maximising rate. For example, to the extent that observed effects on tax revenue are attributable to artificial responses like planning and avoidance, these can be reduced through improved tax design, thereby reshaping the curve and increasing the revenue-maximising rate.

Box 12.2:
Real and artificial responses to tax

There are numerous ways in which individuals may change their behaviour in response to taxes. They can be divided into two main categories:

- 'Real' behavioural responses involve changes in the *substance* of economic and/or social activities. For example:
  - working more/fewer hours, or retiring earlier/later;
  - moving locality, or emigrating;
  - consuming more/less, or consuming different things;
  - saving or investing more/less, or investing in different types of asset;
  - starting or selling/liquidating a business.
- 'Artificial' behavioural responses involve changes in the *appearance* of activities, often through changing their legal structure without changing their economic substance. For example:
  - tax planning to recharacterise activities so that they fall within a different tax base (or outside the scope of tax altogether);
  - tax avoidance schemes, which often rely on artificial steps to achieve an outcome that parliament did not (in a broad sense) intend;
  - tax evasion through non-reporting or misreporting of real economic activities.

Real and artificial responses are often conflated in policy analysis, partly because they can be very difficult to distinguish empirically, using available data. Yet it is important to distinguish them where possible, in particular because their policy implications are often very different.

Recommendations

In the short term

- Communicate a clear intention to increase the share of total tax revenues raised from taxes on wealth relative to existing major tax bases of labour income and consumption and ensure that all taxes on wealth adopt a progressive rate structure.
- Publish a 'road map' for reform that specifies long-term targets (for example, a share of total tax revenues to be raised from taxes on wealth) and initial policy focuses – for example, reforms to allowances/reliefs for capital income and gains.
- Focus initially on reforms to taxes on *returns* on wealth, in particular through measures that increase alignment between effective tax rates

on capital income/gains and effective tax rates (including national insurance contributions) on income from work.

- Prioritise reforms that would achieve both an increase in the redistribution of wealth (so increasing the overall progressivity of the tax system) *and* an increase in economic efficiency (by reducing existing distortions in investment decisions and associated opportunities for tax planning).

In the longer term

- Consider options for more extensive reform of taxes on transfers and holdings of wealth, including (for example) reforms to the tax base for inheritances and gifts, and the tax treatment of owner-occupied housing.

- Where existing tax treatment has become 'capitalised' into asset prices or has otherwise generated legitimate expectations on the part of individual owners, reforms should be implemented gradually and according to a clear timetable.

Notes
1   See further LE Bauluz, *Revised and Extended National Wealth Series: Australia, Canada, France, Germany, Italy, Japan, the UK and the USA*, WID.world Working Paper Series 2017/23, World Inequality Database, 2017, Figure 37
2   See further H Miller and T Pope, *The Changing Composition of UK Tax Revenues*, Institute for Fiscal Studies Briefing Note BN182, 2016, Figure 4, which shows the share of 'capital taxes' unchanged at around 1 per cent of national income. However, this definition excludes council tax (and its predecessors), and income tax on capital income.
3   World Inequality Database: https://wid.world/country/united-kingdom
4   Office for National Statistics, *Wealth in Great Britain Wave 5: 2014 to 2016*, 2018
5   MY Kan and H Laurie, 'Changing patterns in the allocation of savings, investments and debts within couple relationships', *The Sociological Review*, 62(2), 2014; R Joseph and K Rowlingson, 'Her house, his pension? The division of assets among (ex-) couples and the role of policy', *Social Policy and Society*, 11(1), 2011
6   In this book, stamp duty land tax is dealt with in Chapter 15.
7   The concern of this book is with multiple kinds of inequality. Here the focus is on inequality of wealth, but there is overlap with inequality along several other dimensions. For example, those with children are more likely to be poor and women are less likely to be wealthy.
8   P Johnson, 'Tax without design: recent developments in UK tax policy', *Fiscal Studies*, 35(3), 2014, pp243–73
9   Institute for Fiscal Studies and J Mirrlees (eds), *Tax by Design: the Mirrlees Review*, Oxford University Press, 2011; Resolution Foundation, *A New Generational Contract: the final report of the Intergenerational Commission*, 2018; C Roberts, G Blakely and L Murphy, A *Wealth of Difference: reforming the taxation of wealth*, Institute for Public Policy Research, 2018

Thirteen
Taxes on inheritances and gifts
Andrew Summers

Inheritances and gifts totalling over £120 billion are transferred in the UK each year – over 80 per cent is inheritances.[1] The total real value of transfers on death has more than doubled over the past 20 years and is forecast to double again over the next two decades.[2] Inheritances are very unequally distributed. Within the bottom half of the lifetime income distribution, average lifetime inheritance is around £20,000, compared with nearly £100,000 for those in the top fifth (see Figure 13.1).[3] The UK's only tax on gifts and bequests, inheritance tax, collected £5.2 billion in 2018, is equivalent to less than 4 per cent of the total transferred.

Figure 13.1:
Distribution of inheritances

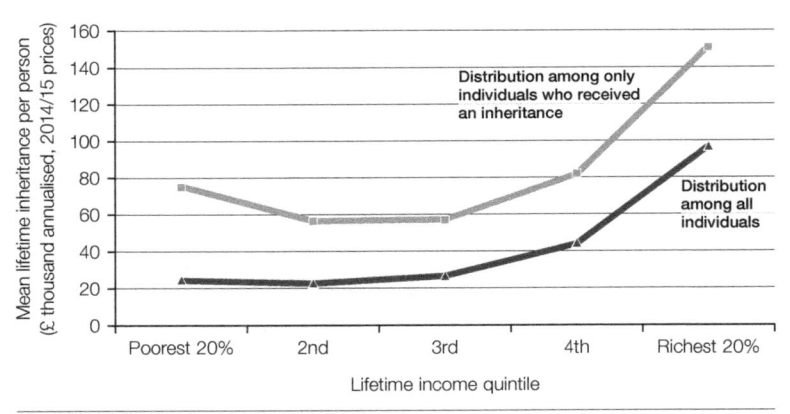

Note: Institute for Fiscal Studies analysis of English Longitudinal Study of Aging (ELSA) data (various waves) and linked administrative data. 'Lifetime income' is the sum of household earnings, state and private pension income; it does not include unearned income or working-age benefits.

Source: A Hood and R Joyce, *Inheritances and Inequality Across and Within Generations*, Institute for Fiscal Studies Briefing Note BN192, 2017, Figure 6

Attitudes towards taxing inheritances raise a puzzle. On the one hand, surveys have shown that the public regard inheritances as the main reason why some people have much greater wealth than others, and express a desire to reduce this inequality.[4] On the other hand, inheritance tax is notoriously unpopular: the public regard it as the UK's most 'unfair' tax.[5] Partly, this unpopularity may be due to the design of the tax and some misunderstanding about its scope. However, it also appears to reveal a deeper conflict between people's desire for a fairer society and the wish to benefit their own family.

Inheritance tax

Overview

Inheritance tax is based on the net value of a person's wealth when s/he dies (known as her/his 'estate'). Lifetime gifts made within seven years of death are added to the value of the deceased's estate to limit the most straightforward way of circumventing the tax. Gifts within three years of death are taxed at the full rate; gifts between three and seven years of death are taxed at a tapered rate.

The tax currently applies to around 4 per cent of estates, and raises £5.2 billion per year, or 0.9 per cent of total tax revenue.[6] This revenue has more than doubled over the past decade,[7] mainly due to the nominal freeze in the tax-free allowance since 2009, coupled with rising house prices over the same period. Nevertheless, the revenue share from taxing inheritances remains low by historical standards: a century ago the estate duty collected nearly 20 per cent of total tax revenues (excluding customs duties).[8]

Each person has a tax-free allowance (known as the 'nil rate band'), set at £325,000 since 2009. Since 2007, any unused allowance has been transferable to the deceased's spouse or civil partner, effectively granting an allowance of £650,000 for couples. In this respect, taxation is not completely 'independent' in the UK, and indeed (as with the marriage allowance, discussed in Chapter 8) has become less independent in recent years.[9] In 2017, an additional allowance was made available where the deceased's home is passed to 'direct descendants': this is currently £300,000 for couples, and is set to rise to £350,000 by 2020, such that the total tax-free allowance for a couple passing their main home to their children will be £1 million.

Inheritance tax is paid at a flat rate of 40 per cent on the value of the estate above the allowance, subject to exemptions and reliefs, which can reduce the effective average rate on large estates to less than 10 per cent (see further below). The legal liability to pay the tax falls on the administrators/executors of the estate, but its economic incidence will almost invariably fall on the inheritors, who receive less as a result of the tax.

Exemptions and reliefs

The main exemption from inheritance tax is for any transfers made to a person's spouse or civil partner, whether during life or upon death.[10] This exemption applied to £11.4 billion of assets in 2016.[11] Together with the transferrable nil rate band, the spousal exemption means that the 'tax unit' for inheritance tax is effectively, albeit not strictly, the couple rather than the individual. Transfers to charities are also exempt: this applied to £3 billion of assets in 2016.[12]

Although lifetime gifts made within seven years of death are generally taxable, there is an annual exemption of £3,000 per year. Less well known, but potentially far more significant, is an additional exemption for 'normal expenditure out of income'. Provided the donor retains enough income to maintain her/his usual standard of living, this exemption effectively allows her/him to give away the rest tax-free. HM Revenue and Customs (HMRC) does not publish statistics on the value of these exemptions.

Pension pots (under defined contribution schemes) are exempt from inheritance tax. Moreover, if someone dies before age 75, there may also in some circumstances be no income tax liability when the pension is withdrawn by the beneficiary. These exemptions are likely to grow in importance following the new 'pension freedoms' introduced in 2015. As the Institute for Fiscal Studies has noted, they have the perverse effect of incentivising people to use everything except their pension to pay for their retirement.[13]

Agricultural and business property benefits from 100 per cent relief from inheritance tax. In 2016, these two reliefs reduced the value of taxable estates by £1 billion and £1.6 billion respectively,[14] at an estimated revenue cost of £1.2 billion.[15] Recent analysis by the Office of Tax Simplification shows that these reliefs disproportionately benefit the very largest estates (see Figure 13.2), reducing the effective average tax rate on estates with net value over £10 million to less than 10 per cent.[16]

Figure 13.2:
Estates benefiting from inheritance tax reliefs

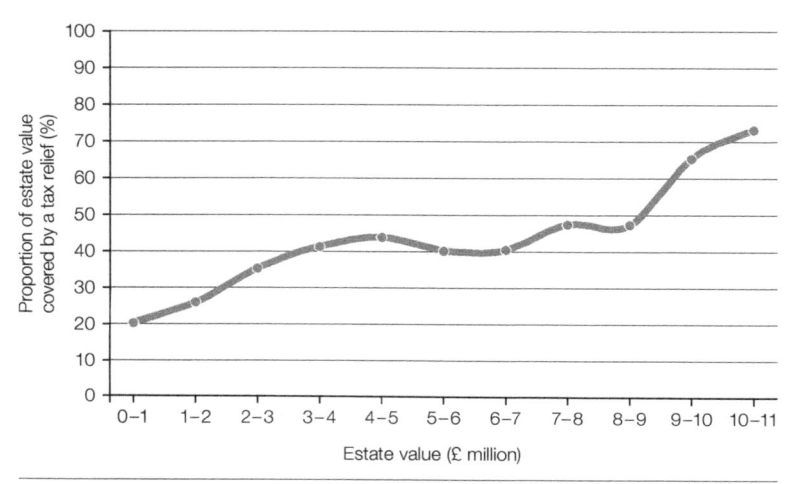

[Line graph showing Proportion of estate value covered by a tax relief (%) on y-axis (0–100) against Estate value (£ million) on x-axis (0–1 through 10–11). Values rise from about 20% at 0–1 to about 72% at 10–11, with a plateau around 40% between 4–5 and 7–8.]

Note: Office of Tax Simplification analysis of HMRC inheritance tax data for 2015/16. 'Tax reliefs' include agricultural property relief and business property relief and exclude nil rate band. 'Estate value' is total assets (including chargeable lifetime gifts) minus liabilities (eg, debts), before reliefs.

Source: Office of Tax Simplification, *Inheritance Tax Review – first report: overview of the tax and dealing with administration*, 2018, p6

Changes to inheritance tax

The UK has had a tax on estates since 1684. The current inheritance tax is modelled closely on the estate duty, which was introduced in 1894. Estate duty similarly taxed the value of estates passing at death, together with gifts made within a few years of death; the main difference from today's inheritance tax was that (until 1972) it included no exemption for transfers between spouses. After 1945, rates were also much higher, peaking in 1969 at a marginal rate of 85 per cent on the top slice of large inheritances.

Between 1974 and 1986, estate duty was replaced with capital transfer tax, which was charged on all lifetime gifts as well as assets transferred at death. Although capital transfer tax served as 'gift tax' as well as an inheritance tax, it remained donor based, rather than applying to the amounts received by each donee. In 1986, it was replaced with today's inheritance tax. Most of the provisions of capital transfer tax were retained, but with the important difference that gifts given more than seven years before death were taken out of tax.

The main changes to inheritance tax in more recent years include the introduction of:

- in 1992, 100 per cent relief for agricultural and business property;
- in 2006, new tax charges for discretionary trusts and other anti-avoidance measures;
- in 2007, the transferable nil rate band for spouses and civil partners; *and*
- in 2017, the additional allowance for main residences passed to direct descendants.

Box 13.1:
Inheritance tax planning

It is often claimed that inheritance tax is only paid by the 'moderately rich', while the 'very rich' can reduce their liability to zero. This is an exaggeration, although tax reliefs do enable some rich individuals to get close. Except for those who can claim 'non-domiciled' status, it is rarely possible for wealthy individuals to avoid inheritance tax altogether. Following a clampdown in the mid-2000s, the days of widely marketed avoidance schemes using complex trust structures have passed, although discretionary trusts do remain an important aspect of dynastic planning.

The easiest way to escape inheritance tax is simply to make gifts more than seven years before death. This opportunity is a feature, not a bug, of the current system: it was the main purpose behind replacing the capital transfer tax in 1986. The consequence of the continued exclusion of most lifetime gifts is greatly to favour those at the very top of the wealth distribution, who are most able to give away property early, without sacrificing their current standard of living. For critics who are concerned that only the 'moderately wealthy' pay under the current system, the answer is surely to extend the existing tax base to cover these gifts, rather than to abolish the tax altogether.

Evaluation

The current inheritance tax is a messy agglomeration of reforms spanning the past century, lacking any systematic rationale. The tax is unpopular for a variety of reasons. Some of these are politically intractable, such as the conflict that many voters would acknowledge between the desire for greater equality of opportunity and the wish to benefit their own family. But the current design of inheritance tax also incorporates some obvious 'own goals' that surely contribute to the perception of unfairness.

The first own goal concerns the widely held and partly justified impression that the tax is easily 'gamed' by the very rich (see Box 13.1).

Since 2006, significant steps have been taken to prevent the most artificial forms of avoidance, but structural features have been retained that invite strategic tax planning by the very rich. These features are both very expensive in terms of foregone revenue, and also undermine public trust in the tax.

The second own goal is that the design of the tax is fundamentally misaligned with its moral and political justifications. Many people are sympathetic to the view that, from the perspective of the recipient, inheritances and gifts are unearned and essentially a matter of luck. And yet, inheritance tax is not framed in this way. Instead, it misdirects attention to the donor, thereby inviting criticisms of unfair 'double taxation' and interference with property rights (see Box 13.2).

Box 13.2:
'Double taxation'

A common argument against inheritance tax is that it involves taxing a person twice: first during her/his lifetime, and then again on death. Several responses can be given:

- The argument tends to be selectively applied. If inheritance tax is double taxation, then so is VAT and the various other taxes that are charged on transactions or activities that taxpayers fund out of their taxed income.

- The argument is often wrong even on its own terms. A large proportion of most taxable estates in the UK consists of house price inflation in the deceased's main home. These gains will have been entirely untaxed during the person's lifetime.

- Inheritance tax clearly involves no double taxation on the *recipient* of the inheritance. However, this point could be emphasised by basing the tax on the amount received by each inheritor, rather than the total amount left by the person who died.

- Most fundamentally, it is not clear why the *number* of separate taxable events should matter in any context. What matters is the effect of the tax system overall. This is a function of the *net amount* of tax payable, whether on one or two (or more) occasions.

Options for reform

Reforming inheritance tax

Within the existing structure of inheritance tax, several reforms could be implemented to broaden the tax base and reduce the current scope for tax planning and avoidance:[17]

- **Abolish or restrict exemptions and reliefs.** The exemptions for pension pots and gifts comprising 'normal expenditure out of income' could be abolished immediately. Agricultural and business reliefs should also be phased out completely (raising up to £1.2 billion per year), but this may need to be done gradually and there ought to be some facility to defer the payment of tax where necessary to prevent the break-up of farms or family businesses. Any changes to the spousal/civil partner rules would be more challenging.

- **Extend taxation of lifetime gifts.** Strategic lifetime giving currently provides an easy way for those with the largest fortunes to pass on their wealth tax-free. Extending the threshold for taxable gifts beyond seven years would go some way towards limiting this practice. However, if the intention was to tax all lifetime gifts, it would be preferable to switch wholesale to a lifetime receipts tax (see below), rather than effectively to reinstate the old donor-based capital transfer tax.

- **Tax treatment of non-domiciled residents.** For most UK-domiciled individuals, the most egregious loopholes in the inheritance tax legislation have now been closed. However, individuals who live in the UK but who can claim that their permanent home is abroad ('non-doms') have been allowed to retain various questionable tax advantages through the use of non-resident trusts and overseas companies. These benefits were only partly curtailed by new legislation implemented in 2017; they require further attention.

Lifetime receipts tax

There are strong arguments for replacing the current donor-based inheritance tax with a recipient-based tax (see Box 13.3). The two main options would be to introduce a 'lifetime receipts tax', or to tax inheritances and gifts as *income* of the recipient. Hybrid approaches are also possible – for example, a lifetime receipts tax where the rate varied according to the recipient's lifetime income from all sources. However, for simplicity of exposition, the options are considered separately here.

A lifetime receipts tax is based on the cumulative total of all inheritances and gifts received by a person over her/his lifetime. Ireland and France both already have taxes of this type. The Resolution Foundation and Institute for Public Policy Research have both recently proposed a new lifetime receipts tax to replace the UK's current inheritance tax.[18] The Resolution Foundation has modelled several variants of its proposal using existing wealth and inheritance data (see Table 13.1).

Box 13.3:
Taxing donors or recipients?

A tax on inheritances could be donor based or recipient based. The UK's current inheritance tax is donor based: it is assessed on the value of the deceased's estate. The USA's (more aptly-named) estate tax also works this way. However, many other countries adopt a recipient-based tax, assessed on the value received by each inheritor. The key difference is in the definition of the tax base, not the legal liability to pay, which usually falls on the administrator/executor of the estate under either system.

From a political perspective, switching to a recipient-based tax may help to *reframe* inheritance tax by aligning it with popular justifications for taxing inheritances, which tend to focus on the unearned windfall of the recipient. A recipient-based tax may also encourage donors to disperse their wealth more widely (since this reduces the total tax payable). However, this effect should not be overstated, since most inheritances and gifts would probably continue to be passed to a small number of close family members.

It is sometimes said that even if inheritance tax was recipient based, it would still unfairly 'interfere' with the right of the donor to determine what happens to her/his property after s/he dies. In this way, however framed, it remains a tax on the deceased. But income tax, corporation tax and VAT (among others) already mean that the amount of money paid over by one person to another is frequently not the amount that the recipient is free to keep, after tax. Taxes on inheritances are no different, in this respect.

Once reframed as a recipient-based tax, there seems no reason to distinguish between inheritances or gifts. Both enhance the recipient's economic resources to the same extent; neither are 'earned' or 'deserved'. It is hard to see how any claim to deservingness by the recipient could vary according to whether the donor is alive or dead. Consequently, most proposals for recipient-based taxes apply equally to both inheritances and gifts.

Under the Resolution Foundation's central proposal, each person would have a lifetime allowance of £125,000. Receipts above this allowance would be taxed at 20 per cent up to £500,000, and 30 per cent above that. Using dynamic modelling that incorporates some (but not all) likely behavioural effects, it is estimated that this policy would raise an extra £4.8 billion per year (in 2020/21) compared with the existing inheritance tax.

The main challenge with switching to a lifetime receipts tax from the UK's current system concerns transitional issues. Revenue would build up gradually at first, as inheritances and gifts would initially be counted towards each recipient's lifetime allowance. If the tax were subsequently abolished following a change of government, this would result in a permanent loss of revenue. A low lifetime allowance helps to mitigate against this risk, but other transitional provisions also need to be considered.

Table 13.1:
Modelling inheritance tax options for reform

	Lifetime allowance	Tax rates	Revenue (2020/21) £ billion	Extra revenue £ billion
Current system			5.9	
Recipient-based taxes				
Flat 40p rate	£500k	40% above that	6.6	0.7
Flat 15p rate	£125k	15% above that	6.9	1.1
Flat 10p rate	£125k	10% above that, with no reliefs or spousal exemption	6.2	0.3
Our recommendation	£125k	20% up to £500k; 30% above that	10.7	4.8
10 x income tax thresholds	£125k	20% up to £500k; 40% up to £1.5m; 45% above that	13.5	7.7
Income tax	Any unused personal allowance. Income tax rates		15.0	9.2
Income tax and national insurance contributions	Any unused personal allowance. Income tax and national insurance contribution rates		16.1	10.2

Note: Resolution Foundation analysis using Wealth and Assets Survey data and Office for Budget Responsibility inheritance tax forecast. Includes a behavioural effect for extra splitting of estates (except in the bottom two scenarios). All include a £3,000 gift allowance.

Source: A Corlett, *Passing On: options for reforming inheritance taxation*, Resolution Foundation, 2018, p30, Table 3

Taxing receipts as income

Inheritances and gifts enhance a person's economic resources just as much as income from work or investments. Consequently, if one wanted to design a tax system that reflected each taxpayer's individual 'ability to pay', there would be no reason to distinguish gratuitous transfers from other sources of income. This insight leads in the direction of taxing inheritances and gifts under income tax (indeed, arguably, national insurance contributions should be applied as well).

Taxing inheritances and gifts as income would involve granting only a very minimal non-taxable allowance (currently £12,500 for 2019/20), and imposing marginal rates up to 45 per cent, or even 61 per cent (if one includes employee and employer national insurance contributions). Compared against our existing system, such a proposal looks rather radical.

On the other hand, this approach has a clear and simple justification (as above), and it could raise three times the current revenue of inheritance tax: an extra £10 billion per year (see Table 13.1).

The main administrative difficulty with taxing gratuitous transfers under income tax concerns the extreme 'lumpiness' of these receipts. Unlike other sources of income, inheritances and gifts tend only to arise once, or at most a few times, in a lifetime. This lumpiness means that someone who spends most of her/his life as a basic rate (20 per cent) income tax payer may still face a 40 per cent or 45 per cent marginal tax rate in the single year when s/he receives an inheritance or gift.

This problem undoubtedly raises a challenge for policy makers, but it should not be overstated. It is not unique to gratuitous transfers; it already affects some types of income from work, investement income and capital gains. For those who would face a higher tax bracket in the year of receipt, various administrative solutions could be adopted, such as backwards averaging (which is already available under the income tax system for some types of income), forwards averaging (by annuity values) or the use of tax reserve certificates.

Recommendations

In the short term

- Immediately abolish the current inheritance tax exemptions for unused private pension pots and 'normal expenditure out of income' that would otherwise constitute a lifetime gift within seven years of death – ie, retain only the fixed annual exemption for gifts.

- Announce the gradual phasing out of the current inheritance tax reliefs for agricultural property and business property. The phasing out of these reliefs should be accompanied by new measures to allow temporary deferral of the tax charge where necessary to avoid the break-up of small farms or businesses.

- Introduce comprehensive measures to prevent non-domiciled residents from avoiding inheritance tax on UK assets through the use of overseas companies (not limited to residential property) and prevent 'deemed domiciled' residents from avoiding inheritance tax on foreign assets through the use of non-resident trusts.

In the longer term

- Consider the options for replacing the existing donor-based inheritance tax with a recipient-based tax on inheritances and lifetime gifts. In particular:
  - Consult on the option of introducing a new lifetime receipts tax in line with Resolution Foundation proposals, with particular attention to resolving transitional and other administrative challenges.
  - Consult on the alternative option of taxing inheritances and gifts as income of the recipient, with particular attention to resolving challenges related to averaging and the lumpiness of receipts.

Notes
1. A Corlett, *Passing On: options for reforming inheritance taxation*, Resolution Foundation, 2018, Figure 1
2. L Gardiner, *The Million Dollar Be-Question: inheritances, gifts and their implications for generational living standards*, Resolution Foundation, 2017
3. A Hood and R Joyce, *Inheritances and Inequality Across and Within Generations*, Institute for Fiscal Studies Briefing Note BN192, 2017, Figure 6
4. K Rowlingson and S McKay, *What do the Public Think About the Wealth Gap?*, University of Birmingham, 2013, Figure 2
5. S Shakespeare, 'Voters in all parties think inheritance tax unfair', YouGov, 19 March 2015, https://yougov.co.uk/topics/politics/articles-reports/2015/03/19/inheritance-tax-most-unfair
6. HM Revenue and Customs, *Inheritance Tax Statistics 2015 to 2016*, July 2018
7. In 2009/10, the tax was paid by less than 3 per cent of estates and raised just £2.5 billion.
8. J Hills, *Changing Tax: how the tax system works and how to change it*, CPAG, 1988, p41
9. See discussion in Low Incomes Tax Reform Group, *Couples in the Tax and Related Welfare Systems: a call for greater clarity*, 2015
10. Not all countries adopt a spousal exemption: for a comparative overview see D Ferguson and R Lipsitz, 'How does UK inheritance tax compare with that in other countries?' the *Guardian*, 17 September 2015
11. HM Revenue and Customs, *Inheritance Tax: exemptions and reliefs*, 2018, Table 12.2, available at www.gov.uk/government/collections/inheritance-tax-statistics
12. HM Revenue and Customs, *Inheritance Tax: exemptions and reliefs*, 2018, Table 12.2, available at www.gov.uk/government/collections/inheritance-tax-statistics
13. S Adam and T Waters, 'Options for raising taxes', in C Emmerson, C Farquharson and P Johnson (eds), *The IFS Green Budget: October 2018*, Institute for Fiscal Studies, 2018, pp179–81
14. HM Revenue and Customs, *Inheritance Tax: exemptions and reliefs*, 2018, Table 12.2, available at www.gov.uk/government/collections/inheritance-tax-statistics
15. HM Revenue and Customs, *Estimated Costs of Principal Tax Reliefs*, January 2018, available at www.gov.uk/government/statistics/main-tax-expenditures-and-structural-reliefs. This is a static estimate that excludes the impact of behavioural responses if the reliefs were abolished.
16. Office of Tax Simplification, *Inheritance Tax Review – first report: overview of the tax and*

dealing with administration, 2018. See also Tax Justice UK, *In Stark Relief: how inheritance tax breaks favour the well off*, 2019

17 For some very recent (and mostly welcome) recommendations, see Office of Tax Simplification, *Inheritance Tax Review – second report: simplifying the design of inheritance tax*, 2019

18 Resolution Foundation, *A New Generational Contract: final report of the Intergenerational Commission*, 2018; C Roberts, G Blakely and L Murphy, *A Wealth of Difference: reforming the taxation of wealth*, Institute for Public Policy Research, 2018

Fourteen
Taxes on investment income and gains
Andrew Summers

Returns on wealth include income from savings and investments ('capital income'), plus the increase in the value of the assets held since their acquisition ('capital gain'). In the UK, these two types of return on wealth are taxed separately, with capital income taxed under income tax, and capital gains taxed (but only upon realisation) under capital gains tax. Some returns on wealth, most notably the income and gains that result from owner-occupation of residential property, are not taxed at all.

Figure 14.1:
Distribution of investment income

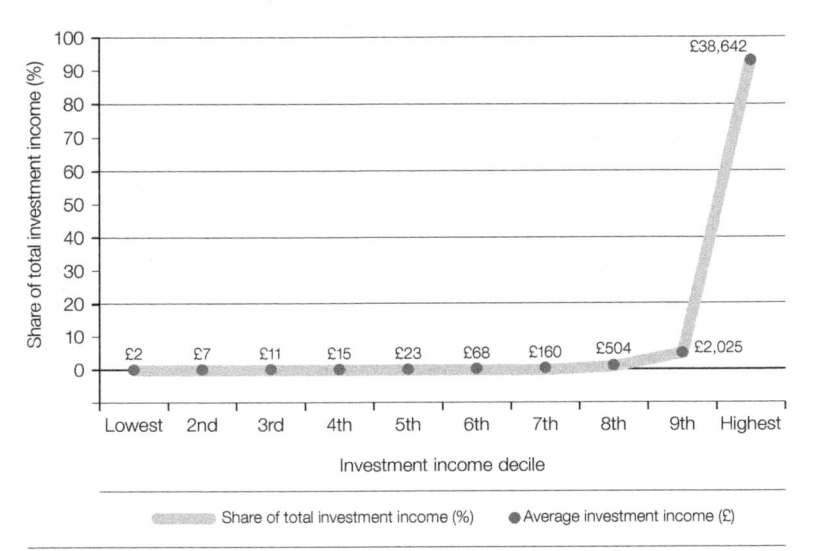

Chart showing share of total investment income (%) and average investment income (£) by investment income decile: Lowest £2, 2nd £7, 3rd £11, 4th £15, 5th £23, 6th £68, 7th £160, 8th £504, 9th £2,025, Highest £38,642.

Note: HMRC analysis using Survey of Personal Incomes data for 2015/16. Excludes tax-exempt investments, and capital gains.

Source: HM Revenue and Customs, Property, Interest, Dividends and Other Investment Income, 2019, Table 13.10

Income tax

Overview

Income tax is paid on income from capital, including interest from savings accounts, dividends from shares, rent from property and other investment income, unless it is exempt. Taxable income from these sources totalled £110 billion in 2015/16, of which 93 per cent (£102 billion) went to just 7 per cent of all income tax payers (see Figure 14.1). Meanwhile, the bottom half of income tax payers received less than £100 *million* between them.[1] It is difficult to calculate precisely the tax revenue attributable to capital income distinct from income from work, but the best available estimate is around 14 per cent of total income tax revenues in 2014, or approximately £22 billion.[2]

Figure 14.2:
Composition of investment income

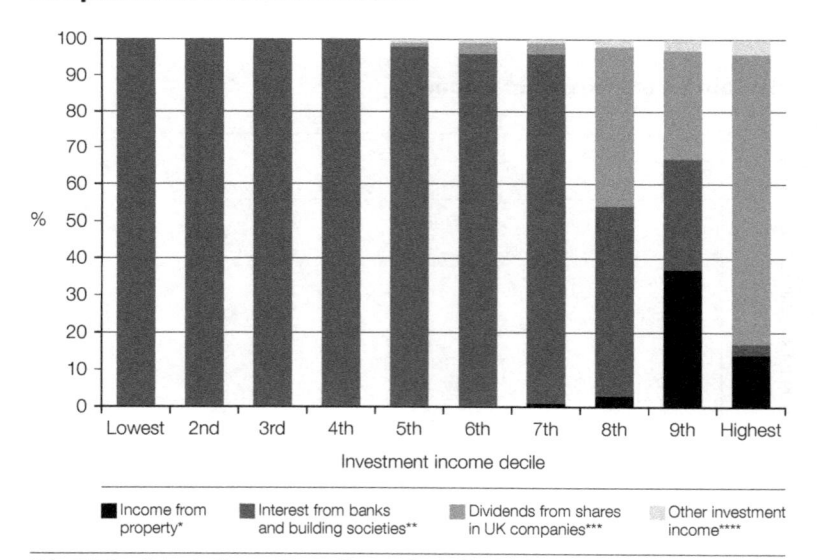

Legend: Income from property* | Interest from banks and building societies** | Dividends from shares in UK companies*** | Other investment income****

Note: HMRC analysis using Survey of Personal Incomes data for 2015/16. Excludes tax-exempt investments, and capital gains.
* Rent from UK and overseas property. Excludes business profits from property businesses.
** Interest from UK banks, building societies and other deposit takers.
*** Dividends from shares in UK companies and unit trusts.
**** Includes interest and dividends from overseas investments.

Source: HM Revenue and Customs, Property, Interest, Dividends and Other Investment Income, 2019, Table 13.10

Types of capital income

Different types of capital income are subject to different treatment under income tax. Several changes have occurred in recent years.

Interest from savings is taxed at normal income tax rates, unless the savings are held in a tax-free savings account. Those whose total income is less than £17,500 (for 2019/20) can receive up to £5,000 in interest tax-free under the 'starting rate' for savings. In 2016, a new personal savings allowance was introduced, under which all basic rate taxpayers can receive the first £1,000 of interest tax-free; this allowance is limited to £500 for higher rate taxpayers and is withdrawn for additional rate taxpayers.

Dividends from shares are taxed at a different rate from other income. A major reform in 2016 replaced the previous system of notional tax credits with a fixed-rate structure: 7.5 per cent for basic rate taxpayers, 32.5 per cent for higher rate and 38.1 per cent for additional rate. A new dividend allowance was also introduced, initially set at £5,000, but later reduced to £2,000 from 2018. Unlike the personal savings allowance, this allowance is retained even for higher and additional rate taxpayers. It cost £1.3 billion in foregone revenue in 2017/18; this is forecast to reduce to £0.7 billion in 2018/19.[3]

Income from property is taxed at normal income tax rates, subject to a new property allowance of £1,000, again introduced in 2016. 'Furnished holiday lettings' receive favourable tax treatment.[4] From 2017, tax relief for finance costs (for example, mortgage interest) is restricted, eventually to the basic rate from 2020. This reform increases tax on higher rate taxpayers who use leverage to invest in buy-to-let properties, but does not affect those who buy outright.

Other investment income is also usually taxed at normal income tax rates, subject to two major exceptions. The first is that returns on private pension funds are not taxed; instead, income tax (but not national insurance contributions) is charged when pension payments (including accumulated returns) are drawn, excluding 25 per cent of the pension pot which can be taken as a tax-free lump sum.[5] The second is that investments within life insurance 'wrappers' are subject to favourable tax treatment.[6]

Box 14.1:
The 'wedge' between taxes on wealth and work

Income and gains from existing wealth are taxed at much lower effective rates than income from work. For capital gains this disparity is obvious, because the headline rates are lower. For capital income, the application of income tax makes it look superficially like these returns are taxed in the same way as labour income. However, that impression is wrong, for several reasons:

- National insurance contributions are not charged on capital income. Consequently, capital income is taxed at an effective rate up to 25.8 per cent lower than an equivalent sum earned through employment.
- Capital income from savings, dividends and rent, as well as capital gains, each benefit from separate additional allowances, not available to those whose only source of income is labour.
- Various forms of savings and investments benefit from tax-free or significantly tax-favoured treatment – for example, ISAs, life insurance wrappers, venture capital schemes and employee benefit schemes.
- Although both labour and capital income are assessed on an individual basis (see Chapter 8), couples can achieve a lower effective tax rate on their capital income and gains by transferring assets to the partner with the lowest tax rate.

These features drive a large 'wedge' between the effective rates of tax on wealth and work. This wedge has grown significantly since the 1980s, particularly due to the abolition of the investment income surcharge and increases in national insurance contributions. The disparity cannot be justified on grounds of either fairness or efficiency. It reinforces that the best way to accumulate wealth is to start with wealth: 'for whosoever hath, to him shall be given'.

Exemptions, allowances and reliefs

The tax-free allowances that were introduced in 2016 for interest, dividends and property income are each available in addition to the main personal allowance, which applies to all types of income. These reforms mean that individuals who are able to diversify their sources of income now effectively receive an additional tax-free allowance of up to £4,000 (until recently £8,000), compared with those who earn all of their income from labour.[7]

In addition, any income received from cash or shares retained in an individual savings account (ISA) is tax-free. HM Revenue and Customs (HMRC) estimates that this exemption costs approximately £3.2 billion in foregone revenue.[8] The limit on annual subscriptions to ISAs has increased significantly over recent years: from £7,000 per year during 1999 to 2007, to £10,200 in 2010, £15,000 in 2014, and £20,000 since

2017. At the end of 2017/18, the total market value of adult ISA holdings stood at £608 billion,[9] the distribution of which is heavily skewed towards those with the highest incomes.[10]

Several schemes offer tax advantages to individuals who buy shares in unlisted companies and social enterprises, either directly or via a venture capital trust.[11] These schemes variously provide income tax and capital gains tax relief on both the initial investment sum and on the investment returns. There are also various employee share schemes that offer tax advantages to employees who invest in shares in their employer.[12]

Figure 14.3:
Effective marginal tax rates on income

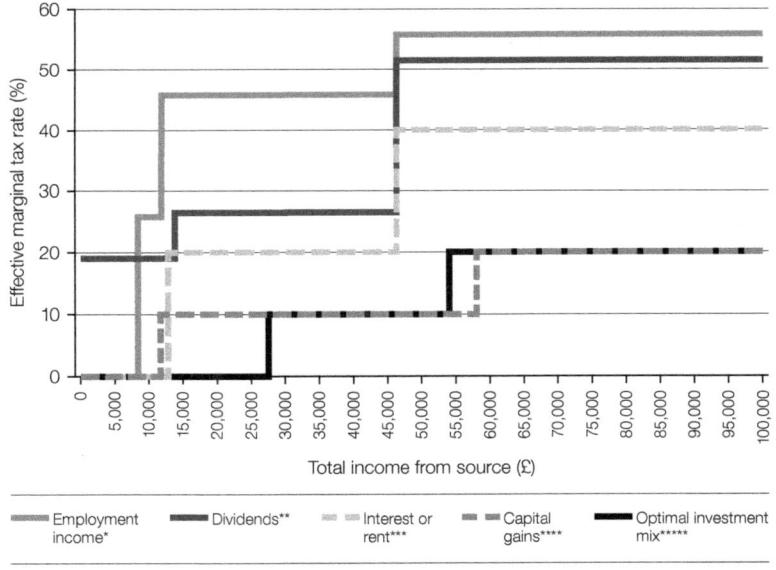

― Employment income* ― Dividends** ― Interest or rent*** ― Capital gains**** ― Optimal investment mix*****

Notes:
* Based on income tax plus employee and employer national insurance contributions (assumes incidence mainly on employee).
** Based on corporation tax on profits prior to distribution (assumes incidence mainly on shareholder), plus income tax at dividend rate.
*** Based on income tax. Does not account for withdrawal of personal savings allowance for higher rate taxpayers.
**** Based on capital gains tax at main rate (not applicable to residential property).
***** Based on income tax and capital gains tax on £13,500 savings interest, £1,000 property income, £2,000 dividends and the remainder capital gains.

Source: Author's estimates based on tax rates and allowances for 2018/19

Capital gains tax

Overview

Capital gains tax is charged on the gain that is realised when an asset that has increased in value is sold (or otherwise 'disposed' of – for example, by gift or exchange). Capital gains tax has undergone a rollercoaster of reforms since its introduction in 1965. Currently, for gains above the annual exempt amount, the main rate for higher rate taxpayers is 20 per cent (28 per cent for gains in residential property), or 10 per cent if the gain qualifies for entrepreneurs' relief.[13]

In 2016/17 (the most recent year available), revenue from capital gains tax totalled £7.7 billion, based on total chargeable gains of £51 billion.[14] Sixty-one per cent of chargeable gains went to individuals who realised gains of £1 million or more in a single year. Capital gains are more unequally distributed than (total) income: whereas only around 1 per cent of income tax payers earn over £150,000 per year, this group represented 12 per cent of capital gains tax payers.

Exemptions, allowances and reliefs

Disposals made to a spouse or civil partner are exempt from capital gains tax, again demonstrating that the tax system is not completely 'independent'; however, the full amount of the gain since the first acquisition remains taxable on any subsequent disposal. By contrast, capital gains tax is entirely written off on death: the deceased's estate does not pay capital gains tax on the gains prior to death, and the inheritors are deemed to have acquired the assets at their market value at the date of death, such that gains prior to death escape tax completely.

Private residence relief provides an exemption from capital gains tax for any gains made on an individual's only or main home. HMRC estimates that the cost of this exemption will be around £28 billion in 2017/18, although this estimate does not account for behavioural responses resulting from the disincentive to move home if the relief was abolished. The other main exempt class of assets is **shares held in an ISA**.

Entrepreneurs' relief provides a reduced rate of 10 per cent capital gains tax on gains in qualifying assets when a person sells her/his business. It was introduced by the Labour government in 2008 at an estimated cost of £200 million per year, but this cost has subsequently ballooned to £2.4

billion in 2017/18 (forecast to rise further to nearly £4 billion by 2023/24).[15] In 2016, a new **investors' relief** was introduced, also at 10 per cent.[16]

There is also a **separate tax-free allowance** for capital gains tax, known as the annual exempt amount, currently £12,000 per year. This allowance effectively serves to double the tax-free income of those who can arrange their financial affairs to realise their gains in tranches each year. Cumulatively, it means that by spreading income across labour, capital income and (short-term) capital gains, an individual can now obtain a total tax-free allowance of over £29,000 per year.[17]

Changes to capital gains tax

There have been a number of significant reforms to capital gains tax since its introduction in 1965. The following table summarises the main changes.

Table 14.1:
Changes to capital gains tax

1965	Capital gains tax is introduced at a flat rate of 30 per cent.
1982	'Indexation allowance' is introduced, under which only gains above inflation (measured by the Retail Price Index) are taxable.
1988	Capital gains tax rates are aligned with income tax (retaining indexation allowance); assets are 'rebased' to their 1982 value, effectively exempting prior gains.
1998	Indexation allowance is replaced with 'taper relief', under which the capital gains tax rate is reduced the longer the asset is held.
2000–2003	Taper relief on business assets is subject to a series of reforms, reducing the taper length from 10 years (from 1998/99) to four years (from 2000/01) to two years (from 2002/03).
2008	A flat capital gains tax rate of 18 per cent is introduced. Entrepreneurs' relief (at 10 per cent) is introduced.
2010	The capital gains tax rate is increased to 28 per cent for higher rate taxpayers.
2016	The capital gains tax rate is cut to 20 per cent for higher rate taxpayers (except for residential property and carried interest). Investors' relief is introduced.

Options for reform

The reforms considered in this section all relate to the aim of reducing or eliminating the current tax preference for returns on wealth over work (see Box 14.1). One could go further, in seeking to tax unearned income and gains at *higher* effective rates than earned income. There may be good arguments for this more radical approach, both in terms of fairness and efficiency. However, from where we are now, moving towards *parity* of tax treatment would be a good start. This approach has the additional advantage of reducing the scope for artificial tax planning (see Box 14.2).

Box 14.2:
The tax planners' charter

The current approach to taxing capital income and gains is a tax planners' charter. Various legal mechanisms invite individuals to lower their effective tax rate by converting their labour income into (what looks like) capital income, and their capital income into (what looks like) capital gains. In many cases, these opportunities result from intentional policy choices, so their exploitation cannot be described as 'tax avoidance', yet in terms of lost revenue, they have the same effect.

Two (simplified) examples illustrate the general point. First, **personal services companies**. Individuals can often choose to supply their services through their own company, instead of as an employee or self-employed trader. This enables them to take their pay as dividends (thereby avoiding national insurance contributions and maximising allowances), or eventually as a capital gain (by rolling up profits inside the company). Where gains are eligible for entrepreneurs' relief, the effective tax rate is more than halved, from over 60 per cent if taken as salary (applying income tax and national insurance contributions) to less than 30 per cent (applying corporation tax and capital gains tax).

Second, **private equity managers** manage investments in private companies on behalf of a fund. By taking some of their remuneration as a share in the profits of the underlying fund ('carried interest'), they can again convert what would otherwise be an effective tax rate of over 60 per cent on labour income, into one less than half that. Indeed, thanks to the taper relief that applied to capital gains tax on carried interest during the mid-2000s, it was true to say private equity managers could achieve lower average tax rates than their cleaners.

Various steps have been taken by successive governments to stem revenue losses in specific areas. For example: the 'IR35' provisions for personal services companies; and the 'base cost shift' and 'income-based carried interest' provisions for private equity. However, the root of the problem runs deeper, and will not be cured by patchwork measures: so long as differences remain between the effective rates of tax on labour income, capital income and capital gains, there will always be ways that legal form can be restructured to minimise tax.

Capital income

The current wedge between the effective rates of tax on capital income compared with labour income is mostly attributable to national insurance contributions, which apply to work, but not to wealth. One way to move towards parity of tax treatment would therefore be to apply national insurance contributions (in addition to income tax) to all capital income.[18] An alternative would be to restore something like the investment income surcharge, which applied to capital income from 1972 to 1985.

Other steps that would help to reduce the tax preference for capital income include abolishing the separate allowances for interest, dividends and rent introduced in 2016; these unfairly advantage those with the financial flexibility to diversify their sources of income. One could also consider fully aligning effective dividend rates with the main income tax rates. However, the implementation of this aim raises complex issues of interaction with corporation tax.

Even a partial shift towards equalising the effective rates of tax on labour and capital income would entail a significant increase in the taxation of savings and investments. This would further increase the relative tax advantage of investing in tax-privileged (or even tax-free) forms, including pension schemes, ISAs, life insurance wrappers, venture capital schemes, employee share schemes, and so on.

What all of these schemes have in common is the aim of using the tax system actively to encourage certain types of savings and investment behaviours. However, tax incentives are a very blunt instrument for this purpose: exemptions and reliefs often provide large windfalls to people who would have saved or invested anyway. They also fail to address various other influences (identified through developments in behavioural science and sociology) such as 'anchoring' or 'loss aversion'.[19]

Consequently, it is essential to scrutinise carefully whether existing savings and investment schemes actually have the incentive effects that they are supposed to have, to what extent, and at what cost relative to alternative (non-tax) strategies for influencing behaviours (see Chapter 9). Successive governments have sadly shown little interest in commissioning or engaging with this type of research, but this should be considered a prerequisite for future reforms.

Capital gains

The effective rate of capital gains tax should also be moved closer to the rates applied to labour income. In the short term, an initial target should be to restore alignment with the rates applied to capital income. The severance of this link in 1998 through the introduction of taper relief does not reflect well on New Labour's approach to the taxation of wealth. The previous system established by Nigel Lawson as Conservative Chancellor in 1988 was preferable; there is a strong case for restoring that approach.

Further issues relating to the design of the tax base for capital gains tax are discussed in Box 14.3 (regarding real and nominal gains, and realised and unrealised gains), and on page 145 in relation to owner-occupied housing. Together, these issues represent the most complex and difficult choices facing policy makers considering major reforms to the taxation of capital gains. However, there are several reforms that could be made relatively straightforwardly, which collectively could almost double the current revenue of capital gains tax.

First, the annual exempt amount for capital gains (currently £12,000) should be abolished. Just as with the separate allowances for interest, dividends and rent, there is no justification for distinguishing between different types of returns on wealth in this way (or indeed, between income from labour and capital). This is especially so, given that the size of the annual exempt amount vastly exceeds anything that could be justified purely on grounds of administrative convenience. The revenue effect of this reform is difficult to estimate, but could raise up to £4 billion.[20]

Second, in line with the recent recommendations from the Institute for Fiscal Studies, Institute for Public Policy Research and Resolution Foundation,[21] entrepreneurs' relief should be abolished. Research commissioned by HMRC already shows that this relief has hardly any prospective incentive effect on entrepreneurial activity;[22] in practice, it is just a (very expensive) additional reward to those who have already made their fortune. Abolishing it now could raise up to £2.4 billion,[23] and the cost of retaining it is forecast to rise in future.

Third, transfers on death should be brought within capital gains tax. The reason most often cited for 'forgiving' capital gains tax on death is that inheritance tax applies instead. However, these two taxes serve different purposes and so one need not displace the other.[24] The simplest reform would be to treat transfers on death as disposals, applying capital gains tax liability to the deceased's estate.[25] Although it is difficult to estimate the revenue effect of this reform, the best available evidence is that it could raise between £0.5 billion and £1 billion.[26]

Box 14.3:
Two key choices for capital gains tax

There are two key choices facing policy makers regarding the tax base for capital gains tax. The first of these also applies to the taxation of capital income.

Real or nominal returns?
Inflation complicates the measure of returns on wealth. If the general price level did not change when an asset initially costing £1,000 yields £50 income, or is sold after increasing in value to £1,050, we could say that the owner is now £50 better off. But if, over the same period, general prices have also risen by 5 per cent, then in *real terms* the owner is no better off now than if s/he had spent the money initially (instead of saving it). Taxing this nominal return would leave the owner worse off, in real terms.

One solution to this problem is to tax only 'real' returns – ie, returns above inflation. This was the approach adopted for capital gains tax between 1982 and 1998, when an 'indexation allowance' (based on the Retail Price Index) was used in calculating the chargeable gain. Another solution, slightly different but with similar effect, would be to tax only income or gains in excess of the 'normal rate of return'; this was the approach favoured in the *Mirrlees Review* (2011). For now, income tax and capital gains tax both remain based on the nominal return, irrespective of inflation or the normal rate of return.

Realised or unrealised gains?
A capital gain is said to be 'realised' when an asset is disposed of for more than it cost. For as long as the asset is retained, without disposal, any gain is said to be 'unrealised'.

One difficulty with taxing unrealised gains is that, even if only the 'real' gain is taxed, this gain may overstate the true benefit to the owner if, in practice, it would be difficult to sell the investment to use the funds for consumption. Two further problems include the need for regular valuations without any market transfer, and concerns about the 'asset-rich/cash-poor'. These issues are discussed further in Chapter 15.

On the other hand, taxing only realised gains creates a distortive 'lock-in' effect that incentivises owners to hold onto assets in order to defer the tax charge. There are ways around this problem,[27] but they have not yet been tried in the UK. Indeed, the taper relief that applied to long-term gains between 1998 and 2008 positively reinforced the lock-in effect.

Taxing returns on owner-occupied housing

Currently, returns on owner-occupied housing go untaxed. Although owner-occupiers derive a large benefit from living in their homes rent-free, this benefit does not generate any income tax liability. Any capital gains realised from owner-occupied housing are also generally exempt from capital gains tax as a result of private residence relief. Although council tax is paid by owner-occupiers, this functions more like a (regressive) tax on the consumption of housing,[28] rather than as a tax on the returns on housing ownership.

There is a strong case for taxing returns on owner-occupied housing somehow, especially because existing distortions in favour of this type of investment would be increased if effective tax rates on returns on other types of wealth were raised while leaving returns on owner-occupation entirely exempt. However, any major reforms to taxes on residential property are difficult, not only politically but also in principle, due to the overlapping functions of housing and the different tax treatment that each of these functions implies.

One option would be to tax the 'imputed rent' on owner-occupied housing, by adding the property's rental value (net of finance costs) to the owner's total income from other sources under income tax. This option has the advantage of reducing the distortion of investment decisions, while co-opting the redistributive function of income tax by applying a progressive rate structure that varies according to the taxpayer's other income. The UK applied this policy until 1963, and it merits reinvestigation.

In relation to capital gains on owner-occupied housing, it is more difficult to see a viable alternative to the current exemption. Taxing gains realised when an individual moves home would create a lock-in effect, in many cases worse even than stamp duty land tax, although a scheme of roll-over relief until death may be feasible to ameliorate this. However, there would in principle be a strong case for taxing housing gains made above the normal rate of return, especially since these are often attributable to economic conditions, local infrastructure development or planning grants, rather than to individual effort.

Recommendations

In the short term

- Immediately abolish:
    - The separate tax-free allowances for interest, dividends, rent and capital gains, retaining a single personal allowance applicable to all forms of income (including capital gains). A strictly limited exemption from the requirement to file a self-assessment return for small amounts of non-employment income and gains could be retained for administrative convenience only.
    - 'Forgiveness' of capital gains tax on death. All transfers on death should be treated as disposals by the deceased for capital gains tax purposes.

- Review the current proliferation of tax preferences for ISAs, venture capital schemes, employee share schemes, entrepreneurs' relief, investors' relief and all other schemes supposedly justified as incentivising savings and investment. Any schemes that lack clear evidence of both effectiveness *and* value for money in achieving the claimed incentive effects should be phased out.
- Align tax rates on capital gains with the rates currently applied to savings income.

In the longer term

- Consider the options for increasing the effective tax rates on capital income and capital gains to align them with the effective rates currently applied to labour income *including* national insurance contributions. In particular:
  - Consult on the option of reintroducing an investment income surcharge on all sources of capital income and capital gains, at a rate equivalent to the effective rate of national insurance contributions (including employer national insurance contributions).
  - Consult on the alternative option of directly adding national insurance contributions (including a component equivalent to employer national insurance contributions) to all sources of capital income and capital gains, with particular attention to implications for the contributory principle.
- Consider reforms to the tax base for capital gains tax, including the options of introducing an indexation allowance or normal-rate-of-return allowance, together with measures to take account of the taxpayer benefit on the deferral of tax on unrealised gains.

Notes

1. HM Revenue and Customs, *Property, Interest, Dividends and Other Investment Income, 2015/16*, 2019, Table 13.10. These figures exclude amounts held in ISAs and other tax-free savings, since these are not reported on tax returns.
2. Directorate-General for Taxation and Customs Union, *Taxation Trends in the European Union: data for the EU member states, Iceland and Norway*, European Commission, 2018, Table F.4
3. HM Revenue and Customs, *Estimated Costs of Principal Tax Reliefs*, 2019. These are static estimates that exclude the impact of behavioural responses if the allowance was abolished.
4. See further HM Revenue and Customs, HS253: *Furnished Holiday Lettings*, 2019

5 See further D Thurley, *Reform of Pension Tax Relief*, House of Commons Briefing Paper CBP–07505, 2018
6 The range of investments that can be held in this way has recently been extended: see V Houlder, 'HMRC relaxes "wrapper" rules on Reits and offshore investments', *Financial Times*, 26 January 2018.
7 This comprises: dividend allowance (£2,000), property allowance (£1,000) and trading allowance (£1,000), which are all available regardless of total income, plus up to £1,000 under the personal savings allowance.
8 HM Revenue and Customs, *Estimated Costs of Principal Tax Reliefs*, January 2019
9 HM Revenue and Customs, *Individual Savings Accounts (ISA) Statistics*, April 2019
10 In 2015/16, 43 per cent of ISA savers on the highest incomes (over £150,000) had ISA holdings of £50,000 or greater (averaging £70,582 each), compared with just 7 per cent of savers with incomes lower than £5,000.
11 See 'Tax relief for investors using venture capital schemes', www.gov.uk/guidance/venture-capital-schemes-tax-relief-for-investors
12 See 'Tax and employee share schemes', www.gov.uk/tax-employee-share-schemes
13 A reduced rate of 10 per cent (or 18 per cent for gains in residential property) applies to gains by basic rate taxpayers.
14 HM Revenue and Customs, *Capital Gains Tax (CGT) Statistics*, December 2018. Revenue in 2016/17 was £0.6 billion less than in 2015/16, despite an increase in the total amount of chargeable gains from £49 billion to £51 billion; this fall is attributable mainly to the 8 per cent cut in the main rates applied from April 2016.
15 HM Revenue and Customs, *Estimated Costs of Principal Tax Reliefs*, January 2019. See further A Corlett, 'Entrepreneurs' Relief has cost £22 billion over the past 10 years. Was it worth it?', Resolution Foundation blog post, 29 August 2018
16 This relief will apply to gains realised after 6 April 2019. See HM Revenue and Customs, *Capital Gains Manual*, www.gov.uk/hmrc-internal-manuals/capital-gains-manual.
17 Personal allowance (£12,500), personal savings allowance (£500), dividend allowance (£2,000), property allowance (£1,000), trading allowance (£1,000), capital gains tax annual exempt amount (£12,000).
18 To achieve full parity, the application of national insurance contributions to capital income ought to include some component equivalent to employer (as well as employee) contributions, reflecting that the long-term incidence of both forms of contribution is likely to fall mainly on employees.
19 See further W Congdon, J Kling and S Mullainathan, 'Behavioral economics and tax policy', *National Tax Journal*, 62(3), 2009, pp375–86
20 HM Revenue and Customs, *Estimated Costs of Principal Tax Reliefs*, 2016. This estimate is likely to represent an 'upper bound' since it excludes the impact of behavioural responses. Since 2016, HMRC has declined to provide any estimate, on the basis that there is insufficient data available.
21 S Adam and T Waters, 'Options for raising taxes', in C Emmerson, C Farquharson and P Johnson (eds), *The IFS Green Budget: October 2018*, Institute for Fiscal Studies, 2018, pp186–87; C Roberts, G Blakely and L Murphy, *A Wealth of Difference: reforming the taxation of wealth*, Institute of Public Policy Research, 2018; 'Scrapping Entrepreneurs' Relief – the UK's worst tax break – would give government a £2.7bn head start in funding its NHS pledge', Resolution Foundation press release, 29 August 2018
22 *Capital Gains Tax Relief: research on entrepreneurs' relief and business asset rollover relief*, Research Report 367, IFF Research for HM Revenue and Customs, 2015
23 HM Revenue and Customs, *Estimated Costs of Principal Tax Reliefs*, 2019

24 See S Adam, C Emmerson and B Roantree, 'Broad shoulders and tight belts: options for taxing the better off', in C Emmerson, P Johnson and H Miller (eds), *The IFS Green Budget: February 2013*, Institute for Fiscal Studies, 2013, pp261–62
25 An alternative would be to treat transfers on death in the same way as disposals to a spouse, such that the transfer was not initially subject to capital gains tax, but the recipient would become liable for the full amount of the gain (including gains prior to death) upon subsequent disposal. This approach is probably less desirable because it exacerbates the lock-in effect.
26 HM Revenue and Customs currently states that it cannot reliably estimate the current cost of capital gains tax forgiveness on death, but in 2012 it was estimated to be £490 million: HM Revenue and Customs, *Main Tax Expenditures and Structural Reliefs*, 2012. Since then, total chargeable gains have risen significantly, so a present estimate is likely to be higher.
27 See especially A J Auerbach, 'Retrospective capital gains taxation', *American Economic Review*, 81(1), 1991, pp167–78
28 See further discussion in Chapters 15 and 18.

Fifteen
Taxes on property and net wealth
Andrew Summers

Total net private wealth in the UK currently stands at around £13 trillion, equivalent to over six times national income. Most of this wealth is in private pensions (42 per cent), followed by property (land and housing – 36 per cent), financial wealth (for example, bank accounts and shares – 13 per cent) and physical wealth (for example, cars and personal possessions – 10 per cent).[1] Financial wealth is by far the most unequally distributed: the top 10 per cent own over 60 per cent, and the bottom half own less than 3 per cent.[2] For comparison, the top 10 per cent own around 40 per cent of property and private pension wealth, where holdings extend somewhat further down the distribution (see Figure 15.1).

The UK currently has no taxes on holdings of wealth. The two closest are stamp duty land tax and council tax. However, neither of these taxes were designed as, and nor do they function as, taxes on holdings of wealth. Although they both apply to property, neither tax is based on the net value of assets owned at any particular point in time; instead, they apply to the purchase or occupation of property, respectively. Aside from stamp duties on shares, there is nothing even approaching a tax on holdings of any other type of wealth.

Taxing holdings of wealth would require policy makers to engage with some distinctive challenges. The most often raised concerns are administrative (see Box 15.2), but an arguably greater constraint concerns public attitudes towards property rights (see Box 15.1). These challenges require careful consideration. Before introducing new taxes on holdings, it would be sensible to explore whether similar objectives could be achieved through reforms to existing taxes on transfers and returns of wealth.

Figure 15.1:
Distribution and composition of private wealth

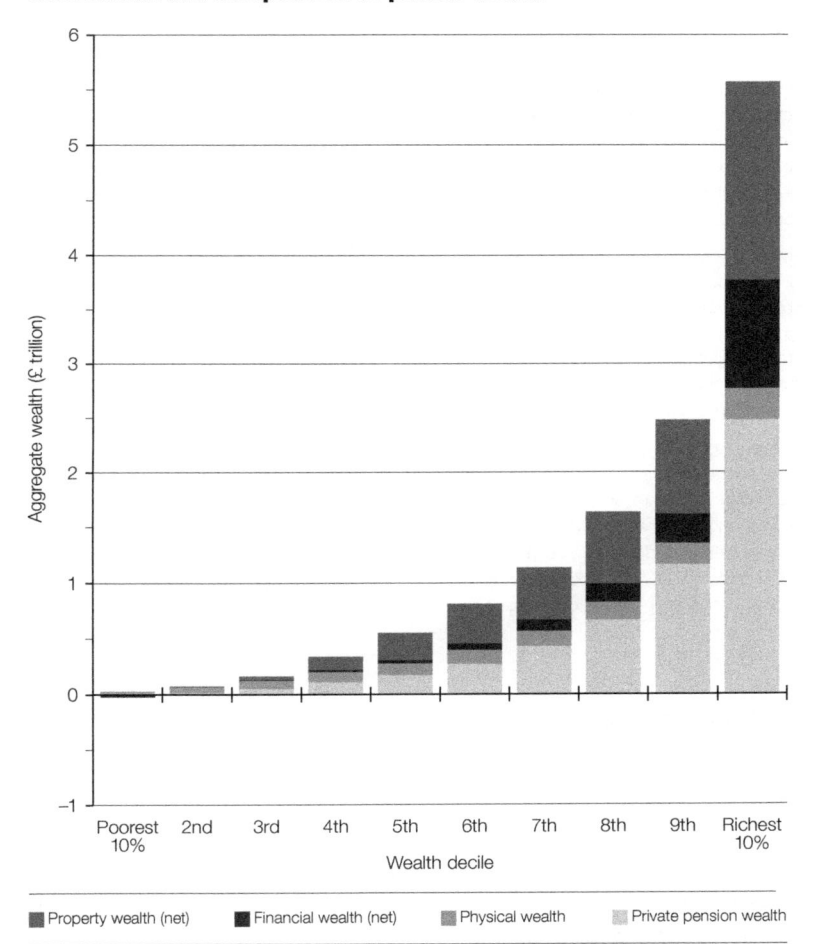

■ Property wealth (net)   ■ Financial wealth (net)   ■ Physical wealth   ▨ Private pension wealth

Note: Office for National Statistics analysis using Wealth and Assets Survey data. 'Private wealth' is net household wealth.

Source: Office for National Statistics, *Wealth in Great Britain Wave 5: 2014 to 2016*, 2018, Figure 5

Box 15.1:
Are wealth taxes 'theft'?

There is a long history of debate about the moral status of property rights and their relation to tax. On the libertarian Right, Rothbard famously claimed that 'all taxation is theft'; on the anarchist Left, Proudhon claimed that '*property* is theft'. The issue turns on whether there is any 'natural' right to private property that precedes, is independent of, and constrains, the state's power to tax. Although in principle this debate could apply to any tax, it excites the greatest passions where liability is imposed solely on the basis of an individual's *ownership* of property, as with taxes on holdings of wealth.

Most philosophers are very sceptical of the idea that there is any natural right to private property independent of the state. Instead, they view the recognition, enforcement and restrictions on private property rights as one of the state's many functions that, together with the tax system, form 'the basic structure of society' and so are up for political (and moral) debate.[3] It is a mistake to think of our rights of ownership as morally more fundamental than the state's power to tax: for one thing, the enforcement of property rights, and the regulation of markets used to allocate property, themselves depend on a tax-funded state.

Nevertheless, in the world in which we live, property rights are all around us. There becomes an understandable tendency to view these rights as somehow natural, even though on careful reflection we should acknowledge that they are not. Liam Murphy and Thomas Nagel refer to this phenomenon as 'everyday libertarianism';[4] it poses a major political challenge to the taxation of wealth, and to the taxation of holdings of wealth in particular. The reality of this challenge is perhaps not fully recognised by proponents of a net wealth tax (or significant increases in tax on residential property), in comparison to more tractable administrative concerns.

Existing taxes

Stamp duty land tax

Stamp duty land tax applies to purchases of residential and non-residential property in England and Northern Ireland. It makes a significant contribution to tax revenues, at nearly £13 billion in 2017/18, of which £9.3 billion was from residential property.[5] However, these revenues are unstable, because they depend not only on the price of property, but also on the volume of transactions – for example, total stamp duty land tax revenue halved from around £10 billion to £5 billion within a single year following the 2008 financial crisis.

Stamp duty land tax is based on the purchase price of the property, with rates varying according to whether the property is residential or non-residential, whether or not the purchaser is a first-time buyer, and whether the property is an 'additional property' – ie, a second home or buy-to-let.[6]

For most residential property transactions, the rate starts at 2 per cent for the value between £125,000 and £250,000, rising steeply to a marginal rate of 12 per cent on the value above £1.5 million.

The distributional effects of stamp duty land tax are highly progressive, but this is just about the only thing that can be said in the tax's favour. From an economic perspective, there is strong evidence that stamp duty land tax distorts people's decisions whether to up- or downsize, move locality, or engage in other mutually beneficial transactions. Consequently, it reduces the efficiency of the housing market and causes what economists call 'deadweight loss', which are effectively distortions that benefit no one.[7]

More fundamentally, stamp duty land tax lacks any coherent underlying rationale. There is no justification in terms of fairness of outcomes or processes (see Chapter 12) for a tax that depends on the number of times that someone chooses (or is required) to move to a new house over her/his lifetime: this factor is arbitrary from a moral point of view. In the conventional tax policy jargon, stamp duty land tax accordingly fails to reflect the goal of 'horizontal equity' between individuals of equivalent means.

Stamp duty land tax is a classic example of a tax that we have only because we have had it for a long time; no one would (credibly) propose it if we were starting from scratch. Its origins lie in the 'stamping' of formal documents, which offered a practical (not principled) opportunity for levying tax: this justification no longer applies in a modern system of tax administration. The fact that the tax has survived for so long, and indeed has become more important in recent years,[8] reflects poorly on the UK's tax policy-making process.

On the other hand, extreme caution is required before proposing the abolition of stamp duty land tax. This is for two main reasons. First, as already mentioned, the tax is at least highly progressive, and (although it is hard to fathom why) seems more widely accepted than many other progressive taxes. Second, the ongoing cost of the tax has now already been taken into account ('capitalised') in property prices, such that its abolition would simply result in an increase in prices and corresponding windfall gain to existing owners.

Consequently, although there is a strong case for phasing out stamp duty land tax, this must only be considered as part of a broader package of reforms to taxes on residential property. In particular, stamp duty land tax on residential property transactions would need to be replaced by an annual tax on housing that is at least as progressive; this would require a radical reform to the rate structure (and other features) of the current council tax.

Council tax

Council tax is considered in detail in Chapter 18. For present purposes, the aim is merely to emphasise that in its current form, council tax does not serve as a tax on wealth.

First, the legal liability to pay council tax is on the *occupier* of residential property, not its owner. In relation to rented property, this means that the real cost of paying the tax (what economists call the 'tax incidence') will fall at least partly (and probably mostly) on tenants, rather than owners, the exact split depending on the extent to which rents adjust in response to the tax.

Second, council tax is based on the *gross* rather than *net* value of the property. Consequently, a person who owns property subject to a mortgage pays the same amount as someone who owns outright, even though the latter has (all else equal) more net wealth. The amount of council tax also depends on other factors, such as the number of occupiers of the property.

Finally, council tax is *highly regressive* with respect to wealth. It is paid by many people who have no net wealth at all – for example, many tenants, as well as owners with negative equity or other large debts. Even among those with positive net wealth, the smallest share of council tax (relative to wealth) is paid by those with the largest fortunes.

These points are important when reflecting on the bigger picture of wealth taxation in the UK. Council tax is often included in international comparisons showing that the UK already raises a relatively large share of revenue through taxes on wealth. Such statistics are misleading: the comparison would look very different if the £35 billion raised by council tax was taken out.

Options for reform

Taxing holdings of housing wealth

One of the many difficulties with proposing reforms to the taxation of residential property is that housing serves several functions, each of which may point to different tax treatment. An owner of housing can use her/his property to live in or rent out, as well as a store of wealth; taxes on residential property may therefore variously be looked at from the perspectives of *consumption* of housing, *returns* on housing, or *holdings* of housing wealth.

Box 15.2:
Administrative challenges

Any tax on the holding of wealth faces two important administrative challenges.

First, the problem of **valuation**. Taxes on holdings of wealth are usually charged on an annual basis, and so may require valuation even where the asset has not been sold. This challenge is not unique: inheritance tax also requires the valuation of assets on death, even where they are passed to inheritors without any sale. However, the problem is more acute for a net wealth tax or a tax on residential property, because ideally these valuations would take place frequently; the current council tax highlights the problems that arise where there are significant gaps between valuations.

The administrative difficulties posed by valuation are easily (and often) overstated. When an annual wealth tax was last proposed in 1974, the need for widespread valuation was a daunting prospect that contributed to the policy's abandonment.[9] Today, big data greatly reduces, if not altogether eliminates, this practical difficulty. To be sure, difficulties remain, especially for assets that are very thinly (if at all) traded, such as private businesses. But this is an area where technological change has shifted the balance of concerns significantly since a net wealth tax was last seriously considered.

Second, there is the problem of dealing fairly with those who are **'asset-rich/cash-poor'**. Unlike most other taxes, a tax on holdings of wealth does not attach to any pre-existing flow of funds. Consequently, some people with significant wealth may not have sufficient income (or liquid assets) to pay the tax. Again, this problem can be overstated, because in practice levels of wealth and income are highly correlated: there are relatively few people who are truly in the position of being asset-rich/cash-poor. Nevertheless, for those affected, this problem calls for a solution.

Fortunately, various administrative solutions are possible. For example, there could be a system of temporary deferral with interest charged at an appropriate rate. Any 'lock-in' effect could further be reduced by ensuring a backstop of payment on death. Alternatively, taxpayers could satisfy the liability immediately by granting an equity stake in the charged property, much like the equity-release schemes offered by banks. Of course, such solutions are not straightforward, but the difficulties are not insurmountable with careful design.

The current council tax resembles something like a tax on the *consumption* of housing (albeit a highly regressive one): it is paid by the occupier and is based on the property's gross value (in 1991), with some concessions. Taxes on *returns* on housing, such as (actual or imputed) rent and capital gains, were discussed in Chapter 14. In this chapter, it remains briefly to consider whether there is any case for introducing a tax on *holdings* of housing wealth.

In principle, there does not seem to be any justification for introducing a tax on holdings of housing wealth *in addition* to reforming taxes on the consumption of housing, and/or returns on housing. If the aim is to redistribute existing holdings of wealth (including housing wealth), it would be better to tax total net wealth across all asset types (ie, to introduce a net wealth tax) than to levy a tax based on housing wealth only.

A land value tax is often proposed as an alternative to the current system of taxes on residential property. The only *definitional* feature of a land value tax that distinguishes it from other property taxes is that it is based on the value of the land only, rather than the value of the land plus any buildings. The main advantage of this approach is said to be that it is less economically distorting, since the supply of land (unlike buildings) is fixed.

Although adopting land value as a tax base has some economic advantages, it would detach the tax from the total value of each property, rendering it less suitable as a tax on either the consumption, returns or holdings of housing wealth. Insofar as the desire for a land value tax coincides with other goals, such as a more progressive rate structure, these could be achieved without switching to a land value base.

A net wealth tax

Another option would be to introduce a new tax based on the total net wealth owned by each individual (or other tax unit), levied at regular intervals. This type of tax is known as a 'net wealth tax' or an 'annual wealth tax' (when charged annually). It is the archetypal tax on holdings of wealth, characterised by a broad base consisting of all marketable assets (typically excluding private pension wealth), net of any debts.

The UK has never had a net wealth tax. One was put forward by the Labour government in 1974, but it was never implemented.[10] However, proposals for a net wealth tax have recently resurfaced, partly due to the mainstream traction provided by Thomas Piketty's *Capital in the Twenty-First Century*, which recommended (as a 'utopian ideal') the introduction of a *global* net wealth tax to tackle wealth inequality.[11]

For proponents, the main attraction of a net wealth tax is its potential (depending on the rates applied) to significantly redistribute existing holdings of wealth within a relatively short timeframe. By contrast, taxes on transfers of wealth and returns on wealth act on (some of) the processes by which wealth is accumulated, and so are more prospective and gradual in their effect on current holdings of wealth.

That said, there are some structural similarities between a net wealth tax and other types of tax on wealth, such that it is important to consider the effects of the whole tax system together rather than assessing the case for a net wealth tax in isolation:

- A comprehensive donor-based tax on gratuitous transfers of wealth (covering both inheritances and gifts) could serve a somewhat similar function to a net wealth tax levied once per generation.

- Income tax on capital income already functions somewhat like a net wealth tax,[12] except that the latter would apply the same rate to all asset types, such that low-yielding assets would face a higher effective tax rate than high-yielding assets.[13]

The most common argument made against the introduction of a net wealth tax in the UK is that it has already been tried elsewhere and failed. It is true that, internationally, net wealth taxes have been in decline. Over the past 30 years, nine countries within the OECD have abolished their net wealth tax (the most recent being France in 2017), leaving only three countries with net wealth taxes still in force: Norway, Spain and Switzerland.[14]

Box 15.3:
Capital flight?

In a globalised world, would increasing taxes on wealth simply result in the very rich moving their assets somewhere else? This concern about 'capital flight' is often raised, but it is (mostly) based on a misconception.

Income tax and capital gains tax currently apply to the *worldwide* income and gains of anyone who spends more than a certain number of days in the UK per year (unless they have 'non-dom' status); likewise, if a net wealth tax was introduced, it would apply to these individuals' *worldwide* assets. So, anyone wishing to escape these taxes (legally) would need to move *themselves* abroad, not just their capital.

Other than for certain highly mobile groups (such as entertainers and sports stars), there is very little evidence of large international migration in response to top tax rates.[15] For a variety of economic and social reasons, the rich tend to remain closely tied to the place where they first made their money.[16] There are, however, two more minor respects in which capital flight may be problematic:

- **Tax evasion.** If people can easily hide their wealth abroad, a net wealth tax might encourage them to expatriate capital to reduce their tax bill illegally. However, recent developments in international co-operation between tax authorities have significantly reduced the scope for this type of evasion.

- **Capital flight by non-residents.** If the tax extended to all domestic assets, regardless of the owners' residence, this may make domestic assets less attractive to foreign investment. This is a valid concern, but it involves a much smaller group than domestic owners, for whom the issue of capital flight is usually raised.

However, caution is required before extrapolating from this international experience. Various reasons have been put forward for the 'failure' of net wealth taxes abroad, but many such explanations lack empirical evidence (see, in particular, concerns about capital flight in Box 15.3). The available evidence indicates that artificial behavioural responses have been far more prevalent than real responses such as divestment or emigration.[17]

For a net wealth tax to be successful, it must therefore apply broadly to *all* asset types, with no exemptions or preferential tax treatment for particular assets.[18] Any other approach is an invitation to tax planning and avoidance, as well as a recipe for distortion of real investment decisions. None of the net wealth taxes so far adopted around the world have adhered to this requirement,[19] and so it remains an open question whether, with proper design and implementation, a net wealth tax could work in the UK.

Recommendations

In the short term

- For immediate reforms to council tax, see Chapter 18.

In the longer term

- Consider the options for more extensive reforms to the tax treatment of owner-occupied housing. In particular:
    - Consult on the option of taxing 'imputed rent' on owner-occupied housing under income tax, with particular attention to the challenges regarding the deduction of interest payments and fairness towards the 'asset-rich/cash-poor'.
    - Consult on the alternative option of a separate tax (to replace or reform council tax) on the consumption of housing by both owner-occupiers and tenants, based on updated property values.
    - Consult on phasing out stamp duty land tax, but *only* in combination with the introduction of a progressive alternative to the taxation of housing (as above).
- Consider the option of introducing a net wealth tax. In particular:
    - Consult on the relationship between a net wealth tax and other

Table 15.1:
International comparison of net wealth tax bases

Category	Assets	France	Norway	Spain	Switzerland	Austria (1994)	Germany (1997)	Finland (2006)	Ireland (1978)	Luxembourg (2006)	Netherlands (2001)	Sweden (2007)
Immovable property	Buildings	T	TP	T	TP	T	T	TP	T	T	T	T
	Main residence	TP	TP	TP	TP	T	X	TP	E	T	E	T
	Woods and forests	TP	TP	TP	TP	T	T	TP	E	T	TP	E
	Land	T	TP	T	TP	T	T	T	E	T	T	E
Movable property	Agricultural or rural assets	TP	TP	TP	TP	T	T	T	TP	T	T	E
	Furniture	T	TP	TP	E	T	X	E	T	T	E	E
	Artwork and antiques	E	TP	TP	TP	T	E	T	E	T	E	E
	Jewellery	T	TP	T	T	T	X	T	T	T	TP	E
	Vehicles	T	TP	T	TP	T	X	E	T	T	T	T
Financial assets	Shares	T	TP	TP	T	T	X	TP	T	TP	T	T
	Life insurance	T	E	T	T	T	X	E	X	T	E	T
	Bonds	T	T	T	T	T	X	E	T	T	T	T
	Liquidities	T	T	T	T	T	X	E	T	TP	T	T
	Intellectual property rights	T	E	E	T	T	E	E	X	E	T	E
	Pension savings	E	E	E	E	T	E	E	E	E	E	E
	Business assets	E	TP	E	TP	T	TP	E	TP	TP	TP	E

Note: Based on OECD Questionnaire on Current and Historical Net Wealth Taxes. T = fully taxed E = fully exempt TP = tax preference (taxed at lower rate) X = no information available

Source: OECD, *The Role and Design of Net Wealth Taxes in the OECD*, OECD Publishing, 2018, Table 4.3

reforms to the taxation of wealth, recognising these reforms as a connected system.
  ○ Consult on potential solutions to the challenges of regular valuation, especially for private businesses and other thinly traded assets.

Notes

1. Office for National Statistics, *Wealth in Great Britain Wave 5: 2014 to 2016*, 2018, Table 1
2. Office for National Statistics, *Wealth in Great Britain Wave 5: 2014 to 2016*, 2018, Tables 2.3 and 2.4
3. J Rawls, *A Theory of Justice*, Belknap Press/Harvard University Press, 1971
4. L Murphy and T Nagel, *The Myth of Ownership: taxes and justice*, Oxford University Press, 2002
5. HM Revenue and Customs, *Annual Stamp Tax Statistics 2017–18*, September 2018
6. The Conservative Party has proposed that there should also be a higher rate of stamp duty land tax if the buyer is non-resident in the UK: see M Selby, 'Higher rate of SDLT for non-resident buyers', *Taxation*, 182(4669), 2018
7. For an estimate of this deadweight loss, see T Besley, N Meads and P Surico, 'The incidence of transaction taxes: evidence from a stamp duty holiday', *Journal of Public Economics*, 119, 2014, pp61–70. See further, C Hilber and T Lyytikäinen, 'Transfer taxes and household mobility: distortion on the housing or labor market?', *Journal of Urban Economics*, 101, 2017, pp57–73
8. Total revenues from stamp duties have quadrupled as a share of GDP since the mid-1990s: HM Revenue and Customs, *Tax and NICs Receipts*, May 2019
9. H Glennerster, 'Why was a wealth tax for the UK abandoned? Lessons for the policy process and tackling wealth inequality', *Journal of Social Policy*, 41(2), 2012, pp233–49
10. See further: H Glennerster, 'Why was a wealth tax for the UK abandoned? Lessons for the policy process and tackling wealth inequality', *Journal of Social Policy*, 41(2), 2012, pp233–49
11. T Piketty, *Capital in the Twenty-First Century*, Belknap Press/Harvard University Press, 2014, Chapter 15
12. For example, for an asset that generates income of 5 per cent, a 2 per cent annual tax on the capital value is equivalent to income tax of 40 per cent.
13. This effect of a net wealth tax (relative to tax on capital income) may not be desirable, given that the wealthiest own a much larger proportion of high-yielding assets (eg, financial assets) compared with those lower down the distribution.
14. OECD, *The Role and Design of Net Wealth Taxes in the OECD*, OECD Publishing, 2018
15. For a recent summary of the literature, see H Kleven, C Landais, M Muñoz and S Stantcheva, *Taxation and Migration: evidence and policy implications*, National Bureau of Economic Research Working Paper No.25740, 2019
16. C Young, *The Myth of Millionaire Tax Flight: how place still matters for the rich*, Stanford University Press, 2017
17. See for example, D Seim, 'Behavioral responses to wealth taxes: evidence from Sweden', *American Economic Journal: Economic Policy*, 9(4), 2017, pp395–421; K Jakobsen and others, *Wealth Taxation and Wealth Accumulation: theory and evidence from Denmark*, National Bureau of Economic Research Working Paper 24371, 2018
18. For a recent proposal in the US context, see E Saez and G Zucman, *How Would a*

Progressive Wealth Tax Work? Evidence from the economics literature, University of California Berkeley, 2019

19 OECD, *The Role and Design of Net Wealth Taxes in the OECD*, OECD Publishing, 2018, Table 4.3. A possible exception revealed by the table is the Austrian wealth tax (abolished in 1994).

Sixteen
Value added tax

Andy Lymer

Value added tax (VAT) was introduced in the UK in the run up to joining the European Community in 1973. It is a requirement of membership for all European Union (EU) states to have a VAT in their tax system. The minimum rate of tax is set by the EU (currently 15 per cent, unless by special dispensation for lower rates) and the rules for its operation are largely required to be common across the EU to minimise trading 'friction' that different taxes (and, therefore, different prices paid by end consumers) would otherwise potentially create.

This fact is, of course, key to how VAT could be reformed in the UK in the future – as the constraint of having this element of our tax system largely run from Brussels will no longer be the issue it currently is (subject, of course, to how far the UK ends up being from the EU over the next few years). This gives us at least the advantage of the option to manipulate this part of our tax system as we may wish – for the first time in over 40 years since it was introduced.

However, it seems unlikely that this tax will disappear as a result of this change in our trading relationships. It is the most important of our indirect taxes in terms of the sums raised, providing the third largest sum for the Treasury of all UK taxes (after income tax and national insurance contributions) at a forecast level in 2019/20 of £136.6 billion.[1] This represents 16.8 per cent of all receipts and is equivalent to around £4,800 per household[2] and 6.2 per cent of national income.

It is predicted to rise at a steady rate for the next few years (Figure 16.1), but only in absolute terms as the Office for Budget Responsibility predicts it will stay at around 6 per cent of GDP (assuming no significant changes to the current system).

Figure 16.1:
VAT receipts forecast

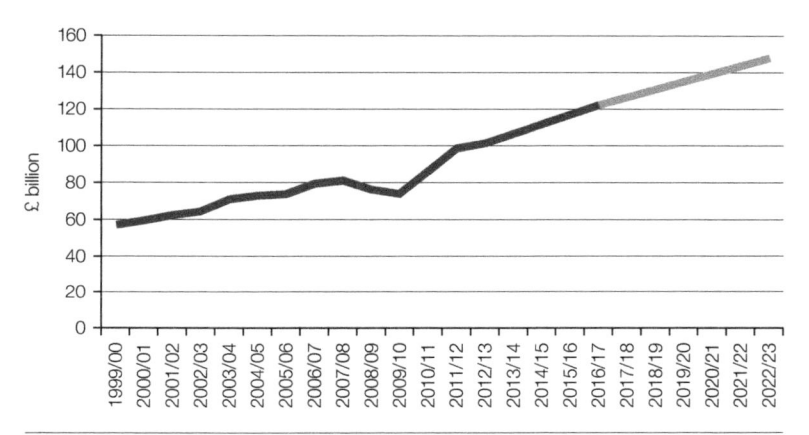

Source: Office for Budget Responsibility forecast at 27 March 2018, available at https://obr.uk/forecasts-in-depth/tax-by-tax-spend-by-spend/vat/

How VAT works

Box 16.1 describes the operation of VAT. As its name suggests, this is done by collecting taxes for the government on the value added at each stage in a production cycle in such a way as to mean it is largely only a cash flow issue for each intermediary stage in the cycle, and only borne by the final consumer of the goods or service. As such, it is classed as a consumption tax – one borne by the consumer. Other forms of consumption tax have been tried around the world in the past, but all had fundamental problems with their operation that limited their application or created knock-on impacts that had to be balanced in other ways to protect those otherwise adversely affected.[3] The UK, in fact, had a purchase tax (tax on final sale only) in the period immediately before VAT was introduced, which was one such system. The USA still operates such a system today, but much of the rest of the world has moved to a value added tax.

Box 16.1:
How VAT operates

Something that is bought in a shop has already been through a series of earlier transactions, during which raw materials have been purchased, components sold to a manufacturer and the finished product passed first to a wholesaler and then to a retailer. At each of these stages, those involved in the item being developed do something – either by physically changing it in some way, or by moving or marketing it – which enables them to charge a higher price than they paid for their input. Their contribution 'adds value' to the product.

The intention of VAT is that tax should be collected at each stage in this process in proportion to the value added by that stage – hence its name. As a very simple example, consider what happens as a piece of crockery, say a mug, goes through this process:

- **Stage one.** Someone extracts clay from the ground and sells it to a pottery business. The price of the clay for one mug is £1 before tax. As VAT on this item will be charged at 20 per cent, the tax to be applied on this value added is 20p. Therefore, the seller of the clay charges the pottery £1 + 20p tax for the clay. S/he retains the £1, but must pay the 20p to the government. S/he simply act as tax collector on the government's behalf for this sum.

- **Stage two.** The pottery business pays £1.20 for this input into its business process (£1 for the clay and 20p VAT). It turns this into a mug, which it sells to a retailer adding £2 to the price. It therefore charges £3 for the mug before tax and must apply 20 per cent VAT – ie, 60p is added in tax. The retailer therefore pays over £3.60 in total. The pottery business only has to pay the VAT on the value it added to the government – ie, 20 per cent x £2, or 40p. This is neatly the difference between the VAT collected on its sale (60p) and the VAT it pays to the clay provider for her/his input (20p).

- **Stage three.** The retailer adds a further mark-up of £1 in selling the mug to a final consumer, taking the pre-tax price to £4. VAT of 80p will now need to be added (ie, 20 per cent x £4), making the selling price in total (including the tax) £4.80. The tax the retailer must pay to the government will be only the VAT on the element it added – at 20 per cent of £1, or 20p. This again is made up of the difference between the VAT charged on the sale of the mug (80p) and the VAT paid for its input to the pottery (60p).

The total amount of tax collected by this process is 80p (20p paid by the clay extractor, 40p paid by the pottery business and 20p paid by the retailer). This is 20 per cent of the £4 that is being paid for the mug itself, before taxes were added. However, note that although the tax is collected at each stage during the production process, only the final consumer actually pays the tax sums. At all other stages, they simply pay to the government the difference between the VAT charged on their sale (outputs) minus the tax paid to their supplier on their inputs. This is achieved as a credit applied at each stage in the process for taxes paid on inputs, the amount of which equals the amount of all the taxes that have been accumulated to that point. If that credit were not applied, the amount eventually collected would be higher the greater numbers of stages there were, a process known as 'cascading' (which has undesirable effects on the way the economy is organised, but was the way these taxes were applied in what was to become the European Community).

A simpler way of achieving the same end result would be for the earlier – intermediate – transactions to be free of tax, but simply to charge 20 per cent on the retailer's full sale price. This is how VAT's predecessor in the UK, called purchase tax, operated, and how the retail sales tax system operates still in the USA. Applying tax at each stage, on the 'value added' at each point, means that tax sums due on a product or service are collected by the government during its production, wholesaling and sale process and not delayed until the point of final sale to a consumer. This means a government gets its tax share earlier in the cycle than might otherwise be the case. It also reduces some of the risks of tax loss that applying tax only at the final stage creates, as tax is collected, in smaller sums, throughout the process.

Worldwide, VAT has largely replaced other forms of general sales taxes as the predominant form of indirect tax. This is, in part, because VAT has advantages in enforcement. Under a retail sales tax system, transactions take place free of tax until the final, retail, stage bringing a danger that goods may slip through to the consumer tax-free as the system relies heavily on the honesty and accurate accounting of the retailer. Although more complex to administer, collecting relatively small sums from several people appears to be less open to evasion than leaving it all in the hands of a single person, the retailer. In the UK however, VAT's introduction had more to do with the requirement of the European Community which had adopted a VAT system over a cascade tax.

Where could VAT reform take us?

The example above is simplified as, in reality, VAT operates in a somewhat more complex way. This has been a key issue for its operation since its introduction, so much so that the Office of Tax Simplification was commissioned by the government to look for ways of reforming the system in the *Autumn Statement* in 2016.[4] Its report (produced in November 2017[5]) highlighted various areas in which it argued simplification should be explored. These included:

- **Reviewing the thresholds that required traders to engage with VAT.** All traders are required to start to charge VAT above a threshold point of turnover (set at £85,000 for 2019/20). Businesses operating with turnovers below this point can choose to register to charge VAT to their customers if they so wish (and make eligible supplies), but must do so once their turnover exceeds that year's threshold at any point during their trading year.

  This creates 'bunching' of business turnover levels just below the threshold limit. The reasons for this are likely to be that some businesses choose to operate to stay below this threshold limit – likely when they are doing business with final consumers, for whom their registration would then increase their costs. The use of staged registration points might smooth out this process and result in extra tax revenues.

  The UK also has particularly high threshold rates and while many businesses below this threshold rate do register for VAT, even though they are not required to do so,[6] this represents significant VAT foregone compared with other VAT-operating countries, which typically use much lower VAT registration thresholds.[7]

- **Reducing the number of special rates.** At present, VAT is not just charged at 20 per cent in the UK, it is actually charged at four different rates – a 5 per cent rate, zero rate (0 per cent) and exempt rate (no charge for VAT is made). The latter two rates both mean that no VAT is added to the price of the goods or services being bought, but the zero rate charge use allows the seller to still offset their input taxes paid and produces a refund from the government for this sum. The seller of exempt goods or services cannot reclaim these input taxes – in effect, they become the end consumer for these products and have to bear the VAT against their profits.

The presence of lower rates of VAT in the system, and the exempting of various items from VAT altogether, enables some support to be provided to those who may otherwise suffer the regressive impacts of any tax on consumption, such as a VAT. This arises where those spending a higher proportion of their income (typically those on lower incomes who must spend more of their earnings, and therefore pay VAT on a higher percentage of their take-home pay[8]) pay higher levels of tax as a proportion of their incomes than those spending a lower proportion (typically those on higher incomes who are not consuming all their income each pay period). Use of reduced rates for goods or services that those on lower incomes will be likely to need to purchase (such as uncooked food items and children's clothing) means that the impact of this regressive nature is reduced somewhat in practice.

However, the use of multiple rates, and the somewhat odd application of different rates to different items,[9] leads to complexity in the system and there may be other ways to target support to those on lower incomes to balance this regressive impact than through reduced rates in the VAT system that, in effect, provide benefit to all who buy reduced-rate items. This would reflect how systems of VAT operate in other countries, such as in New Zealand, where there are almost no exemptions for any goods or services and limited reduced rates of tax.

While this may reduce the complexity of the system, the removal of zero-rating may be conceding ground which would not be equalised elsewhere, or may not be equalised into the medium term, even if provided initially, with further impact on the reduction of progressivity in the overall tax system, detailed elsewhere in this book. Indeed, there has been some pressure recently to extend exemptions, in particular to sanitary products for women. While this has not been conceded, there has been concern about 'period poverty', leading to schemes to provide these in schools, and the government has agreed to pass on the revenue from VAT on tampons to fund women's organisations.

In addition to the above review that looked at possible simplification reforms, Brexit also provides us with a key opportunity to more fundamentally re-examine the role of a consumption tax in our tax system. One key anomaly that could be re-explored is the exemption of all financial services to VAT. This is a large area of service and product-selling activity that could produce significant VAT revenue[10] if applied suitably to at least some aspects of such service provision.[11] However, the application of VAT to such services has, in the past, proven to be a difficult issue – and hence why it has to date been exempt.[12]

Recommendations

In the short term

If a government were minded to look again at how VAT could raise further revenues, the most suitable place to start may be with addressing the levels of the VAT registration threshold.[13] Bringing this down (perhaps closer to the averages of other VAT-using countries, which is somewhat closer to £20,000[14]) would bring more activity into the reach of VAT. While this would add extra administrative burdens to those running relatively small businesses which may be caught by this lower registration level, keeping a low threshold of say £20,000 could still exclude the very smallest of businesses from having to account for VAT, and the cost implications this would create for their customers. HM Revenue and Customs estimates[15] suggest that 45 per cent of VAT-charging businesses actually operate under the threshold already – as they are allowed to voluntarily engage in the VAT system, even if below the compulsory registration threshold. This suggests that requiring more businesses to register compulsorily would not necessarily be an undue burden on many businesses which are currently operating below this threshold point.[16]

An Office of Tax Simplification estimate for a radical reduction of the VAT registration threshold suggests a cut to £43,000 would affect between 400,000 and 600,000 businesses and would raise between £1 billion and £1.5 billion a year.[17]

In the longer term

Questions of the breadth of the VAT base should occupy a review for medium to longer-term changes to this part of the UK's taxation of consumption. Some care would need to be applied to ensure continued, but perhaps more clearly justified, support is maintained to essential items through zero-rating. However, it is arguably time to re-examine, on an item-by-item basis, why specific goods and services are reduced-rated, zero-rated or exempt from VAT to ensure the reasons they were so classified historically are still valid in the current environment. This exercise could also look to confirm that the current use of reduced rates of VAT is indeed the best way to ensure the effects of any regressivity from this general consumption tax are rebalanced, rather than through the greater use of more targeted mechanisms (which may therefore be cheaper to the Exchequer, releasing funds for other uses). In light of the experiences of several other countries that have adopted VAT more recently than the UK, but which allow many fewer exemptions and address related regressivity in different ways elsewhere in their tax and particularly benefits systems, this could be a timely and appropriate change for the UK. This is particularly the case in a post-Brexit world where more flexible changes to VAT are made more possible – changes that could enable an updating of the older 'EU-style' VAT system currently required of the UK's system.[18]

Further analysis for such a review may suggest that the case for the financial services exemption, at least the full exemption as it is at present, is one that should be revisited – albeit this is an area that does not yet have widely agreed practical solutions for taxing appropriately at present. It may also be the case that blanket exemptions for medical services and education should also be re-explored on the same basis. This would help to ensure that any continued exempted status these services receive is appropriate for the way they are now provided. It might also assist in creating a clearer case that the foregone VAT revenue created by exempting these services is indeed a suitable way to support those that actually need the resulting pricing reductions to enable them to enjoy appropriate consumption levels of these services.

Brexit also provides the opportunity to think again about the possibility for a devolved basis for indirect taxation – currently not possible under EU regulations. The potential for different consumption taxes at a more local level could also provide opportunities for local adjustments that could provide extra income sources for cash-strapped councils or regional governments. This change would also allow them to broaden their base of taxation where they are currently overly reliant on property taxation (locally) and income taxes (in the case of Scotland), to extend large central government support. A longer-term policy review of the possibilities for devolved taxation, to potentially now include not just direct but also indirect taxation, should perhaps also therefore be on the government's agenda for possible revenue-raising potential where currently this is not possible.

Notes

1. Office for Budget Responsibility, *Economic and Fiscal Outlook*, CP50, 2019
2. Figure 2.4 shows how this sum varies between quintiles within the income distribution such that the poorest 20% pays on average £3,984 of their income to indirect tax (of which VAT is the larger part) and the richest 20% £10,307. Given that this only represents a 2.5 times difference, against the remaining income after taxes of four times difference, it illustrates the heavier burden VAT places proportionally on those on lower incomes. The impact of this regressivity is explored further later in this chapter and brings into question the role of indirect taxes, as currently structured, as a suitable way to spread the tax burden fairly in our economy. The role of other indirect taxes in furthering this issue is discussed in Chapter 17.
3. See further details on these systems, and the issues they created, in C Evans and others, *Comparative Taxation: why tax systems differ*, Fiscal Publications, 2017, Chapter 7
4. Office of Tax Simplification, 'OTS review of value added tax', 2016, available at www.gov.uk/government/collections/ots-review-of-value-added-tax
5. Office of Tax Simplification, *Value Added Tax: routes to simplification*, 2017
6. It is estimated that around 44 per cent of businesses operating below the threshold do, in fact, register for VAT, despite not being required to do so: Office of Tax Simplification, *Value Added Tax: routes to simplification*, 2017
7. The average threshold for EU countries is £20,000.
8. As has been illustrated in Figure 2.4 and discussed further in note 2, highlighting the significant difference between the VAT burden impact on average earnings of the lowest and highest quintile of earners.
9. Historic cases of such allocation anomalies have been: the Jaffa Cake – determined to be zero-rated as a cake, rather than standard-rated as a biscuit; children's colouring books (zero-rated) versus the recently popular growth of adult colouring books (standard-rated); ebooks (standard-rated) versus print books (zero-rated); and the infamous pasty tax proposal – where VAT is charged on hot items, such as pasties, but not on cold items.
10. *Mirrlees Review* computations based on HMRC data suggest upwards of £10 billion could be so raised by approaches they outline, although this may be partly offset by reductions in other taxes on businesses that might cease with VAT imposition. See Institute for Fiscal Studies and J Mirrlees (eds), *Tax by Design: the Mirrlees Review*, Oxford University Press, 2011, Chapter 8
11. South Africa, for example, charges VAT on selected banking services that customers are expressly charged for.
12. A possible way to address this with extensions to VAT or as a separate tax not directly linked to VAT has been most recently revisited in the *Mirrlees Review*. See Institute for Fiscal Studies and J Mirrlees (eds), *Tax by Design: the Mirrlees Review*, Oxford University Press, 2011, Chapter 8
13. Recent government announcements (29 October 2018) suggest the current government is

not minded to change this position radically until the implications of EU withdrawal are clearer – see HM Revenue and Customs, *VAT: maintain thresholds for two years from 1 April 2020*, 29 October 2018

14 This number is obtained from the Office of Tax Simplification, *Review of Value Added Tax: progress report and call for evidence*, 2017, and is repeated in the full consultation report, *Value Added Tax: routes to simplification*, 2017
15 HM Revenue and Customs, *Annual UK VAT Statistics: commentary and tables 2017/18*
16 The requirement for all VAT returns to be made electronically (from April 2019) may create further reductions in compliance costs for this tax.
17 See Office of Tax Simplification, *Value Added Tax: routes to simplification*, 2017, p9. This report does note that some extra administrative and compliance costs would be created for both government and affected businesses as a result of this change, which would reduce the overall net gain to some extent.
18 For a fuller discussion of different VAT systems currently operating around the world, see C Evans and others, *Comparative Taxation: why tax systems differ*, Fiscal Publications, 2017, Chapter 7

Seventeen
Drinking, driving and smoking
Alan Marsh

Like VAT, excise duties are taxes on consumption. In the UK, those who buy alcohol, tobacco, motor cars and the fuel to run them contribute additionally to the government's income. There are other small excise duties on betting companies' profits and air travel and other indirect taxes on insurance premiums, landfill use, customs duties and a climate change levy on commercial carbon emissions. Most recently, manufacturers of soft drinks must pay a levy on the sugar content of their products. But duties on fuel, alcohol and tobacco are the three largest items and each impacts directly on individual consumers.

The combined rates of duty and tax make up about three-quarters of the sale price of tobacco and fuel,[1] two-thirds of the price of spirits, though less than a third of the price of a pint of beer (Table 17.1). The duty on tobacco consists of a fixed amount per packet plus an *ad valorem* of 16.5 per cent of the retail price. VAT at 20 per cent is then applied to this total – a tax on a tax. Fuel duty is a fixed charge per litre (57.95p) plus VAT. Duty on alcohol is related to the pure alcohol content, but the VAT is again related to the price – rare wines attract the same duty, but more VAT.

Together, excise duties contribute almost £55 billion to the UK government's income, almost half of that coming from fuel duty alone. This, though, is a relatively small percentage of the government's total revenue – about 7 to 8 per cent – which is less than half the £126 billion contributed by VAT, for example. On the other hand, excise duties in the UK make up a larger share of GDP – almost 3 per cent – compared with excise duties in most other OECD countries and is the second highest of the G7 nations, behind Italy.[2]

Trends

Overall, UK revenues from excise duties have fallen as a proportion of government income, from about 10 per cent in the 1970s, and will continue to fall to about 6 per cent in 2021. The rates of duty themselves, however, have moved in different directions. Annual budget decisions about the rates of excise duties have to take account of general price inflation and the sometimes quite rapid changes in the supply and demand for fuel, alcohol and tobacco.

Fuel

Revenues from fuel duty have fallen the most, due mainly to the policy since 2011 of freezing the rate in response to the rise in the supply price of oil, despite a short-lived fall in 2014/15. Before then, Labour and Conservative governments both accelerated and then decelerated the rate of increase in fuel duty, reversing direction when the combined price of oil, fuel duty and VAT met strong consumer resistance. Although the number of vehicles has increased, better fuel efficiency has also held down fuel consumption. HM Revenue and Customs (HMRC) now foregoes £9 billion a year that would accrue had the pre-2011 policy of accelerated increases remained in place.[3]

Alcohol

Duty on beer has remained at levels paid in the late 1970s, while duty on wine has fallen to about three-quarters of the earlier real values and duty on spirits to about half. Average adult consumption rose steadily each year to a peak of 11.6 litres of pure alcohol a year in 2004, falling now to 9.7 litres.[4]

Smoking

In real terms, the duty on a pack of 20 cigarettes (disregarding the VAT) has increased more than threefold since the 1970s, from less than £2 per packet of 20 to between £5.50 and £7, following the policy of raising the rate of duty each year at typically twice the rate of inflation. For this and many other reasons, smoking in the UK has decreased markedly. Fifty-four per cent of men and 41 per cent of women smoked in 1974, falling to 17 and 13 per cent in 2017.[5] This decline is likely to continue since the proportion of young people smoking is falling fastest.[6] The Institute for Fiscal Studies estimates that '… revenues from tobacco duties are expected to fall in real terms to £8.5 billion in 2020/21.'[7]

Table 17.1:
Excise duties and other indirect taxes, 2017/18

		Duty and VAT as a percentage of sale price	Total tax raised in 2018/19 £ billion	Percentage of total UK government revenue
Excise duties	Fuel	71%	£27.9	3.7%
	Vehicle duty	Rates fixed to CO_2 emmisions	£6.2	0.8%
	Alcohol	30–65%	£11.6	1.5%
	Tobacco	76%	£8.8	1.2%
All excise duties			£54.5	7.2%
Other indirect taxes	Insurance premium tax		£5.9	0.8%
	Climate change levy		£1.9	0.3%
	Air passenger duty		£3.4	0.5%
	Other		£7.7	1.0%

Note: Other indirect taxes include landfill tax, aggregates levy, betting and gaming duties, customs duties and diverted profits tax.

Source: Office for Budget Responsibility, *Economic and Fiscal Outlook*, March 2019, Table 4.3

Fairness: regressive and progressive taxation

A test of the acceptability of any tax is the extent to which it is thought fair. Direct taxes are fair insofar as those earning more pay more, though as a fraction of income, the richest 20 per cent pay only twice the income tax paid by the poorest (23 per cent versus 11 per cent). Excise duties, by contrast, are paid at the same rate by everyone buying the commodity taxed, regardless of their income. Table 17.2 shows that the percentage of disposable income paid in excise duties by the poorest 20 per cent of the UK population is nearly three times greater than that paid by the richest 20 per cent.

Table 17.2:
Percentage of disposable incomes taken by the three main excise duties

	Poorest 20%	Second	Third	Fourth	Richest 20%	All households
Duty on alcohol	1.4%	1.1%	1.1%	1.0%	0.8%	1.0%
Duty on tobacco	2.2%	1.8%	1.4%	0.7%	0.3%	0.9%
Duty on hydrocarbon oils and vehicle excise duty	3.0%	2.2%	2.3%	1.4%	1.4%	1.9%
Total	6.6%	5.1%	4.8%	3.1%	2.5%	3.8%

Note: Disposable incomes are net of taxes and benefits, and equivalised by the number of adults and children living in each household and the children's ages.

Source: Office for National Statistics, *Effects of Taxes and Benefits on UK Household Income: financial year ending 2016*, April 2017, Figure 6

The poorest fifth actually buy *less* alcohol and fuel than better-off households, but this takes a higher proportion of their much smaller incomes. For example, the Office for National Statistics reports that more than eight out of 10 workers earning more than £40,000 a year drank in the week before the survey interview and drank more in volume, compared with about four out of 10 among those earning less than £10,000 a year.[8]

This satisfies another test of fairness: being 'luxuries', it is fair that those who can afford them more should pay more tax as they consume them. This makes these duties on alcohol and fuel quite 'progressive' – the better off pay more. On the other hand, fuel duties were introduced when driving was a luxury enjoyed by higher income households. It is now a necessity for people who live and work in places where public transport is no longer plentiful. It does, however, retain some of the fairness of any 'user charge', in that those who place the greater burden on road maintenance and traffic control pay most towards its costs. On the other hand, the duty paid by haulage firms finds its way into the retail prices of all the goods carried into the shops and bought by everyone regardless of their income.

While smoking has decreased among all social groups, it has decreased least among low-income households, who still buy far more tobacco than better-off households buy. In doing so, they surrender in duty seven times the fraction of their income compared with richer households, which makes tobacco duties the most 'regressive' tax we have – the poor pay most:[9]

In the UK, around 1 in 4 (25.9%) [of] people in routine and manual occupations smoked, compared with just 1 in 10 people (10.2%) in managerial and professional occupations.

Thirty per cent of people unemployed and seeking work smoke, which means that those among them smoking the national average of 11 cigarettes a day will return almost a third of a single adult's allowance from their universal credit back to the Treasury in tobacco duty and VAT.[10] On the other hand, it has been argued that high rates of tobacco duty so compress consumption among smokers that they spend less than they would if duty were much lower, because cigarettes are one of those commodities that are prone to overconsumption.

Intended and unintended consequences

Excise duties are difficult to justify solely on revenue terms – smokers, drinkers and drivers can feel to a degree victimised. Some duties are obviously targeting behaviour in favourable ways, such as the new sugary drinks levy aimed at reducing obesity, particularly among children. Duties on wine, unknown in several European countries, act as a hidden tariff on imported goods, favouring both the balance of payments and the more lightly taxed domestic beer and cider production. Vehicle excise duty increases sharply for vehicles emitting greater amounts of CO_2, favouring climate change targets, but is not related to use, so fuel duty becomes more important, both in constraining mileage and reducing atmospheric pollution.

Generally, then, duties are aimed at products that have other costs, which can be costs both to the government and to the individual consumer. Smoking raises costs to the NHS and to the health and lifespans of both smokers and the adults and children who live with them, so tobacco duties are an undisguised deterrent to smoking.[11] This, though, has some unintended consequences. Deterrent pricing of a product whose consumption among smokers is almost non-discretionary provokes evasive behaviour. Low-income smokers can switch to cheaper hand-rolling tobacco and seek out cheaper imported or actually smuggled or stolen supplies. By 2000, tobacco smuggling had reached an alarming volume, causing the authorities to put considerable new resources into tackling it. The latest HMRC report claimed success in:[12]

... reducing the illicit cigarette trade from 22% (in 2000 to 2001) to 15% today, and from 61% to 28% for hand-rolling tobacco. In the same period the revenue lost has reduced from £3.4 billion to £2.5 billion per annum.

However, the sharpest policy dilemma associated with tobacco duty is its impact on poverty. Not only is smoking concentrated among low-income households, within those households the poorest smoke the most. A combined measure of low income and six other indices of socio-economic deprivation showed that the most deprived were four times more likely to smoke compared to the least (61 per cent, compared with 15 per cent).[13] Thus, each increase in duty deepens their hardship for them and their families. Using several survey sources, Charmaine Belvin and others estimated that, in 2011, half of all UK children in income poverty lived with a least one parent who smoked.[14] They would be joined by a further 400,000 if the cost of their parents' smoking were deducted from their household income.[15]

The main problem with a policy of tobacco taxation is that smokers give up smoking for optimistic reasons and people living in poverty in the UK are justifiably short of optimism. So, whereas low-income households are usually expected to be sensitive to pricing, they are reluctant to give up the one anodyne they feel helps them cope with the stress and discouragement that poverty brings. Given that so much of their benefits and tax credits are returned in duty to the Treasury – hundreds of millions each year – there is a strong case to use at least some of this money in redoubled efforts to help them quit. As well as clinical interventions and nicotine substitutes, simply raising the incomes of the lowest-income families would lessen the kinds of stress most associated with difficulties in quitting smoking.

By contrast, the harm associated with alcohol is less a linear function of the amount drunk. The abuse levels are somewhat different. Moderate drinking remains relatively harmless, while the serious health and social costs of drinking accelerate at high levels of consumption. It is difficult to fine tune alcohol duty to disproportionately target harmful binge drinking: just 9 per cent of people aged 16 and over said they exceeded recommended limits on at least one day in the previous week.[16] This may be achieved in part by the higher rate of duty payable on more concentrated drinks, especially strong spirits, which may be more likely to be consumed to abuse levels by dependent drinkers. This may be improved by raising the base duty on all alcohol and Scotland is currently experimenting with a minimum price policy of 50p per unit, whose effects are yet to be evaluated.

The paradox of policy towards excise duties is that, on the one hand, they are an attractive 'soft tax' that will raise easy revenue for the Chancellor, because consumers are thought to be relatively *insensitive* to price. On the other hand, they are justified by the intention to reduce harmful behaviour, because consumers are thought to be relatively *sensitive* to price. They cannot be both.

Recommendations

- The freeze on annual fuel duty increases should end.
- Tobacco tax returned to the Treasury from low-income smokers should fund wide-ranging interventions to assist them to give up smoking.

Notes
1   There are numerous exceptions and rebates available for fuel for domestic heating and for diesel fuel for agricultural construction vehicles.
2   OECD, *Consumption Tax Trends 2014: VAT/GST and excise rates, trends and policy issues*, OECD Publishing, 2014. See also P Levell, M O'Connell and K Smith, 'Excise duties', in C Emmerson, P Johnson and R Joyce (eds), *The IFS Green Budget: February 2016*, Institute for Fiscal Studies, 2016, Figure 9.2
3   S Adam, 'Motoring Taxation Today and the Case for Change', presentation at a BVRLA/RAC Foundation roundtable, Institute for Fiscal Studies, 3 September 2018
4   Institute of Alcohol Studies, *Consumption of Alcohol: factsheets*, 2018; Office for National Statistics, *Adult Drinking Habits in Great Britain: 2017*, 2018
5   Office for National Statistics, *Adult Smoking Habits in the UK: 2017*, 2018
6   At the other end of the age range, non-smokers are surviving much longer than they used to; smokers less so.
7   P Levell, M O'Connell and K Smith, 'Excise duties', in C Emmerson, P Johnson and R Joyce (eds), *The IFS Green Budget: February 2016*, Institute for Fiscal Studies, 2016, citing HM Treasury, *Spending Review and Autumn Statement 2015*, Cm 9162, November 2015
8   Office for National Statistics, *Adult Drinking Habits in Great Britain: 2017*, 2018. These comparisons can be weakened to the extent that they rely on respondents to ONS surveys reporting income and expenditure at the time of interviews; they are not an annual assessment.
9   Office for National Statistics, *Adult Smoking Habits in the UK: 2017*, 2018
10 Assuming they buy the cheapest brands at £8 per pack of 20. Thus, 11 cigarettes are £4.40 so the tax is £4.40 x 0.76 = £3.30 per day, or £23.41 per week. The single over-25 rate of universal credit is £73.34 per week. It is fair to add that many smokers on universal credit will use rolling tobacco or otherwise try to limit their expenditure, but accurate data are not available.
11 The excess mortality attributed solely to smoking is hard to measure and harder to forecast, but most estimates range between five and 10 lost years. While this results in costs for the

NHS in treatment, it has been pointed out, perhaps unkindly, that there is a greater saving for government in foregone state pensions and the avoidance of late-life care.
12 HM Revenue and Customs, *Tackling Tobacco Smuggling: outputs for April 2016 to March 2018*, 10 January 2019
13 R Hiscock and others, 'Smoking and socioeconomic status in England: the rise of the never smoker and the disadvantaged smoker', *Journal of Public Health*, 34(3), 2012, pp390–96
14 C Belvin and others, 'Parental smoking and child poverty in the UK: an analysis of national survey data', *BMC Public Health*, 15(507), 2015
15 C Belvin and others, 'Parental smoking and child poverty in the UK: an analysis of national survey data', *BMC Public Health*, 15(507), 2015
16 Exceeding 12 units for men in a day and nine for women: Office for National Statistics, *Opinions and Lifestyle Survey*, 2018

Eighteen
Council tax

Michael Orton

The development of local taxation in Britain

Local taxation in Britain began with the establishment of locally determined rates to fund individual projects such as bridge building. By the early nineteenth century, a series of separate rates were being levied for purposes ranging from highways to building workhouses. A long process of merging these numerous individual rates began in the 1830s and was largely (though not fully) completed in the 1920s, leading to the establishment of the general rates regime which remained in place through to the 1980s.

General rates

General rates were a property tax, based on the individual value of a dwelling. There was concern from the early twentieth century that the tax was regressive. The incidence of rates was distributed unevenly across the population and a higher proportion of the income of the poor was spent on rates than was the case for the middle class. However, it was not until the *Allen Committee Report* of 1965 that clear evidence of the regressivity of general rates was established. This led to the introduction of a means-tested rebate system and, by the time of its abolition in 1989/90, rates were no longer regressive and were broadly neutral in their impact.

Poll tax

Poll tax (or to use its proper name, community charge) replaced general rates in 1989/90, covering England, Scotland and Wales. Northern Ireland retained general rates. Poll tax was a flat-rate tax and, as such, was highly regressive. Its impact was dramatic in benefiting those with higher incomes over people on lower incomes. The change from general rates to poll tax led to households with a net weekly income of under £100 losing £1.30 a week; households with a net weekly income of £200 to £250 lost even more (£3.85 a week) because rebates ran out at that stage. In contrast, households with a weekly net income of £600 to £1,000 gained £4.04 a week, while the greatest benefit went to those on the highest incomes – households which had a weekly income of over £1,000 gained £6.50 a week. Poll tax met with widespread protest and an extensive campaign of non-payment, leading to its rapid demise. In 1993, poll tax was replaced by council tax.

The council tax scheme

Council tax has been the system of local taxation in England, Scotland and Wales since 1993. Northern Ireland is different, having still retained general rates.

Council tax is primarily, though not wholly, a property tax. Its introduction involved (domestic) properties being valued and then placed in one of eight valuation bands, A to H (H is the highest band). The valuation bands were based on 1991 prices. A revaluation of properties was undertaken in Wales in 2003 and an additional band (I) was added (in Wales only). In England and Scotland a revaluation has never been undertaken.

Table 18.1:
Council tax bands

Band	Property value England and Scotland (1991 prices)	Property value Wales (2003 prices)
A	Up to and including £27,000	Up to and including £44,000
B	£27,001 to £35,000	£44,001 to £65,000
C	£35,001 to £45,000	£65,001 to £91,000
D	£45,001 to £58,000	£91,001 to £123,000
E	£58,001 to £80,000	£123,001 to £162,000
F	£80,001 to £106,000	£162,001 to £223,000
G	£106,001 to £212,000	£223,001 to £324,000
H	£212,001 and above	£324,001 to £424,000
I	Not applicable	£424,001 and above

Source: Compiled from Valuation Office Agency information: www.gov.uk/guidance/understand-how-council-tax-bands-are-assessed

A different amount of tax is payable for each valuation band, with the liability for a band H property being three times that of a band A property – a ratio of 3:1. Thus, the value of an individual property determines the council tax band in which it is placed, but the amount of council tax that has to be paid depends on the council tax band, not the actual property value.

Council tax is not a pure property tax as liability also depends on additional criteria. In particular, council tax includes a system of discounts. For example, single householders receive an automatic 25 per cent reduction (the single-occupier discount). Other discounts, which are dependent on meeting certain criteria, can be applied for by people including apprentices, carers and students. Discounts are part of the structure of the council tax scheme and separate to the means-tested council tax benefit which operated from 1993 but was abolished in 2013, since when each local authority has been responsible for determining its own council tax reduction scheme. In practice, both council tax benefit and council tax reduction are rebates, reducing the amount of council tax that a person has to pay rather than providing a benefit.

Council tax and regressivity

Council tax is highly regressive. This is demonstrated in Table 18.2, which shows the percentage of household income accounted for by local taxation (net of discounts and rebates). From Table 18.2 it can be seen that the proportion of household income accounted for by local taxation rises with each income quintile – ie, in the latest year for which data are available (2016/17) local taxation accounts for 5.4 per cent of household income for those in the lowest 20 per cent of the economic distribution, but only 1.7 per cent for those in the top. Table 18.2 also shows figures for 2003/04, the first year for which this data is available in the present form, and it can be seen that the regressive impact has intensified. While the proportion of household income accounted for by local taxation has remained stable for the richest 20 per cent, it has increased for the other 80 per cent of households and in particular, for the poorest 20 per cent. In a report in 2015, the charity StepChange noted that its clients coming for advice about council tax debt were more likely to be families with children, women and single parents.[1]

Table 18.2:
Local tax in the UK as a percentage of gross household income, net of discounts and rebates, 2003/04 and 2016/17

	Poorest 20%	Second	Third	Fourth	Richest 20%
2003/04	4.9%	3.6%	3.0%	2.5%	1.7%
2016/17	5.4%	3.8%	3.2%	2.6%	1.7%

Note: Council tax (England, Scotland and Wales) and Northern Ireland rates after deducting discounts, council tax benefit/reduction and rate rebates.

Source: compiled from Office for National Statistics dataset, 'Effects of taxes and benefits on household income', 2014, www.ons.gov.uk/peoplepopulationandcommunity/personalandhouseholdfinances/incomeandwealth

In 2005, the New Policy Institute found there were a quarter of a million households whose income fell below the poverty line (60 per cent of median income) by an amount less than they paid in council tax, meaning 'the council tax they pay may be said to be the immediate cause of their being in poverty'.[2] At the same time, and consistent with changes in income tax and national insurance rules that took place in the 1980s, the council tax banding system means there is a strict ceiling put on the amount of local taxation that has to be paid, irrespective of how high an income a person has or the extent of her/his wealth.

The key cause of this regressivity is the ratio between council tax bands and the relationship between the bands and the amount of tax that has to be paid. The importance of the ratio between council tax bands is demonstrated in Table 18.3. The table shows the impact of three different ratios: the actual 3:1 ratio (as noted above) and hypothetical ratios of 5:1 and 10:1. The results are dramatic. For example, a 10:1 ratio would reduce liability in band A by 34 per cent and increase it for band H by over 100 per cent.

In 2017, the Scottish government revised the ratios for the four higher bands, as shown in Table 18.4 (and applying to Scotland only). Liability for a band E property increased from 122 per cent of the band D liability to 131 per cent; band H liability increased from 200 per cent of band D liability to 245 per cent. This increases the council tax yield, but the precise impact on regressivity remains to be seen.

Table 18.3:
Estimated average council tax bill with different ratios, 2007 figures (England only)

Band	Estimated average bill			Change			
	3:1 £	5:1 £	10:1 £	5:1 £	5:1 %	10:1 £	10:1 %
A	1,846	1,764	1,555	-82	-9.7	-291	-34.4
B	1,987	1,955	1,833	-32	-3.2	-154	-15.6
C	1,128	1,050	1,111	-78	-6.9	-17	-1.5
D	1,269	1,367	1,388	98	7.7	119	9.4
E	1,551	1,623	1,666	72	4.6	115	7.4
F	1,833	1,910	2,221	77	4.2	388	21.2
G	2,115	2,483	3,054	368	17.4	939	44.4
H	2,538	3,820	5,553	1,282	50.5	3,015	118.8

Source: M Lyons, *Place-Shaping: a shared ambition for the future of local government*, Lyons Inquiry into Local Government, 2007, Annexes, Table C3

Table 18.4:
Revised council tax ratios (Scotland only)

Band	Council tax as percentage of band D charge (before 1 April 2017)	Council tax as percentage of band D charge (from 1 April 2017)
A	67%	67%
B	78%	78%
C	89%	89%
D	100%	100%
E	122%	131%
F	144%	163%
G	167%	196%
H	200%	245%

Source: www.gov.scot/counciltax

Options for reform

In terms of options for reform of council tax, the changes to the ratios made by the Scottish government show one possible way forward. Other changes to ratios could be made, and revising the values of the bands themselves is another option. The Liberal Democrats and Labour have at different times made proposals for increasing taxation on high-value properties, invariably dubbed a 'mansion tax', but these have not developed. A revaluation of properties would be likely to have significant impact.

A recurring theme in consideration of council tax is not just its reform, but whether it should be abolished and replaced by a different form of local taxation. The *Lyons Inquiry*[3] considered options such as a local sales tax, land value tax, greater use of fees and charges and a local income tax. Introduction of the latter was suggested by John Hills in the original version of this book, *Changing Tax*.[4] Hills was writing as the poll tax was being introduced and before council tax had been conceived. His view then was that general rates should be restored, but with a lower yield and supplemented by a local income tax. A local income tax has the potential to be highly progressive, but, as Hills and Lyons both acknowledged, it would require major administrative changes and a fundamentally new approach to local tax unseen in the UK previously. More recently, an interesting proposal has been made for introduction of a new local property tax as will now be discussed.

A new local property tax

The proposal for a new local property tax has been made in reports by the Resolution Foundation and Institute for Public Policy Research.[5] The former argues that as time has passed, council tax has come to have only a very weak link to real property values and is beginning to look a lot like poll tax in its impact. Examples to support this are provided, including: a search of property comparison websites shows that a three-bedroom flat for sale for £2.1 million in south London has a council tax bill of £700 per year while just one mile away another three-bedroom flat for sale at £400,000 (less than one fifth of the price) has a council tax liability of £1,160 per year (two-thirds higher); in 2015/16, the typical net council tax bill was around 10 per cent higher in London than in the North East, but typical property values were 220 per cent higher.

The Resolution Foundation report models five options for a possible new property tax. The first two are:

- a proportional tax of 0.5 per cent of capital value of domestic properties (boosting annual yield by £1.6 billion compared to council tax);
- a slightly higher proportional tax of 0.7 per cent (boosting annual yield by £12.7 billion).

Other options add elements such as exempting properties under £100,000 but with a 1 per cent tax rate above that, and regionally specific tax-free allowances.

The Institute for Public Policy Research report adopts the first of the above options – ie, a proportional tax of 0.5 per cent of capital value of domestic properties. It argues that this would be far more progressive than council tax and would effectively capture increases in house prices which the current system fails to do. This means the proposed new tax would act as both a property tax and a tax on consumption. The vast majority (80 per cent) of households would benefit from the tax change and for those in the bottom half of the income distribution disposable income would rise.

Both reports contain considerable further detail. This includes consideration of a mechanism to help the cash-poor/asset-rich, scope for local discretion, use of new technologies to enable regular revaluations, developing the new tax to replace not only council tax but stamp duty as well, and a land value tax to replace non-domestic rates.

The politics of local taxation

We have so far considered what are largely technical matters, but it is important to recognise the importance of the politics of local taxation – not simply in terms of ideological preferences for different types of tax but that:[6]

> Council tax is considered by many to be in the 'too difficult to touch' box when it comes to reform. Haunted by memories of the poll tax, which is widely perceived to have contributed to the fall of Margaret Thatcher, the majority of national politicians daren't even speak of reform, let alone propose any change, for fear of the political consequences.

With a more journalistic flourish, media commentator Simon Jenkins wrote over a decade ago that:[7]

> Mention council tax to Gordon Brown or David Cameron and their faces turn white... Local taxes are the devil's work. Even to suggest their reform has ghosts howling in the graveyard.

The outcome, however, is a tax based on badly outdated property valuations and which demands more of those on middle and low incomes than those on high incomes, with regressive impact intensifying over time.

Conclusion

The Introduction to this book set out a number of objectives. These include identifying ways to raise additional revenue to reverse cuts in spending and ensuring progressivity. Council tax has some relevance to the former, but is primarily about the latter.

There are three basic choices regarding council tax:

- Do nothing and continue with regressivity and demanding more of those on middle and lower incomes than those with high incomes.
- Make it a little less bad, with changes in Scotland and Wales serving as examples, but leave in place the fundamentally problematic design of the tax.
- Abolish council tax and replace it with a new property tax.

Given the objective of ensuring progressivity, the recommendation arising from this chapter is that council tax should be abolished and replaced by a new local property tax at a proportional rate of 0.5 per cent of the capital value of domestic properties. This would benefit the vast majority (80 per cent) of households, include a mechanism to help the small number of cash-poor/asset-rich households affected, and keep up to date with regular revaluations using new technologies.

Box 18.1:
Business rates

Non-domestic rates (or business rates) are a property tax paid by occupants of non-domestic properties. The basic rates bill is determined by multiplying the rateable value of a property (a 'hereditament') by the 'multiplier'. The multiplier is expressed in pence per pound of rateable value. In November 2018, the UK government announced provisional multipliers for 2019/20 in England: a standard multiplier of 50.4p, and a small business multiplier of 49p. It is set by the UK government in England and by the Scottish and Welsh governments in Scotland and Wales. In Northern Ireland, both the Northern Ireland Executive and the district councils set separate rating multipliers, with the full rate liability collected by Land and Property Services. Business rates are devolved in Scotland, Wales and Northern Ireland. In England, district and unitary councils collect business rates. The revenue is partly pooled at central government level and redistributed, and part is retained locally. Various reductions in liability for business rates are available, including for small businesses, charities and some rural properties. The autumn 2018 Budget announced reliefs for smaller retail properties.

Notes
1. R de Santos, *Council Tax Debts: how to deal with the growing arrears crisis tipping families into problem debt*, StepChange, 2015
2. New Policy Institute, *Council Tax Benefit for Working-age Households: a review of the problems and some options for reform*, 2005
3. Lyons Inquiry into Local Government, 2007
4. J Hills, *Changing Tax: how the tax system works and how to change it*, CPAG, 1988
5. L Murphy and others, *A Poor Tax – Council Tax in London: time for reform*, Institute for Public Policy Research, 2018; A Corlett and L Gardiner, *Home Affairs: options for reforming property taxation*, Resolution Foundation, 2018
6. L Murphy and others, *A Poor Tax – Council Tax in London: time for reform*, Institute for Public Policy Research, 2018, p3
7. S Jenkins, 'Politicians are too terrified to devolve power to the people', the *Guardian*, 14 November 2007, available at www.theguardian.com/commentisfree/2007/nov/14/comment.politics

Nineteen
Taxing companies
Andy Lymer

The taxation of companies raises many complex issues, which go be beyond the scope of this book. Indeed, John Head writes '[c]company taxation has long been among the most controversial and inconclusive areas in the public finance literature'.[1] The intention of this chapter is therefore to simply outline the current system and some of its main features, and to lay out some of the key challenges with pinning taxes on companies and particularly addressing the challenges of international competition for corporate tax revenues, rather than to explore it in detail and to make detailed policy development recommendations.

Some aspects of taxing companies are covered in other chapters – including the payment of national insurance contributions by companies (Chapter 7) and in the chapter on escaping taxation (Chapter 20). These issues will therefore not feature again here.

There were 4.1 million companies in the UK at the end of December 2018.[2] As Table 19.1 shows (for the 2.67 million VAT and pay as you earn (PAYE) registered (ie, mostly larger) of these businesses), the vast majority (90.8 per cent) of these are quite small and are created most often to (legitimately and legally) shield the private assets of the owners from their business endeavours – so called 'limited liability'. Without the formation of a company to trade through, those engaged in business activity are otherwise exposed personally to any and all liabilities of their businesses. This significant advantage for those wishing to engage in business activity has been a feature of the UK legal and commercial systems for over 150 years. Some argue that this alone is a key justification for why companies should pay tax themselves – a cost for being provided with this protection in law to do business within – even though they are not the owners of their own assets (their shareholders are) and therefore are artificial entities in essence.[3]

Table 19.1:
Number of VAT- and/or PAYE-based enterprises by turnover, 2018

Turnover band	Number of companies	Percentage of total
Below £100,000	1,055,080	39.5%
£100,000–£499,999	1,179,955	44.2%
£500,000–£999,999	190,280	7.1%
£1–5 million	183,265	6.9%
£5–10 million	28,080	1.1%
£10–50 million	24,785	0.9%
Above £50 million	7,995	0.3%
Total	2,669,440	100%

Source: Office for National Statistics, *UK Business: Activity, Size and Location, dataset*, 2018, Table 7

However, the fact that companies are not the ultimate owners of their assets creates a number of important difficulties for pinning taxes onto them, as the next chapter explores. As such, the UK, like many other so-called 'developed' countries, has been careful not to become too reliant on taxing company profits as a key revenue source. In 2019/20, for example, corporation tax is forecast to raise £60 billion[4] of the total receipts to the UK government of £810 billion (ie, only 7.4 per cent), compared with personal income taxes of £193 billion (23.8 per cent) – more than three times as large a contributor.[5] The UK has consistently been a lower user of corporation tax than some other OECD countries, although above levels typically found across Europe. For example, the average percentage of UK tax receipts that comes from corporation tax was 8.9 per cent across the period 1990 to 2015 (see Table 19.2). Countries including New Zealand (at 11.9 per cent average over the same period) and Australia (at 17 per cent average over the same period) are consistently much more reliant on their companies in absolute taxes paid terms, whereas countries such as France (at 5.5 per cent average over the same period) and Germany (at 4.8 per cent average over the same period) are much less so.

Table 19.2:
Taxes on corporate income as percentage of total tax revenue

	1990	2000	2010	2014	2016
Australia	14.1%	20.3%	17.9%	16.4%	16.5%
New Zealand	6.5%	12.4%	12.2%	13.1%	15.5%
United Kingdom	9.9%	10.6%	8.9%	7.8%	7.5%
France	5.3%	6.9%	5.6%	5.1%	4.5%
Germany	4.8%	4.8%	4.3%	4.7%	5.2%

Source: OECD, *Revenue Statistics 2017* and *2018*, Table 3.9

There are, in fact, four main kinds of tax levied on companies in the UK:

- **Corporation tax** levied on the profits of 'incorporated' companies – ie, those where the liability of the owners or shareholders is normally limited to their investment.

- **Employer national insurance contributions** charged on the wages and salaries paid by all employers (whether companies or not, although those self-employed currently have different rules).[6]

- **Non-domestic rates** paid via local authorities and charged on most commercial and industrial property (although currently an exemption exists in part against these payments for properties occupied by small business).[7]

- **North Sea taxes** charged on companies involved in oil and gas extraction.[8]

Companies will also pay other taxes, depending on their circumstances and the market sector in which they operate, including non-recoverable VAT, environmental taxes and duties and, for those operating in the banking sector, the bank levy and banking surcharge. Their profits are used to pay their workers, whose salaries and wages are taxed, and so some argue that their activity can also be said to be the basis for these taxes too.[9]

Problem of incidence

To many, it may seem obvious that companies should be taxed. Companies make up over 70 per cent of the total number of businesses in the UK,[10] control large parts of the economy, own a large part of the country's assets (albeit on behalf of their shareholders) and many of the larger ones make large profits on very significant levels of turnover. They can therefore surely be reasonably asked to bear 'their share' of the tax burden is the argument. However, as a company is only a collection of the assets of its owners and is not the ultimate consumer of services and products, it does not really bear anything directly itself – imposing tax on it will actually affect the people involved in its activities, not just the company itself.

The most obvious effect of a tax on corporates is that their profits – and hence the dividends paid to the company's owners, its shareholders – would be reduced. This is, of course, the same premise as for all taxes where the associated costs reduce at least the direct returns available to their owners. But, unlike with many other taxpayers, the tax might not necessarily stick at the corporate/shareholder level as the company might respond to taxation by raising its prices, leaving its profits unaffected and instead shifting the *incidence* of the tax to the *consumers* of its products or services. Equally, the effect of the tax might be that less would be available for wages – the *employees* would therefore bear the tax; or it might pay less to its *suppliers*; or its *managers* might be provided with fewer perks.

Furthermore, where the company is part of a larger group structure of interconnected companies (as the majority of the large ones are), there is the possibility to pass profits in one part of the group to offset losses in another part of the group. This reduces the overall taxes the group then pays. If parts of the group are outside the UK, this may mean passing taxes that would be paid to the UK tax authority either to other authorities or to no one at all (where losses elsewhere cancel out profits made in the UK).[11]

Without direct regulation to pin taxes onto companies and prevent them passing it on, which is costly and can be difficult to do, all company taxes are therefore open to the problem of 'shifting' and to difficulties in determining who really ends up paying them. While this is not just a problem for company taxation – it applies to all business taxes – it is particularly an issue in this case, given the range and breadth of a company's ability to spread the incidence of taxes it is asked to pay.

If the shareholders ultimately bear the tax, it will be highly progressive as shareholders are typically among the wealthier in society (although many others would also be affected where their pension funds, for example, are shareholders). If consumers bear it, its effects will be like those of indirect taxes and will be much less progressive, and maybe even regressive.[12] As the economy is now very internationalised, the latter may become more likely as foreign investors will demand the same after-tax rate of return as they can obtain in other countries. Prices and levels of investment will tend therefore to adjust until this is achieved. On the other hand, it may become more difficult for domestic producers to change the price at which internationally traded goods and services are sold, in which case consumers may be protected.[13]

Why tax companies at all?

In view of this uncertainty about who would actually end up paying corporation taxes, it might seem better to avoid such taxation and instead apply tax directly on the intended target: taxes on dividends if shareholders are the target; taxes on high salaries and fringe benefits/benefits in kind if managers are the target; or indirect taxes if consumers are the target. Nonetheless, there are good reasons for retaining a system of company tax:

- Some argue the provision of limited liability by society alone is a key justification for why companies should pay tax themselves – a payment for being provided with this protection in law to do business within – even though they are not the beneficial owners of their own assets and therefore are artificial entities in essence.[14]

- If companies were not taxed, they would provide a tax-free 'shelter' for the wealthy. Instead of saving in taxable forms, they would accumulate their savings within a company, not pay out dividends to create a taxable activity, and pay no tax until money was needed (when shares are sold and releasing a capital gains tax charge, or a currently tax-advantaged dividend-related income tax charge if funds are withdrawn as income). This would not matter so much if capital gains tax could be made an effective tax, but, as discussed in Chapter 12, it is hard to make capital gains tax really effective in practice. A key role of a tax on company profits is therefore as a way of catching undistributed (so called 'retained') profits that might otherwise not be taxed for some time, if at all.

- Companies offer a convenient 'tax handle' for tax collectors to grab hold of – there are relatively few of them to deal with compared with individual taxpayers or even retailers. This therefore offers an increase in the efficiency of tax collection costs over other possible alternatives.

- Most other countries have company taxes and their effects are built into the whole structure of international finance and into 'double taxation' agreements between countries.[15] The rules of some of these arrangements can have the effect that where a foreign company generates profits in the UK, it will end up paying the same tax overall across both jurisdictions (at least at the rate set in its home country) regardless of the level of UK tax (for payments of which the home government gives a 'credit'). If the UK charged such companies less tax, the beneficiaries would be foreign governments, not the foreign companies themselves (or those they pass tax savings on to). The resulting credit for the UK taxes would simply shrink against the fixed tax rate in the home country applied to the returns in bringing profits home. So there would not necessarily even be a greater incentive for them to invest in the UK from these lower taxes – the UK is simply foregoing taxes it would otherwise be able to collect. The 'tax credit' basis is, however, a model of double tax relief operation globally that is losing favour more recently with countries exchanging their basis for relieving foreign taxes paid by this crediting process with an exemption process – where foreign profits are just not taxed at all in the home country. Where this occurs, lower company taxes in the UK could produce the desired effect then to stimulate investment (or to reduce reductions to returns created by taxation for other stakeholders where these are passed on by the company).

- Domestic financial markets have also adjusted to the existence of company taxes – abolishing them (or even reducing their rates) might simply deliver windfall gains to those who had already allowed for the tax. Recent drops in the rate of UK corporation tax (heading now for 17 per cent from 52 per cent a limited number of years ago) could perhaps be argued to be providing just such a windfall gain and perhaps is an area to be looked at to examine who the real beneficiaries are of such falls in the tax rate.

- Taxes are also not solely used by governments for revenue-raising purposes. A further reason to maintain taxation at the corporate level is to provide the government with the mechanism for changing behaviour and as a source of indirect regulation (albeit indirectly and fairly crudely).[16] The removal of taxation at a corporate level would therefore reduce the leverage governments have to regulate corporate activity.

These are considerations of principle. The major reason for the continued existence of company tax may be somewhat less honourable and perhaps less justifiable therefore. Company taxes are much less visible than direct taxes on individuals or indirect taxes like VAT (again mostly paid by individuals, although somewhat less well recognised as taxes by the population it seems). Precisely because it is unclear who really ends up paying them, taxes on corporations offer a convenient way for governments to raise revenue with less protest than might otherwise be the case. There are many examples of tax reforms in countries around the world where lowering the burdens on individuals and increasing in the burdens on companies is presented as a positive move for fairer shares being borne by corporations. As has been illustrated above, however, the underlying reality may be less clear on the overall impact of the burden sharing than these appearances suggest are the case.

Corporation tax charges

For a number of years until 1982/83, the rate of corporation tax had been 52 per cent,[17] the rate dropped to 35 per cent for many years in the later 1980s and has more recently been dropping further again. At the time of writing, the current government is proposing that this will be only 17 per cent by 2020 from a current rate of 19 per cent.[18] This will be the lowest rate of taxation on corporations of any comparable developed country in the world (other than the current rates in Ireland at 12.5 per cent, Hong Kong at 16.5 per cent and the same for Singapore). While some may argue this is key for the UK to find a place as the location for international business in a post-Brexit world, this is quite a bold departure from the trends in other comparable nations. It is arguable whether the rate needs to be quite this low to achieve the desired objectives of keeping companies based or headquartered in the UK who might otherwise leave, and to encourage those companies that are so domiciled to bring their overseas income back to the UK.

Figure 19.1:
Rates of UK corporate tax, 1971 to 2020

Source: www.figurewizard.com/list-uk-corporation-tax-rates.html; https://tradingeconomics.com/united-kingdom/corporate-tax-rate

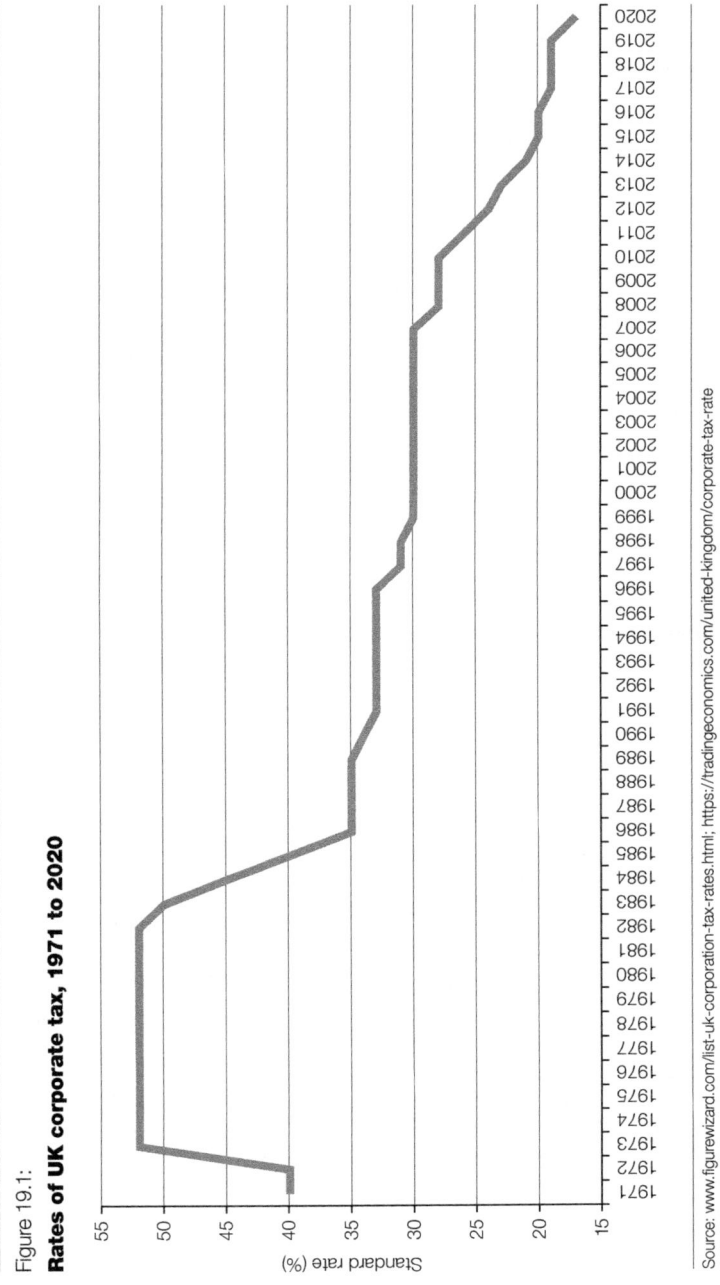

While the proposed rate for after 2020 at 17 per cent is only one-third of the rate in the UK throughout much of the 1970s and early-1980s (see Figure 19.1), supporters of this move argue that this can be justified on the basis that, at the same time, the base for this tax (the profitable activities on which it is applied) has increased and corporations have become considerably more profitable over this period to compensate for these reductions. Furthermore, there is evidence that taxable activity has been stimulated by these reductions (including a dramatic 21 per cent increase in revenues from corporation tax in 2017/18 compared with the previous year). Of course, it is very difficult to unpick what is motivating these changes in the balance between rates and tax take when other factors are also changing at the same time in the wider economy, in the global setting in which UK companies operate and in the underlying rules on how such taxes are computed and paid. It is also near impossible to know what would have happened to corporation tax takes had these reductions in rates not occurred, or occurred to the same extent, with other events still occurring over this period.

Figure 19.2:

Comparative corporate tax rates showing UK and averages for Asia, North America, Europe and Latin America, 2006 to 2019

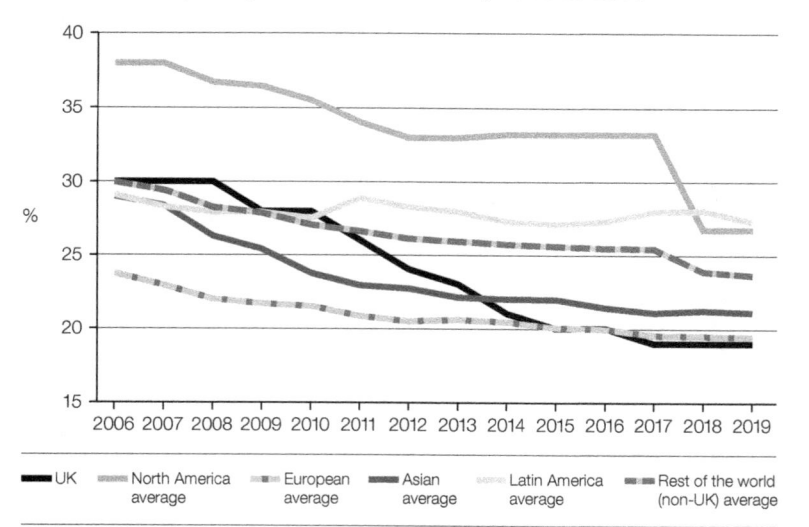

Source: KPMG corporate tax rates, https://home.kpmg/xx/en/home/services/tax/tax-tools-and-resources/tax-rates-online.html

Figure 19.2 illustrates how the fall in the UK rate compares to recent changes on average across the rest of the world for the years following the period immediately before and during the global financial crisis in 2007 and 2008. As this data illustrate, the UK has been out of step with the average moves around the world in pursuing a much more aggressive strategy of lowering its corporate tax rates at a faster rate.

Table 19.3 illustrates how UK corporation tax rates have changed compared with corporation tax revenues. It illustrates how tax revenues have risen significantly at the same time as rates of tax have been falling. This represents a 164 per cent rise in tax revenues from corporation tax (unadjusted for inflation) – although for comparison, personal income tax increases over the same period are 190 per cent, social security receipts are 253 per cent, and VAT is 293 per cent (on the same computational basis).[19] The third column of Table 19.3 illustrates that corporation tax has become a smaller percentage of GDP over time and also a falling percentage of the total tax revenues received by the government (column four). Cuts to corporation tax rates announced between 2010 and 2016 are estimated to have reduced revenues by at least £16.5 billion a year in the short to medium run, albeit reduced to an estimate of £12.5 billion once changes to rules associated with tax avoidance are taken into account.[20] Helen Miller comments that 'changes to corporate tax have represented some of the largest giveaways in both parliaments since 2010'.[21] As such, while total revenues in absolute terms have increased significantly over this period, the reliance that the government places on corporate taxes has been falling in the last 20 years.

Table 19.3:

Corporate tax revenues, unadjusted for inflation, 1990 to 2016

Year	UK corporation tax income £ billion	Percentage of GDP	Percentage of tax revenues
1990	£20.1	3.3%	9.9%
2000	£38.1	3.5%	10.6%
2010	£45.6	2.9%	8.9%
2015	£46.0	2.4%	7.5%
2016	£53.4	2.7%	8.3%

Source: OECD, *Revenue Statistics 2018*, 2018, Table 4.69

In addition to falling rates of tax and lower reliance on corporate tax as a part of the mix of taxes received by the UK government, companies are also privileged with various allowances and reliefs that they can apply to lower their tax bills. These are argued to be tax expenditures that help to stimulate ongoing entrepreneurial investment in UK businesses.[22] Examples of such reliefs include very generous deductions for research and development costs, for the purchase of assets (via the annual investment allowance) and deductions for intangible assets usage.

On the other hand, regulations have also been imposed periodically to reduce the ability of companies to shift profits to reduce tax completely at will. These include recently:

- changes to the way in which profits can be left in group companies that are offshore in low tax jurisdictions that might be otherwise deemed to be owned by a UK-based parent company (the so-called 'controlled foreign corporation tax principles');
- interest deductibility curtailment to prevent the ability of companies to use internal tax-deductible loans between group members to move profits around into lower taxed deductions; *and*
- limitations on the use of transfer pricing to do likewise with other costs incurred to buy and sell goods and services within a group of related companies at favourable rates.

Examination of the extent to which these, and similar, regulations have the effect of bringing back, or keeping, otherwise taxable activity in the UK is the source of much debate and study. Similarly, time will tell whether reducing the rates of corporate taxation to historically, and internationally, very low rates will stimulate future taxable activity and pass further rewards to stakeholders beyond a limited number of wealthy shareholders – it is therefore important to keep this under close scrutiny. The government's own analysis (albeit carried out before the latest rounds of further reductions in corporation tax rates) suggests the cost to the UK of these policies is around 45 per cent to 60 per cent of the actual foregone revenues – once behavioural responses that might be predicted, such as increased levels of investments made as the direct result of lower taxes on returns from those investments, have been taken into account.[23] This is, however, likely to be an area in which further reform is needed as the impact of these rules and rate changes becomes clearer over time.

Recommendations

In the medium term, the UK government should commission a study of the impact of the reductions in corporation tax over the last 30 years to develop its 2013 study further and make more publicly available a justification for why this policy of operating very low rates of tax on corporate profits remains suitable in the current climate in order to enable this policy choice to be more subject to public debate.

Notes
1. J Head, 'Company tax systems: from theory to policy', in J Head and R Krever (eds), *Company Tax Systems*, Australian Tax Research Foundation, 1997, pp1–48
2. Office for National Statistics, *Incorporated Companies in the UK: October to December 2018*, 2019
3. A fuller exploration of the justification for taxing companies can also be found in C Evans and others, *Comparative Taxation: why tax systems differ*, Fiscal Publications, 2017, Chapter 5
4. HM Treasury, *Budget 2018*, HC 1629, October 2018, p20, Chart 2: Public sector current receipts 2019/20, p5
5. This reflects a similar position found in other OECD countries where approximately 9 per cent of government tax receipts come from taxes on company profits and capital gains – which has been consistently the case since the OECD started to collect this data in 1965: OECD, *Revenue Statistics 2017*, OECD Publishing, 2017, Table 3.9
6. The nature and possible reform of these 'taxes' are discussed in more details in Chapter 7 and therefore not expanded on further in this chapter.
7. Non-domestic business rates are discussed briefly in Chapter 18.
8. These taxes are not explored further in this book because they now form a very limited revenue source for the UK government. See H Miller, *What's Been Happening to Corporation Tax?*, Institute for Fiscal Studies Briefing Note BN206, 2017
9. This is a reasoning often put forward for why company profits taxes are relatively low. However, the provision of labour is arguably what is actually being taxed here, not the profits of the company per se – a hotly debated issue in some quarters.
10. Office for National Statistics, *UK Business; activity, size and location: 2018*, October 2018
11. This process of profit shifting is part of a large international initiative currently underway to look again at the principles of taxing international business. See the OECD-led Base Erosion and Profit Shifting initiative for further details at www.oecd.org/tax/beps
12. See Chapter 16 for a discussion of the regressivity of VAT, for example.
13. For a fuller review of corporate tax incidence, see A Auerbach, 'Who bears the corporate tax? A review of what we know', in J Poterba (ed), *Tax Policy and the Economy*, Volume 20, National Bureau of Economic Research, 2006
14. A fuller exploration of the justification for taxing companies can also be found in C Evans and others, *Comparative Taxation: why tax systems differ*, Fiscal Publications, 2017, Chapter 5
15. Double tax agreements are contracts between country states to manage the possibilities of taxation being charged on the same activities by more than one jurisdiction where the activ-

ity that produces the returns being taxed can be said to be arising from, or belonging to, entities that have taxable presence in more than one jurisdiction.

16 A fuller description of the regulatory role for corporate taxation and the advantages and limitations of the use of taxation in this process can be found in C Evans and others, *Comparative Taxation: why tax systems differ*, Fiscal Publications, 2017, pp81–90. See also A Auerbach, M Devereux and H Simpson, 'Taxing corporate income', in Institute for Fiscal Studies (ed), *Dimensions of Tax Design: the Mirrlees Review*, Oxford University Press, 2010

17 The rate of corporation tax rose to 52 per cent in 1973 and had been at that level until it began to be reduced over the following 30+ years from 1982/83. The longest period since that time without a fall in rate was between 1991/92 and 1996/97, when the rate remained at 33 per cent. No increases in rates have occurred in any period over this window.

18 This reduction was first proposed by George Osborne in the 2015 Budget, but recently endorsed by Philip Hammond as still current government policy (see HM Revenue and Customs, *Corporation Tax to 17% in 2020*, March 2016). This suggests it remains part of the strategy of the current UK government to make the UK corporation tax system one of the 'most competitive' in the developed world as part of its announced corporate tax road map that was released under the previous coalition government (in November 2010) – see HM Treasury, *The Corporate Tax Road Map*, 2010.

19 OECD, *Revenue Statistics 2018*, OECD Publishing, 2018, Table 4.69 – UK tax revenue by selected tax revenue category

20 H Miller, *What's Been Happening to Corporation Tax?*, Institute for Fiscal Studies Briefing Note BN206, 2017

21 H Miller, *What's Been Happening to Corporation Tax?*, Institute for Fiscal Studies Briefing Note BN206, 2017

22 Tax reliefs and tax expenditures are explored further in Chapter 9.

23 See HM Revenue and Customs and HM Treasury, *Analysis of the Dynamic Effects of Corporation Tax Reductions*, 2013

Twenty
Escaping tax
Alan Buckle

While the majority of people simply pay their taxes, there are those who work hard to reduce their tax bill either legally or illegally, and there are others who advise and assist them.

The opportunity to reduce taxes is open mainly to the wealthy, who buy advice and have diverse sources of income, along with large companies which are able to reduce their taxes through complex structuring and planning, supported by well-staffed tax departments and external advisers.

While HM Revenue and Customs (HMRC) has focused on avoidance with some success, its efforts are undermined by the complexity of the tax system, the difficulty in changing it and the reluctance of successive governments to do so. This chapter is noticeably longer than others in this book, not least because the complexities of our tax system (which is said to run to 17,000 pages of legislation) allow for a wide variety of avoidance.

Box 20.1:
Definitions

Until quite recently, the distinction was drawn between illegal tax evasion and legal tax avoidance. More recently, three terms are commonly used:[1]

- **Tax evasion** is the illegal concealment of taxable income, either in the UK's 'hidden economy' or offshore.
- **Tax avoidance** is working within the law to gain a tax advantage, by following the letter of the law, but not its spirit. This often involves complex and artificial arrangements which are devised by tax advisers.
- **Tax planning** involves using tax reliefs and allowances in the way that they were intended.

The boundary between avoidance and planning is highly contested. As the House of Lords Economic Affairs Committee put it, the definition of tax planning as within the spirit of the law: 'Depends on the existence of a common interpretation of what the original lawmakers had in mind.'[2] For example, when PEPs, the predecessors of ISAs, were introduced in 1986, they were intended to widen share ownership, whereas over time they have evolved into an opportunity for tax-free investment for high net worth individuals, at times reaching more than a million pounds of tax-free assets. Who knows whether this is, was or will continue to be intended?

The debate about tax avoidance

There is a continuing debate about the morality of tax and, indeed, whether it is appropriate to discuss tax as a moral issue. At the two ends of the spectrum there are those who are 'anti-tax', who believe that taxes are an imposition, to be avoided in any way that is permissible within the law, and those who are 'pro-tax', who see taxes as an obligation of citizenship and therefore to be paid without any planning to reduce one's liability.

The prevention of tax avoidance and evasion are a clear focus for recent governments. They are concerned to ensure that taxes are collected effectively, that all who should contribute to public expenditure do so and that illegal evasion is prevented. They do not attempt to curtail, or even fully monitor, the cost of tax planning, which is seen by some as just as reprehensible as avoidance.

There would also appear to be rising public concern about avoidance, led by campaigning NGOs.

The problem with the tax system

The best way to reduce loss of taxes is to design a system which is simple to administer and hard to manipulate. This is far better than papering over the cracks of a complex regime which tends towards an arms race between avoiders and the authorities, which the authorities will continue to lose. Prevention is better than cure.

As the *Mirrlees Review* puts it:[3]

> If activities were taxed in similar ways there would be no (or at least much less) incentive for taxpayers to dress up one activity as another – and there would correspondingly little or no loss to the Exchequer if they did so.

The UK tax system has at least five ways of potentially taxing the same income, depending on the tax status of the individual and the characterisation of the income:

- An individual may be **an employee** taxed through the pay as you earn (PAYE) system and, along with the employer, also paying national insurance. Even in this case, there is the opportunity to 'sacrifice' part of one's salary and receive other benefits instead, thereby avoiding national insurance. But, in general, there are fewer loopholes and the tax is relatively easy to collect.

- If someone is a **self-employed supplier** to a business, there is more opportunity for tax deductions, national insurance is paid through a different and more advantageous regime and is avoided by the company. The 'gig economy' makes self-employment more common. Definitions are difficult and the government has worked hard to avoid companies treating its employees as self-employed.

- A step beyond this is for the individual to **incorporate**. This has various tax advantages: national insurance is potentially avoided, income tax is deferred until dividends are paid, family members may be 'employed' to perform duties which are hard for the tax authorities to scrutinise, and additional cost deductions are possible. In 2017, HMRC started a clampdown on 'personal service companies', which can be used unfairly to enable the avoidance of the PAYE/national insurance contributions regime. While the use of personal service companies by the rich and famous attracts media attention, they have also been widely used by relatively low-paid people in sectors such as IT, education and health.

- Taxes will be lower if applied to **capital gains** rather than income. Many tax planning schemes have been based on turning income into capital, where typically rates are lower, and generous tax breaks are available. Lower capital gains tax rates have also increased the benefits for private equity ownership rather than public ownership of companies.

- Finally, **gifts** are received tax-free and only taxed if the giver dies within seven years.

The UK system grew up piecemeal and is rooted in a world before global companies, complex financing arrangements, intangible assets, mobile citizens, digital technology and a highly effective tax planning industry. It has never been overhauled in a systemic way. Successive governments have built a tax system which is highly complex and, therefore, harder to administer, harder to comply with and easier to game.

Various proposals have been made over the years to simplify the tax system which would result in fewer opportunities for abuse and be easier to administer. However, little progress has been made. Governments are reluctant to change, as there will be losers whose negative reaction will outweigh the positivity of the winners.

In 2017, the Budget proposed closing part of the gap between self-employed and employed status by bringing national insurance for the self-employed into line with employed people. However, the government hastily withdrew, as the 'losers' included the increasing army of self-employed as well as small businesses.

If anything, recent changes in rates and regimes have widened the cracks between different taxes and encouraged abuse. In 2016, rates of capital gains tax were reduced to 10 per cent, and for additional rate taxpayers to 20 per cent, well below the rates of income tax. And corporation tax rates have fallen to 19 per cent, again well below income tax levels.

The system for tax collection is highly complex and anything but user-friendly. Even the basic tax return is difficult for a normally tax-literate person to follow – 81 sections with plenty of terminology – so errors are inevitable. However, the complexity of the form is a consequence of the complexity of the UK's tax legislation. There are more than a thousand reliefs and allowances.

Work by the Behavioural Insights Team (the formerly government-controlled group, colloquially known as the 'nudge unit') suggests that complexity could be a significant cause of evasion and error. Its work suggests that if websites were simpler, forms easier and the customer interface with HMRC friendly, compliance would increase.

The Swedish tax authorities are often held out as an exemplar in tax collection: a very high proportion of people complete tax returns online, there are financial incentives to do so, much of the required information is already held by the tax authorities and each person has a personal contact at the tax authority. For most people, the tax form is four pages long and pre-populated with most of the information – not least because there are few tax allowances, the system is simple.

HMRC is working hard to make itself more 'customer focused' and to make the system simpler including pre-population of information and a long-held aspiration to abolish the paper form as part of its programme to 'make tax digital'. However, the project has been subject to delays and it is questionable whether HMRC is being given the necessary resources to complete this work.

The UK's ability to collect tax is intertwined with the tax regimes of other countries. The global tax system was designed at a time when companies were rarely international and, if they were, they had largely national supply chains and overseas affiliates mainly to support exports of finished goods and import of raw materials. Companies were therefore taxed locally, and international rules were in place to avoid manipulation by insisting on arm's length pricing between countries. The countries set corporation tax rates for local reasons, 'tax competition' between nations was unheard of and tax havens barely existed. Similarly, it was far more difficult for individuals to take advantage of international complexities, as the infrastructure did not exist to move assets and income across tax jurisdictions.

The scale of the problem

HMRC defines the tax gap as 'the difference between the amount of tax that should, in theory, be paid to HMRC and what is actually paid'.

The official view in the 2018 edition of HMRC's tax gap report is that the tax gap is around £33 billion, which represents 5.7 per cent of tax liabilities. The absolute amount has been more or less static since the analysis was first undertaken in 2005/06, when the gap represented 7.3 per cent of total tax liabilities.

The figures are surprising, given the public debate about tax which is focused on tax avoidance by large global corporations and wealthy individuals. The largest customer group is small businesses rather than large, tax avoidance is only £1.7 billion (only 5 per cent of the gap) and corporation tax is only just over 10 per cent of the total gap.

Figure 20.1:
Value of the tax gap, 2016/17

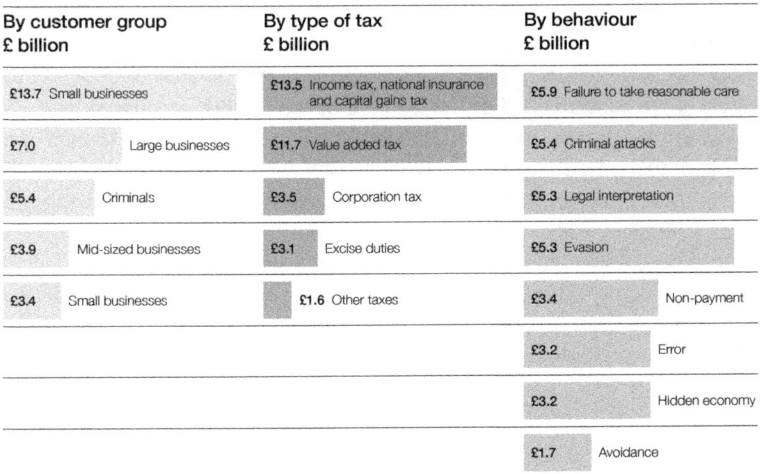

By customer group £ billion	By type of tax £ billion	By behaviour £ billion
£13.7 Small businesses	£13.5 Income tax, national insurance and capital gains tax	£5.9 Failure to take reasonable care
£7.0 Large businesses	£11.7 Value added tax	£5.4 Criminal attacks
£5.4 Criminals	£3.5 Corporation tax	£5.3 Legal interpretation
£3.9 Mid-sized businesses	£3.1 Excise duties	£5.3 Evasion
£3.4 Small businesses	£1.6 Other taxes	£3.4 Non-payment
		£3.2 Error
		£3.2 Hidden economy
		£1.7 Avoidance

Source: HM Revenue and Customs, *Measuring Tax Gaps 2018 Edition: tax gap estimates for 2016/17*, 2018

The tax gap analysis is to be applauded, so far as it goes, and attracts international praise. It has been prepared using consistent methodologies for 12 years and is clearly presented. It allows focused discussion of tax gaps which, regardless of politics, most wish to see closed. And it enables comparisons with others who prepare reports on a similar basis.

The report has been criticised for underestimating the scale of the black economy, and therefore of evasion. By definition, evasion is difficult to quantify. HMRC's tax estimates for tax lost through evasion (including criminal attacks) would suggest a relatively small figure.[4] However, for example, a report by Tax Research UK in 2014 for the Public and Commercial Services Union disputed the credibility of many of the estimates; it estimated the tax gap as £70–100 billion.[5] This figure was revised up to £122 billion with respect to 2014/15. In part, this is due to a wider definition of avoidance. It would be helpful for HMRC to rebut or explain these suggestions.

The greatest problem with the tax gap report is that it excludes tax planning. From an HMRC perspective, this is reasonable – it is not HMRC's role to force people to pay more taxes than the law requires, and neither is it HMRC's role to finally determine tax policy. That is for the politicians.

However, this means that the tax gap report, which is the only comprehensive report on the tax gaps, cannot be used to assess the total leakage from the system of all forms of tax reduction. Furthermore, we have seen how difficult it is to draw the line between avoidance (which the government is clamping down on) and planning (which it encourages).

The impact of tax planning, particularly through the use of allowances, is huge and not analysed in a single report. The cost of only those tax expenditures which aim to change behaviour is more than £100 billion. If we included half of the reliefs that are partially to change behaviour, the cost heads toward £150 billion. This huge amount dwarfs the whole of the tax debate and is subject to little scrutiny. In the case of both capital gains tax and inheritance tax, the reliefs almost eliminate the tax raised – reliefs were almost four times the capital gains tax take and almost seven times in the case of inheritance tax.

The scale of tax reliefs was illustrated by the Resolution Foundation in a different way by comparing individual reliefs to whole government department budgets as Figure 20.2 shows.

Figure 20.2:
Cost comparisons of selected tax expenditures and government departments, 2014/15

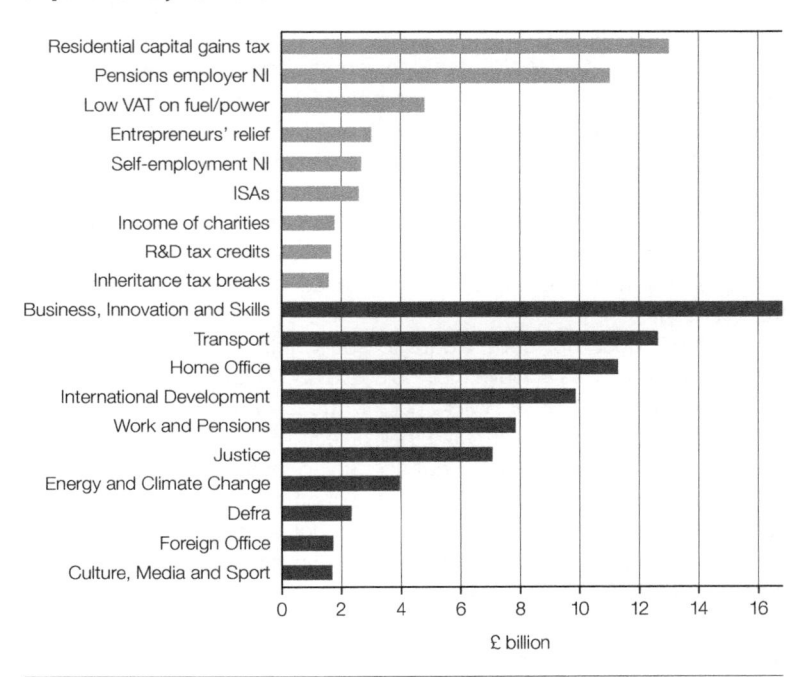

Category	£ billion
Residential capital gains tax	~13
Pensions employer NI	~11
Low VAT on fuel/power	~5
Entrepreneurs' relief	~3
Self-employment NI	~3
ISAs	~3
Income of charities	~2
R&D tax credits	~2
Inheritance tax breaks	~2
Business, Innovation and Skills	~17
Transport	~13
Home Office	~11
International Development	~10
Work and Pensions	~8
Justice	~7
Energy and Climate Change	~4
Defra	~2
Foreign Office	~2
Culture, Media and Sport	~2

Source: A Corlett, *Finding Some Relief: the case for applying fiscal discipline to tax expenditures*, Resolution Foundation, 2015

As well as the official reliefs, many taxes are ineffective by dint of reliefs which are not recorded. This includes, for example:

- lifetime gifts before death which are not subject to inheritance tax;
- activities which are deemed to be non-taxable, but are contentious – for example, public school education; *and*
- UK tax which is unpaid by global companies or citizens as a result of their structuring and internal financial planning.

The position of governments is unhelpful. While they enthusiastically introduce tax allowances that make the opportunity for planning ever wider, they are unwilling to shine a light on the cost. And they explicitly encourage the use of planning – to the extent that the government's Money Advice Centre publishes advice on *Using a Trust to Cut Your Inheritance Tax*.[6]

Additionally, the HMRC tax gap report is quite clear that its gap 'does not include international tax arrangements... which will be tackled multilaterally through the OECD'. As result, by HMRC's definition, avoidance is only £1.7 billion, a long way behind simple error, which is £3.2 billion.

The tax gap analysis should therefore, at best, be seen as a tool for measuring HMRC's success and not as a measure of the overall leakage from the tax system and the opportunity for increasing tax receipts. The lack of such a measure is one reason for a lack of focus and scrutiny of the tax take.

HMRC does not collect data to see whether reliefs which have behavioural objectives achieve their objective and neither does it carry out such an evaluation. Neither HMRC nor HM Treasury reports to parliament on whether tax reliefs are achieving their objective, so that a huge value of what is effectively expenditure is not accounted for to parliament.

It is salutary to compare the scrutiny of other areas of public expenditure with that applied to tax allowances. If, for example, entrepreneurs' relief, which gives tax breaks to those who sell businesses, was a grant to businesses start-ups, it would be scrutinised by the Department for Business Energy and Industrial Strategy (for which it would constitute a large proportion of the budget) and would be given as much attention by parliament (for example, via the scrutiny of the Business, Energy and Industrial Strategy Committee) as any other item of expenditure. Higher scrutiny would have benefits for the economy as well as simply for the tax take – so, for example, the subsidies that are given to the pharmaceutical and film industries through tax breaks would be assessed within the overall industrial strategy for the country.

There would seem to be a role for the Office for Budget Responsibility to report on the size of the overall tax gap, using various definitions as well as on the effectiveness of tax allowances. There is also a role for the National Audit Office to consider whether tax incentives offer value for money, in the same way as other public expenditure.

The consequences of tax planning

We have discussed earlier in this book the various tax reliefs and allowances made available by the government. There are good reasons for tax allowances:

- Fairness. For example, the zero-rating of food and children's clothes for VAT is of great benefit to poorer families, though arguably the money could be targeted better by giving it directly to them.
- To deal with differences between companies' cash flow and profits – for example, capital allowances.
- Administrative benefit, including a *de minimis* amount which does not need to be declared.
- At least in theory, tax allowances can be a way to change behaviour so as to create beneficial effects for the economy – for example, by encouraging saving.
- To achieve a wider policy objective. A recent example is the marriage allowance, which was introduced in 2015 to 'recognise marriage' (see Chapter 8).[7]

However, tax allowances create difficulties in a number of ways. They reinforce the view that tax is a bad thing, create an environment where reducing tax bills is seen as normal, create loopholes, bring complexity and therefore more likelihood of error. Tax reliefs are too often an opportunity for momentary political messaging, accompanied by an unresearched wish to change behaviour. Each new relief is a potential entry drug to aggressive planning.

It is hard to understand quite why successive governments use tax reliefs so much, when in cases such as energy saving, the government has used grants effectively, and its own 'nudge unit' has a range of ideas for behavioural change.

The main individual reliefs illustrate the problems:

- **Scale.** The largest reliefs by far are the £24 billion income tax reliefs on private pensions (net of tax collected on pensions in payment) and £16.9 billion on national insurance contributions to these pensions.[8] The amount has continued to rise each year and the vast majority of the benefit accrues to higher earners, despite the restrictions. It has been estimated that 50 per cent of the benefit of income tax breaks for pensions goes to the highest 10 per cent of earners, who would probably make financial provision for retirement in any case.[9]

- **Fairness.** The second largest item by far is the exemption of capital gains arising on the disposal of a principle private residence. This is also regressive, as it enables the wealthy to roll up tax-free gains in a large home which can then be released tax-free in later life as they downsize. In 2013/14, the cost was £20.5 billion, and by 2018 was forecast to be £27.8 billion – largely as the result of property price increases. One can envisage this being reformed via a cap (perhaps at the value of the average home) or some kind of rollover of the tax.

- **Effectiveness.** The entrepreneurs' relief is a perfect illustration of the risk of spending money for no benefit. HMRC commissioned IFF Research to consider the behavioural change that came from the annual expenditure of around £2.7 billion. It found that only 5 per cent of those starting businesses were aware of the relief when they started and only 13 per cent at the time of disposal. The average claimant is a 57-year-old man. It may be that the relief encourages 'angel investors', but this is unproven.

- **Clarity of purpose.** Tax-free or tax-reduced savings (principally ISAs, but also venture capital trusts and enterprise investment schemes) cost £3.5 billion. There is no evidence that such allowances achieve a clear economic objective.

- **Status.** Contributions to charities cost the state £2 billion. This amount is simply the tax benefit on donations and takes no account of the tax-free status of charities. Clearly, the tax status of charities, such as private schools, is a political issue.

- **Complexity.** Inevitably in such a complex system there will be contradictions which undermine the system – for example, £1.1 billion of relief for national insurance to those employed over the state retirement age, who nonetheless can continue to receive tax deductions for pension contributions.

Reliefs are cumulative in the sense that the wider your assets and sources of income, the greater the tax savings. Independent financial advisers will tell their clients that a well-off person after retirement with an income of around £100,000 should expect to pay around 10 per cent tax on a well-managed retirement portfolio simply by making use of the various tax-free limits and allowances. This might include making full use of the personal allowance, the capital gains tax allowance, the 25 per cent of pension withdrawals which are tax-free and tax-free capital withdrawals from an ISA portfolio. Similarly, high-paid working people can accumulate a wide variety of reliefs that are out of reach of the vast majority of people.

There is a multigenerational benefit in obvious and obscure ways. We have already discussed the overall ineffectiveness of inheritance tax. A less obvious relief is the ability to leave a personal pension to one's children who can continue to roll up tax-free benefits and potentially pass these on to their forebears.

The National Audit Office[10] and a subsequent review in 2015 by the Public Accounts Committee[11] recommended significant changes to the way that tax reliefs are reported and managed. There have been no significant changes as a result of those reviews.

International tax planning

While the largest leakage from the tax system is from tax reliefs, the highest profile is aggressive tax planning by large multinationals.

Focus recently has been on the big five technology companies: Amazon, Facebook, Microsoft, Apple and Google, which have become a lightning rod for governments, the media and tax campaigners.

The allegation is that they avoid UK tax in two ways. First, they reduce UK profits, and therefore UK corporation tax, by making charges against UK tax for the use of intellectual property, management time, systems and finance costs. These charges are made by companies in lower tax jurisdictions – sometimes tax havens, but also in other European Union (EU) countries such as Ireland and Luxembourg. Therefore, profits are shifting to low or zero tax jurisdictions. Secondly, they supply goods from outside the UK and therefore pay lower rates of VAT or avoid it completely. This is familiar to those who shop online and receive goods that are invoiced or despatched from unexpected countries.

There is an undercurrent in the criticisms of these companies that what they are doing is underhand or illegal. What is more likely is that they tread a very fine and well documented line, supported by highly paid advisers, that in court would support their case that what they are doing is legitimate tax planning to achieve the best result for their shareholders. For example, ownership of intangible assets, such as rights or know-how, will be located in tax havens, job descriptions will be carefully drawn, and the physical location of final decision makers decided carefully.

While there is a case for these companies to answer, the problem is systemic rather than specific. These are simply the latest generation to legally take advantage of an out-of-date international tax regime. So, in a sense it is unfair to single them out. Indeed, some of the big tech companies – as reported in their public filings – have reasonably high global tax rates.

In 2017, Google had a global corporate tax rate of more than 50 per cent. This was unusual and resulted from a one-off hit as a result of the USA's new repatriation tax. Even without this, in 2016 it paid around 19 per cent. Microsoft had a similar profile in 2018 and 2017. Amazon, Apple and Facebook had 2017 rates in the range 20 per cent to 25 per cent.

Amazon's global tax paid was only $769 million on $178 billion of sales, of which only $11 billion was in UK. However, of course, corporation taxes are levied on profits, not sales, and Amazon's pre-tax profits are low ($3.8 billion in 2017), partly because, unlike some of the purely digital companies, it is still growing fast and investing in new businesses.

The proportion of overseas tax versus US tax is certainly low in some cases, but there is a case that these companies are singled out because of their market dominance and for political convenience, rather than because of their tax behaviour per se. It is difficult for the UK to criticise US companies' tax rates when its own corporation tax rate has reduced to 19 per cent and is planned to reduce further to 17 per cent.

Before tech companies came into focus, the international tax regime was used by pharmaceutical companies who owned drug patents in low-cost countries, soft drinks companies who supplied key ingredients from low-tax countries and by highly leveraged private equity-owned companies who located their finance arm in a low-cost jurisdiction. This all continues.

Retail chains are a current user of now familiar techniques. For example, Caffè Nero pays no UK corporation tax.[12] Whole sectors have slipped into private ownership and are able to exploit the rules in the same way. Quite apart from the loss of tax revenues, this situation is damaging to competition. So, for example, while Nero paid no UK tax, Costa – its biggest rival – had a reported tax rate of 24 per cent – above the UK headline rate.

The private equity sector has effectively created a new class of 'zero-taxable' companies. While they are often domestic companies in that their operations are entirely in the UK, they are owned by offshore companies and avoid taxes through high interest charges and other charges. This is likely to grow and become more significant still as interest rates increase.

Two solutions have been suggested.

The purest would be a 'unitary' method, where a global tax calculation is made based on worldwide profits and then allocated nationally based on activity. A long global negotiation is being led by the OECD through its BEPS (base erosion and profit shifting) project, which, while not envisaging the full move to a unitary system, aims to close off the worst manifestations of the current system. The OECD is specifically reviewing the implications of digital business and considering a move away from the arm's length system. While the OECD has had one notable success in agreeing that multinationals should disclose tax paid in different jurisdictions, known as country-by-country reporting, it is unlikely that major countries would agree to a unitary system.[13]

The alternative which is less pure, but allows for unilateral action, is to supplement taxes on company profits with taxes on sales. The most highly developed version is called 'destination-based cash flow tax', which taxes sales after deducting costs of sales. It has many advantages: unlike VAT, it arises on the point of delivery rather supply; unlike corporation tax, it does not allow deductions for intellectual property or finance costs.

A unilateral wholesale shift to such a system would be extremely difficult and would be likely to add to international tax competition. However, the recent announcements of sales levies in the UK and EU are a tentative step towards this. The UK is planning a 2 per cent sales levy tax from 2020, which interestingly will be reviewed in 2025 – presumably anticipating international progress. The EU has aimed for 3 per cent, though its internal battle against countries such as Ireland and Luxembourg, as well as a US challenge, perhaps show the value in unilateral action. France has recently moved alone.

The sales levy could also be a starting point in addressing VAT avoidance by multinationals. VAT is reduced in two ways. First, orders are booked through companies in low-tax jurisdictions such as Luxembourg so that lower rates are paid. Secondly digital 'marketplaces' make it difficult to ensure that VAT is charged when, for example, a small supply is made by a third party using a digital platform; as well as avoiding tax, this allows UK retailers to be undercut by companies from, for example, China selling via eBay or Amazon.

International tax planning is not restricted to companies. A quirk of the UK system as regards individuals is 'non-domicile' status, whereby someone who lives here for a long time (and may have been born here and always lived here) can legally pay tax on only their UK income plus overseas income remitted to the UK. The practice originates from a scheme introduced in 1799 by William Pitt the Younger to protect British and Irish people working in the colonies from new taxes which might discourage them from returning home.

In recent years, one can retain the non-domicile status by paying a fee of up to £60,000. It is estimated that there are over 90,000 'non-doms' and several thousand have agreed to pay the fee. The approach of recent governments seems to have been based on pragmatism rather than principles, judging that the fees collected will outweigh the tax that might be recovered if the status was withdrawn.[14]

HMRC action against UK tax avoidance

There is no question that HMRC has had some success in fighting tax avoidance in recent years. While the official tax gap has not reduced in absolute terms, it is a far smaller proportion of the total potential liability.

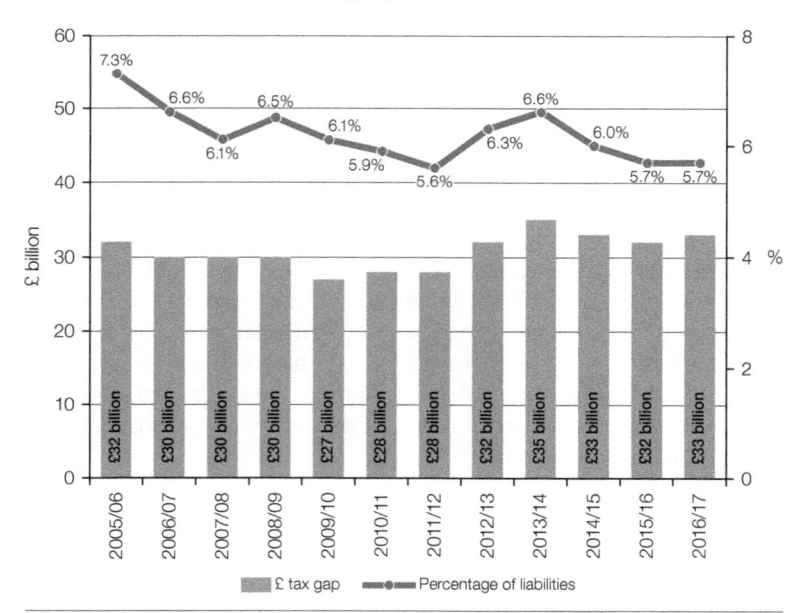

Figure 20.3:
HMRC's estimates of the tax gap, 2005/06 to 2016/17

Year	£ tax gap	Percentage of liabilities
2005/06	£32 billion	7.3%
2006/07	£30 billion	6.6%
2007/08	£30 billion	6.1%
2008/09	£30 billion	6.5%
2009/10	£27 billion	6.1%
2010/11	£28 billion	5.9%
2011/12	£28 billion	5.6%
2012/13	£32 billion	6.3%
2013/14	£35 billion	6.6%
2014/15	£33 billion	6.0%
2015/16	£32 billion	5.7%
2016/17	£33 billion	5.7%

Source: HM Revenue and Customs, *Measuring Tax Gaps 2018 Edition: tax gap estimates for 2016/17*, 2018

And this has occurred during a period when capital, companies and people have been ever more mobile, and ingenious in reducing taxes.

HMRC has made a number of important changes to the rules relating to tax planning.

A turning point was the introduction in 2004 of rules on the disclosure of tax avoidance schemes (DOTAS), which require promoters of tax planning schemes to pre-clear them with HMRC. As well as enabling HMRC to close down the individual schemes, this gives HMRC early warning of new tax planning ideas, enabling it to introduce rules to block further similar ideas. DOTAS was extended to VAT in 2017. DOTAS and the changes that have followed have contributed to behavioural change: advisers have been more cautious about the schemes they promote, and their customers more cautious when signing up.

In 2013, after many years of discussion, the government introduced general anti-avoidance rules, which aimed to clamp down on 'unreasonable' tax arrangements. The new rules have been seen by some as too soft and so far few cases have been brought. However, the rules are a starting point, and were strengthened in 2016 to make them easier for HMRC to apply.

DOTAS was supplemented in 2014 by advanced payment notices, which require taxpayers using a notified avoidance scheme to pay, up front, the full amount of tax that is avoided. HMRC is then obliged to repay any amount that turns out to be overpaid. This gives HMRC the upper hand in disputes and focuses the mind of the taxpayer. It has reduced the backlog of 65,000 outstanding cases. These notices were supplemented by follower notices, which are sent to all who have used similar schemes. In 2015, penalties were increased along with the introduction of the naming and shaming of offenders.

The tightening of the screw on avoidance in 2014 demonstrated the need for persistence and courage. The measures were bold and controversial with legal and technical challenges – particularly claims that they were retrospective. Despite extensive lobbying by, for example, the Institute of Chartered Accountants and the Chartered Institute of Taxation (which judged the actions to be 'disproportionate'), objections from backbenchers from both sides and legal challenges, the government successfully argued its case.

The 2014 Budget announced the supplementing of DOTAS with POTAS – rules on the promotion of tax avoidance schemes. POTAS enables HMRC to warn advisers about their conduct and to impose financial penalties. While it is unclear whether POTAS has had much effect, it is a rare departure from the government's reluctance to regulate tax advisers.

While many professions and trades are regulated, tax advisers are not. It is hard to discern why this, and other tools, are not used to tilt the playing field in favour of the tax collectors, rather than the tax avoiders.

As well as rule changes, HMRC has done a number of things during the last 20 years to raise its game operationally. It has improved its use of technology to pinpoint likely groups of tax avoiders, it has reorganised its people into specialist teams so that it is able to focus on specific groups, and it has laid the path for the digitisation of tax returns.

UK tax evasion

Evasion is defined by HMRC as where 'individuals or businesses deliberately omit, conceal or misrepresent information in order to reduce their tax liability'. HMRC distinguishes evasion from the hidden economy where the whole of the income is hidden. This is done by 'ghosts' who simply are not in the tax system and 'moonlighters' who have sources of income that they do not declare. What evasion and the hidden economy have in common is that their activities are straightforwardly illegal.

While the definition of evasion is easy to agree, the cost of evasion is extremely hard to estimate and there are wide differences of view. HMRC estimates the cost of evasion at around £5 billion, and the cost of the hidden economy at around £3 billion.[15] As mentioned above there are much higher estimates of the value of the black economy.

While it is difficult to put a number on the hidden economy, the causes are fairly clear: a willingness to both pay and accept payment in cash. This culture of cash-in-hand is encouraged by the media and, at convenient times, politicians. For example, in the run-up to the 2015 election, the then shadow Chancellor Ed Balls suggested that it was right to ask for a receipt for minor household services. He was strongly criticised by the press and politicians. For example, Iain Duncan Smith – who was then Secretary of State for Work and Pensions – said on BBC radio that it was, 'absurd that one would be punished for failing to keep a receipt for a taxable item'. A curious comment from the minister leading the reduction in social security payments.

HMRC has made significant progress in identifying unreported income, especially through its increasingly sophisticated used of technology whereby, for example, its 'Connect' system draws on a wide range of data sources to expose under-reporting and to enable blanket investigations of sectors or issues. However, the cash economy persists.

HMRC is trialling 'making tax digital for business', with a view to roll out in 2019, but this will only apply to companies above the VAT threshold. The VAT threshold may itself be a problem – a lower threshold might bring more businesses into the wider tax net.

Encouragingly, the Treasury has consulted (in March 2018) on how digital payments can help to reduced tax evasion.[16] Only 2.7 million people in UK are entirely reliant on cash. And all those who claim benefits – the poorest in the country – are obliged to claim electronically. So, it should not be too difficult to require all businesses to request payment online and to only accept cash with good reason. At the same time, purchasers could be obliged to request electronic payment or a receipt for cash.

HMRC and offshore tax evasion

International tax evasion involves moving UK gains, income or assets offshore to conceal them from HMRC; not declaring taxable income or gains that arise offshore, or taxable assets kept overseas; and using complex structures to hide beneficial ownership of assets income and gains. It presents greater challenges, as it has become easier to move funds around the world and there are more legitimate reasons to do so as investment is increasingly a global activity. The tax avoidance industry has become global.

HMRC's strategy sees three priorities: make the international tax system work better, increase the chance of being caught and increase the penalties for being caught. We have seen how hard it is to achieve change through international agreement, though progress has been made with the other two priorities.

The scale of the problem was highlighted by the release of the 'Panama Papers'. In 2015 an anonymous source leaked 11.5 million documents from Panamanian law firm Mossack Fonseca that detail financial and legal information for more than 214,488 offshore entities. The Panama Papers themselves have had an impact. The UK government set up a task force to specifically deal with the information.

In recent years, the UK government has spoken of taking international leadership against tax evasion, but it lacks credibility. UK Crown Dependencies and Overseas Territories include a number of tax havens; London is seen by some as a laundry for 'dirty money'; and the UK is seen as a leading player in the tax competition game, both for individuals, with 'non-dom' status and for companies with ever decreasing tax rates. The

Panama Papers identified the UK as the country with the second largest number (after Hong Kong) of intermediaries for tax avoidance and the British Virgin Islands was by far the most frequently used tax haven.

Despite these challenges, HMRC has introduced a wide number of measures in recent years to tighten the screws on international tax evaders.

Figure 20.4:
Panama Papers: Top ten countries where intermediaries operate

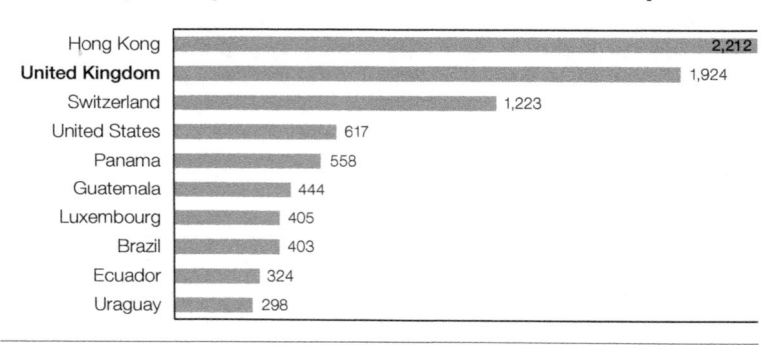

Country	Value
Hong Kong	2,212
United Kingdom	1,924
Switzerland	1,223
United States	617
Panama	558
Guatemala	444
Luxembourg	405
Brazil	403
Ecuador	324
Uruguay	298

Note: Intermediaries include banks, law firms, accountants and company incorporators who worked with Mossack Fonseca.

Source: ICIJ, h/t Quartz

Figure 20.5:
Panama Papers: Top ten most popular tax havens

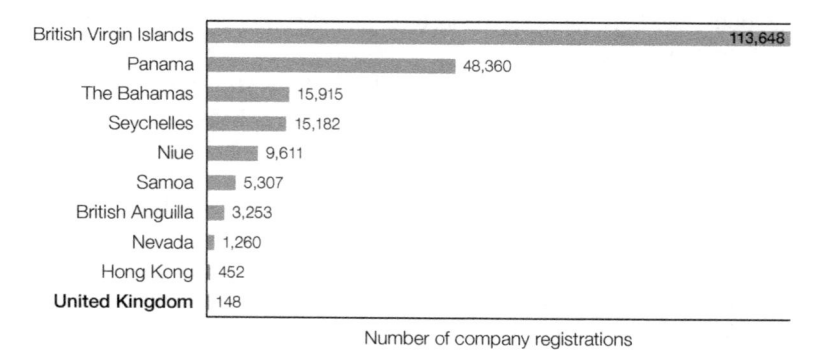

Country	Value
British Virgin Islands	113,648
Panama	48,360
The Bahamas	15,915
Seychelles	15,182
Niue	9,611
Samoa	5,307
British Anguilla	3,253
Nevada	1,260
Hong Kong	452
United Kingdom	148

Number of company registrations

Note: The table shows the country of registration of the companies appearing in the Panama Papers.

Source: ICIJ, h/t Quartz

The turning point may be the introduction in 2015 – driven by the OECD and now adopted by more than 100 countries – of the common reporting standard, which provides for an annual exchange of large volumes of information between national tax authorities. A few years earlier, the UK agreed disclosure with many Crown Dependencies and Overseas Territories, and also with France, Germany, Italy and Spain. While some countries – most notably the USA – have not signed up, tax evaders can now assume that their activities will come to light at some point. A number of important countries – including Switzerland, Singapore and Hong Kong – were 'late adopters' of the common reporting standard and their information will only arrive from 30 September 2018.

At the same time, the UK government tightened the penalties regime. The government effectively set 30 September 2018 as a final date for disclosure (known as 'requirement to correct'), after which harsher penalties would apply and there would be no incentive to voluntarily disclose. This show of confidence from HMRC suggests that the combination of information flow, fear of more leaks, data analysis through HMRC's systems and the harsher penalties had shifted the balance of power from the avoiders towards HMRC. Effectively, HMRC has moved from carrot to stick, as it can now more easily see who it has to beat.

As with UK evasion, the government has begun to focus on the advisers, including introducing in 2017 new offences of 'enabling' tax evasion by acting as an intermediary, building infrastructure (bank accounts and so on) and giving advice.

At the same time, the government introduced new requirements from 2017 for UK companies to take action to ensure that their employees were not facilitating tax evasion, including a new criminal offence.

While progress has been made, there is still much to do. For example, progress on disclosure of beneficial ownership has been slow. Without this, it is difficult to track assets and income to individuals or companies. As a direct result of the Panama Papers, the UK created a register to show who has a beneficial interest in which UK companies. In July 2017, it created a similar register of the beneficial ownership of trusts. Unfortunately, this register does not cover non-resident trusts controlled by UK residents, and so may have the perverse consequence of encouraging the movement of trusts offshore.

Three criticisms continue to be levelled at the government's work: too much advice coming from the anti-tax lobby, a lack of credibility of the UK in the international community and a lack of HMRC resources.

Conclusion

If you were to design a tax system that was difficult to avoid, you would not start from here. It is too complex, has too many taxes, too many loopholes and too many reliefs. The world has changed in ways that make taxes easier to avoid.

As a result, a large percentage of the tax take is lost through evasion, avoidance and planning. The benefit accrues mainly to those who are meant to pay the most and can afford to do so.

Progress has been made in some of the most difficult areas: complex schemes and international evasion. HMRC has worked hard within its remit and, at times, politicians have had the courage to override vested interests. Yet the system is in need of an overhaul of both our tax rules and our tax culture.

There is an opportunity for a progressive government to increase the tax take in both the short and longer term by taking further action.

Recommendations

In the short term

Tax incentives. Immediately remove or restrict tax incentives where there is little evidence that they achieve their behavioural objectives, or where they are simply not affordable. This might include:

- Ending entrepreneurs' relief, the transferable tax allowance for married couples and civil partnerships, and any other reliefs that seem to serve little or no purpose.
- Reducing the capital gains tax annual allowance to an administrative *de minimis* or merging it with the income tax personal allowance.
- Further reducing the value of the pension annual allowance and setting a far lower lifetime allowance.

Sales levy. Introduce the sales levy that was heralded in the last Budget, but apply it to a wider range of companies that pay little or no tax because of their international structure and/or their capital structure. Consideration should also be given to a 3 per cent rate as proposed by the EU, or a sliding scale of up to 5 per cent as in France, rather than the UK's 2 per cent.

In the longer term

Tax incentives. Establish a road map and programme, so that during the life of the next parliament each of the more than a thousand tax allowances is tested to ensure that it meets its purpose and does this more effectively than alternatives such as grants or behavioural 'nudges'. This should include:

- So far as possible each non-structural allowance should be reviewed by a 'spending department', so that its effectiveness in achieving a policy objective is properly evaluated. So, for example, the Department for Business Energy and Industrial Strategy could consider the value of the entrepreneurs' relief alongside its own spending budgets.

- Consideration should be given in each case as to alternative mechanisms – financial or other – to achieve behavioural change, and a cost-benefit analysis undertaken of alternatives to tax relief. This might mean grants or behavioural 'nudges', rather than tax breaks. If new reliefs are deemed necessary in the future, they should be introduced with a 'sunset clause'.

- Where there *is* considered to be an economic benefit to a tax incentive, consideration should be given to lower annual and lifetime caps for each remaining benefit. For example, *if* ISAs are proved to encourage people to save for retirement (and are more effective than other methods), a limit of say £200,000 per person in total ISA protected savings might be sufficient.

- Consideration should be given to setting an overall limit to the total reliefs that can be claimed in a single year, as opposed to the current regime where reliefs are accumulated by those with a wide range of significant income sources.

Visibility and scrutiny. HMRC's tax report is clear, granular but partial. The report should be supplemented by a report of the same clarity which includes all tax expenditures and reliefs so that the full cost of planning, avoidance and evasion can be seen. HM Treasury should be required to account for the economic benefit that has accrued from each tax allowance or expenditure.

- HM Treasury should each year publish the overall tax paid by income level in the population and each Budget should be accompanied by an impact assessment by income level. This should sit alongside the

impact of changes to social security and changes to poverty levels, and should always include an equality impact assessment, disaggregating the statistics by gender wherever possible.
- Tax is a necessary component of civil life and should be communicated as such. Governments should provide clear information about who pays specific taxes – wealth taxes and taxes of transfers are feared by the public at large, most of whom will in no circumstances pay them.
- It is time to open up for public scrutiny the tax affairs of individuals who take public appointments or receive honours.

Continue the fight against avoidance and evasion. HMRC has made strides to reduce avoidance and evasion. However, the balance of power, influence and resources is strongly in favour of the anti-tax lobby. We recommend the following:

- The government should consider reinforcing the progress made against aggressive tax planning by regulating tax advisers, rather than relying on HMRC's code of conduct.
- The register of beneficial ownership should be extended to non-resident trusts with UK resident beneficiaries.
- Tax allowances for interest deductions should be restricted so that highly leveraged companies owned from low-tax jurisdictions pay their fair share of tax.
- Non-domicile status should end. A wide review of tax status is overdue.
- All businesses, including sole traders, should be required to ask their customers to pay them by bank transfer or if they do not have a bank account, should be required to give them written receipts. It should be a criminal offence to offer discounts for cash payment.
- In general, the UK government should take a more responsible approach to tax havens among UK dependent territories.

Simplification. The complexity of the tax system makes it far easier for income to fall between the cracks of the various taxes, hampers scrutiny, wastes HMRC resources and decreases the motivation to comply with the system. We recommend the following:

- Align the taxation of employed, self-employed, and incorporated businesses as closely as possible so as to remove anomalies and prevent avoidance.
- Fully resource the HMRC programme to 'make tax digital'.

Notes
1. For example, HM Treasury, *Tackling Tax Evasion and Avoidance*, Cm 9047, 2015 p5
2. House of Lords Select Committee on Economic Affairs, *The Draft Finance Bill 2013*, HL Paper 139, March 2013, para 12
3. Institute for Fiscal Studies (ed), *Dimensions of Tax Design: the Mirrlees Review*, Oxford University Press, 2010
4. HM Revenue and Customs, *Measuring Tax Gaps 2018 Edition: tax gap estimates for 2016/17*, 2018, p5
5. R Murphy (Tax Research UK), *The Tax Gap: tax evasion in 2014 – and what can be done about it*, Public and Commercial Services Union, 2014
6. Money Advice Service, 'Using a trust to cut your inheritance tax', www.moneyadviceservice.org.uk/en/articles/using-a-trust-to-cut-your-inheritance-tax
7. A Seely, *Tax, Marriage and Transferable Allowances*, House of Commons Briefing Paper SN04392, 2019
8. www.gov.uk/government/statistics/main-tax-expenditures-and-structural-reliefs. Figures are actual for 2017 and forecast for 2018 as presented in January 2018
9. House of Commons Treasury Committee, *Household Finances: income, saving and debt*, HC 565, 26 July 2018, Chart 5.1
10. National Audit Office, *Tax Reliefs*, HC 1256, 2014
11. House of Commons Committee of Public Accounts, *The Effective Management of Tax Reliefs*, HC 892, 2015
12. As reported in its UK accounts. For a more detailed explanation, see P Sikka, 'Here's how Caffè Nero made £2bn in sales but did not pay a penny in corporation tax', 12 March 2018, https://leftfootforward.org/2018/03/heres-how-caffe-nero-made-2bn-in-sales-but-did-not-pay-a-penny-in-corporation-tax
13. For a recent OECD status report, see OECD, *Tax Challenges Arising from Digitalisation – Interim Report 2018: inclusive framework on BEPS*, OECD Publishing, 2018
14. HM Revenue and Customs, *Statistics on Non-domiciled Taxpayers in the UK 2007/08 to 2016/17*, 2018
15. HM Revenue and Customs, *Measuring Tax Gaps 2018 Edition: tax gap estimates for 2016/17*, 2018
16. HM Treasury, *Cash and Digital Payments in the New Economy: call for evidence*, March 2018

Twenty-one
Devolved taxation: Scotland
David Eiser

The Scottish government now has extensive control over the taxation of both property and income in Scotland (Table 21.1). It can use its powers to vary the progressivity of these taxes, and to raise additional revenues to support public services.

Indeed, in each of the first three of five budgets that the government will set in this parliamentary session (which runs from 2017/18 to 2021/22), the Scottish government has sought to raise additional revenue by increasing the average income tax rate faced by Scottish taxpayers in the upper half of the income distribution, relative to what those individuals would pay if they lived in the rest of the UK. Moreover, it announced an increase in the council tax liability of homes in bands E, F, G and H in 2017/18, relative to those in bands A to D.

These tax changes underpin the Scottish government's claim that Scotland is 'the fairest taxed part of the UK'.[1] But it could be argued that many of the changes are relatively marginal, and that the Scottish government has been reluctant to take forward more substantive reforms, particularly around property taxation and the calls for local government to have greater revenue raising autonomy. At the same time, the objective to raise additional revenue through increasing personal taxation has coincided with a reduction in the burden of business taxation through non-domestic (business) rates.

This chapter reviews the tax policy choices that have been made by the Scottish government in recent years, and considers whether the claim to be 'the fairest taxed part of the UK' can be justified.

Table 21.1:
Taxes contributing to the budget of Scottish government and/or Scottish local authorities

	Revenue forecast 2019/20 £ million	Date of transfer to Scottish Parliament	Degree of control
Council tax	2,088	1999	Full
Non-domestic rates	2,785	1999	Full
Land and buildings transactions tax	643	2015	Full
Landfill tax	104	2015	Full
Income tax	11,684	2017	Ability to vary rates and bands only – UK government determines tax base, allowances and reliefs
Air passenger duty	312	TBC	Full
Aggregates levy	56	TBC	Full
VAT assignment	5,801	TBC	None – assignment of revenues but not policy control

Source: Revenue forecasts for aggregates levy: Office for Budget Responsibility, *Devolved Taxes Forecast*, October 2018; Council tax forecast: *Local Government Circular* 8/2018; all other forecasts: Scottish Fiscal Commission, *Economic and Fiscal Forecasts*, December 2018

Income tax

Revenues from non-savings, non-dividend income tax in Scotland were transferred to the Scottish budget in April 2017. The Scottish government is able to vary the rates and bands of tax without constraint, although setting the personal allowance and all reliefs is determined by the UK government.

Non-savings, non-dividend income tax is forecast to raise £11.7 billion in Scotland in 2019/20, according to the Scottish Fiscal Commission's December 2018 forecasts. However, the impact on the Scottish budget is complicated. Ultimately, the Scottish budget is 'better off' (than it would have been without tax devolution) to the extent that income tax revenues *per capita* in Scotland grow more quickly than the equivalent revenues in the rest of the UK. This could happen if either the Scottish government sets a tax policy that raises proportionately more revenue than in the rest of the UK, or if the underlying determinants of tax revenues (such as earnings and employment) grow more quickly in Scotland.

Scottish income tax policy has diverged from the UK government's income tax policy in each of the three Scottish Budgets since the power was devolved. In 2017/18, the higher rate threshold was frozen at £43,000 in Scotland, while it increased to £45,000 in the rest of the UK. This meant that Scottish higher rate taxpayers paid £400 more income tax than their counterparts in the rest of the UK – a policy forecast to raise around £70 million.

In 2018/19, the Scottish government introduced a new five-band income tax schedule. There was a new starter rate of 19 per cent on the first £2,000 of income above the personal allowance, and a new intermediate rate of 21 per cent on income between £24,000 and the higher rate threshold. The higher rate was increased by one percentage point to 41 per cent, and the higher rate threshold was increased by 1 per cent, further widening the gap with the rest of the UK (where the threshold had increased by 3 per cent). The additional rate was increased by one percentage point to 46 per cent.

The 2019/20 Budget proposed to maintain the five-band structure, but to freeze the higher rate threshold at £43,430. In the rest of the UK, the threshold will increase to £50,000.

The income tax structures for 2019/20 are shown in Table 21.2.

Table 21.2:
Scottish and rest of UK income tax policy, 2019/20

	Rest of UK	Scotland
Personal allowance	£12,500	£12,500
Starter rate	–	19%: £12,501–£14,549
Basic rate	20%: £12,501–£50,000	20%: £14,550–£24,944
Intermediate rate	–	21%: £24,945–£43,430
Higher rate	40%: £50,001–£150,000	41%: £43,431–£150,000
Additional rate (now known as the top rate in Scotland)	45%: above £150,000	46%: above £150,000

Source: HM Revenue and Customs and Scottish government

The difference in tax liability for individual income tax payers is shown in Figure 21.1. The introduction of the 19 per cent starter rate in Scotland means that taxpayers with income below £27,000 pay less tax in Scotland than they would do in the rest of the UK. This should benefit women in particular, as they are more likely to have lower incomes.[2] Income of

£27,000 corresponds to the median taxpayer income in Scotland, and so the Scottish government is able to state that half of taxpayers pay less than they would do if they lived in the rest of the UK. However, the maximum that any Scottish taxpayer can be 'better off' is just over £20 annually.

At incomes above £27,000, Scottish income tax payers are liable for more income tax than their counterparts in the rest of the UK. At an income of £40,000, Scottish taxpayers face additional liabilities of £130 (an extra 0.33 per cent in tax as a percentage of income). As a percentage of income, the difference is highest at an income of £50,000, when Scottish taxpayers face liabilities of £1,544 more than those in the rest of the UK on the same income. After this point, the difference in liability continues to rise in cash terms, but falls as a percentage of income (so, for example, someone earning £100,000 in Scotland will face liabilities that are £2,044 higher than in the rest of the UK, which is 2.04 per cent as a percentage of income).

The Scottish government justifies its differential tax policy in relation both to notions of fairness and progressivity, but also on the importance of raising additional revenues to support public services.

Figure 21.1:

Difference in average tax rate, Scotland and rest of UK, 2019/20

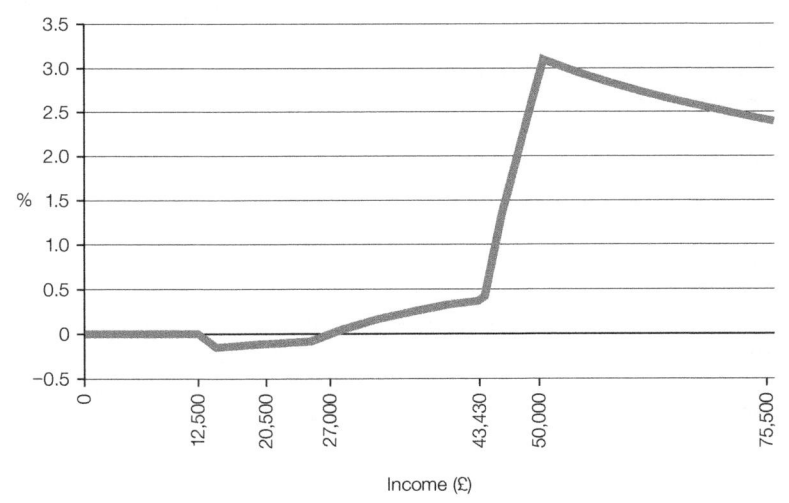

Source: Author's calculations

The Scottish government estimates that Scottish income tax revenues in 2019/20 will be £500 million higher than they would have been had the Scottish government followed the rest of the UK policy. Its 2018/19 Budget states:

> The provision of high quality universal services, combined with progressive taxation represents a strong social contract between the government and the people of Scotland. This contract supports the economy of Scotland, reduces inequality and boosts intergenerational fairness. It gives everyone a stake in our public services and the economy.

Unfortunately, the latest tax forecasts suggest that the Scottish budget will no higher higher in 2019/20 than it would have been without tax devolution. This is because the Scottish economy (and more particularly, Scottish earnings) are forecast to grow more slowly than in the rest of the UK, wiping out the revenue effects of the tax increases.

Taxes on property

Three taxes on property are determined in Scotland. Council tax and non-domestic rates operate on a similar basis as in England and, although rates and bands do differ somewhat from those in other parts of the UK, the Scottish government would, in principle, be able to vary these taxes in any way it saw fit. Stamp duty land tax was devolved to Scotland in April 2015 and replaced with the land and buildings transactions tax – which follows a similar structure, but with different rates and bands.

Council tax

The limitations of Scotland's council tax have been extensively documented. Most recently, the cross-party Commission on Local Tax Reform highlighted the apparent unfairness inherent in the system: council tax liability is not at all well related to property value. As discussed in Chapter 18, this is partly because the spread of ratios between council tax bands is not nearly as broad as the spread of property values (so that council tax is charged at a much lower percentage of property value for high-value properties than for low-value properties), and partly because there has been no revaluation of properties since 1991, with the result that many properties are now in the 'wrong' band.

The Commission on Local Tax Reform recommended that council tax be replaced by a 'fairer' tax, with options considered including a local property or land tax based on up-to-date property values, a local income tax and a reformed council tax based on up-to-date property valuations and revised banding structure.

The Commission reported in December 2015, and both Scottish Labour and the Scottish Greens proposed major reforms of council tax in their manifestos for the 2016 Holyrood elections. However, the minority SNP government took forward more modest reforms for the 2017/18 financial year. These amounted to a relative increase in liability for properties in bands E, F, G and H – a reform that was expected to raise around £110 million for local government spending, and improve slightly the relationship between property value and tax liability (Table 21.3). However, the Scottish government refused to countenance the idea of property revaluation, arguing that this would be too costly and time-consuming.

Table 21.3:
The implications of the 2017 council tax reform

	Ratio to band D		Difference in liability 2019/20 (£)	Difference in liability 2019/20 (%)
	Pre-2017	Post-reform		
Band E	1.22	1.31	£113	7%
Band F	1.44	1.63	£239	13%
Band G	1.67	1.96	£364	17%
Band H	2.00	2.45	£565	23%

Source: Scottish government and author's analysis

This is not the first time that momentum for reform has been thwarted. In 2006, the *Burt Review* recommended replacing council tax with a tax of 1 per cent of property value. But this was rejected by the incumbent Labour-Liberal Democrat coalition. In 2009, the SNP minority government failed to implement its manifesto commitment to replace council tax with a 3 per cent local income tax.

There had been some expectation that the Scottish Budget for 2019/20 would propose steps towards further local property tax reform. This expectation was driven by the fact that the Scottish Greens – whose political support the minority SNP government relies on to pass the Budget

Bill – had indicated that progress on more fundamental reform of council tax would be a prerequisite of their support for the 2019/20 Budget.[3]

However, the only commitment that the government has made is to establish yet another cross-party review of council tax in 2019. If these talks result in agreement, then legislation will be published by the end of this parliament and taken forward in the next (post 2021).

Non-domestic rates

Non-domestic rates work in broadly the same way in Scotland as in England. There are differences in the reliefs available; perhaps most notably in terms of more generous reliefs for small businesses in Scotland – businesses occupying premises with a rateable value of less than £15,000 qualify for 100 per cent relief in Scotland, against a threshold of £12,000 in England. Scotland also has a 'large business supplement', which charges a 2.6p supplement on the 'poundage' of businesses occupying premises with a rateable value in excess of £51,000.

In the 2019/20 Budget, the Scottish government announced that the business rates poundage would increase by 1p less than Consumer Price Index inflation. This enabled it to say that 90 per cent of Scottish business (all businesses other than those liable for the large business supplement) pay a lower rate of non-domestic rates than a business occupying premises of equivalent value in England.

The Scottish government has been very keen to point out the generosity of the non-domestic rate relief system in Scotland, and the generally lower tax rate that applies in Scotland. Its 2019/20 Budget points out that the value of reliefs is now £750 million annually. While many of these reliefs are clearly justifiable – particularly those for charities, places of worship, and so on – the scale of reliefs offered to businesses is arguably somewhat at odds with the government's wider narrative about the importance of revenue raising to support more generous public services and the social contract. The slower than inflationary increase of the non-domestic rates poundage in 2019/20 will cost £35 million in foregone revenues, and was perhaps motivated largely by the desire to make a political point about the lower tax liability for most Scottish businesses. Non-domestic rate reliefs introduced in 2018/19 cost over £80 million.

The Scottish government commissioned the *Barclay Review* of non-domestic rates, which reported in August 2017. The Commission was constrained to make policy recommendations that were revenue neutral in aggregate, although the Scottish government has so far made more progress in implementing the recommendations relating to the expansion of reliefs than it has on the recommendations relating to where reliefs should be restricted.

Land and buildings transactions tax

Like stamp duty land tax in England, land and buildings transactions tax is a tax on property transactions that applies to both the residential and non-residential parts of the property market.

On the residential side, Scotland has a more 'progressive' rates structure – properties transacting for less than £333,000 pay somewhat less tax in Scotland than they would in England, but those transacting for more than £333,000 pay more. Scotland introduced an 'additional dwelling supplement' for people buying a second home in 2016, following the announcement of the equivalent UK policy, and the Scottish government has recently announced that this will increase from 3 per cent to 4 per cent in 2019, expected to raise £25 million in 2019/20.

Non-residential land and buildings transactions tax rates are very similar in Scotland to those in England and Northern Ireland, although transactions are taxed at 1 per cent between £150,000 and £250,000 in Scotland, compared with 2 per cent in England.

Taxes proposed or in the pipeline

Various other taxes are in the pipeline to be transferred to Scotland. In revenue terms, the assignation of around half of the revenues raised from VAT is the most significant, but as an assigned tax it will provide no policy tools to the Scottish government (but the size of the Scottish budget will become linked to VAT revenue growth).

The Scottish government had put in place legislation to replace air passenger duty with a new air departure tax from April 2018. Its stated policy had been to reduce the rate of the tax by 50 per cent during the course of this parliament, with a view to abolishing the tax altogether in the long run. The government published analysis arguing that a reduction in the rate of air passenger duty would boost economic activity, although the analysis was based on optimistic assumptions rather than a robust evidence base.

However, the Scottish government announced in May 2019 that it has abandoned its Manifesto commitment to halve air passenger duty (a commitment likely to have cost around £150 million), on the grounds that the policy would not have been compatible with its aspirations to be seen as a world leader in tackling climate change.

There is growing in interest in the potential for land value taxation in Scotland. A report published in December 2018 for the Scottish Land Commission argued that a land value tax could help diversify land ownership and improve productive use of the land.[4] But it also highlighted political and administrative challenges. The Scottish Land Commission is taking the findings forward through further consultation and research.

There is also growing impetus to allow local authorities to introduce one or more new taxes in their areas to raise additional revenue and manage various externalities. As part of the agreement reached with the Scottish Greens to support the 2019/20 Budget, the government has committed to consult on the principles for a 'transient visitor levy' or 'tourist tax', with a view to introducing legislation later in this parliament. Also as part of the Budget deal, the government has agreed to allow local authorities to introduce workplace parking levies should they wish (a tax on the provision of parking spaces at places of work or study, similar to the scheme that already operates in Nottingham).

While further revenue-raising autonomy for local authorities would be welcome, tourist taxes and parking levies will raise relatively little revenue for most councils. Careful consideration will also need to be given as to how the devolution of unequally distributed tax bases will affect inequalities in local government resources.

Conclusions

If a theme emerges from the Scottish government's tax policy choices of recent years, it is of setting tax structures that the government can frame as being more progressive, and hence fairer, than the equivalent taxes in the rest of the UK.

This is most obviously the case with income tax, where (very marginal) reductions in tax liabilities for those in the bottom half of the income distribution have been combined with more substantial increases in tax liability for those in the upper half.

The aspiration to set more progressive tax policy is also seen in terms of the rates of land and buildings transactions tax (where the

Scottish government can argue that 90 per cent of Scottish residential properties pay less transactions tax than an equivalent property in the rest of the UK), council tax (where the distribution of ratios between tax bands is more pronounced than in the rest of the UK) and non-domestic rates (given the large business supplement).

With the exception of income tax however, the difference between Scottish tax policy and the equivalent policy in the rest of the UK tends to be fairly marginal. Indeed, the Scottish government has been somewhat conservative in its policy on property taxation and local tax reform more generally. It appears reluctant to take serious steps towards addressing the inherent weaknesses in council tax, despite something approaching cross-party consensus that reform is necessary (the Commission on Local Tax Reform was supported by all Holyrood parties, with the exception of the Scottish Conservatives). It is not clear how the announcement, in January 2019, of a further cross-party investigation will resolve the impasse – politicians appear to recognise the need for change, but are reluctant to be the ones to implement it.

The Scottish government has justified its income tax policy choices on the basis of the requirement to raise revenues to support the 'social contract' – Scotland's more generous provision of universal public services compared with other parts of the UK. Scottish income tax revenues are estimated to be £500 million higher than they would be if the rest of the UK policy was followed in 2019/20, while the council tax reform of 2017 raised £100 million for local authorities. (To put these numbers in some perspective, the Scottish government's resource budget for 2019/20 is £27 billion).

But the increasing personal taxation burden sits somewhat uneasily alongside the continued expansion of non-domestic rate reliefs. These now cost £750 million annually, and while a large proportion of these reliefs is justified (for example, for nurseries, charities and places of worship), no serious evaluation has ever been conducted of the benefits of the small business bonus scheme. Furthermore, unlike in Wales, there has been no discussion in Scotland about the possibility of introducing new taxes to raise further revenues.[5]

In summary then, the Scottish government has been more willing than many had expected to allow income tax policy to diverge with the rest of the UK. However, the revenue effects of the current policy divergence equate to less than 2 per cent of the government's resource budget (£500 million out of £27 billion). In net terms, the government's tax policy choices raise less than this once the expansion of non-domestic rates reliefs are considered.

It remains to be seen whether, and by how much, tax policy continues to diverge in Scotland relative to the rest of the UK throughout the remainder of the parliament. It also remains unclear the extent to which meaningful reform of property taxation will take place – or simply be the subject of further inquiries and debates.

Recommendations for the Scottish government

In the short term

- Undertake a robust evaluation of the system of reliefs in non-domestic rates, in order to assess whether their benefits justify the £750 million opportunity cost.
- Ensure that commitments to give local authorities the ability to introduce taxes on workplace parking spaces and transient visitors result in meaningful uplifts to local government budgets, and that the policies do not increase the funding disparities between economically stronger and weaker authorities.

In the longer term

- Commit to replacing council tax with a tax more closely related to property value by the middle of the next parliament. In the longer term, investigate the revenues and distributional implications of abolishing all existing property taxes in Scotland and replacing them with a tax on land value.
- Under the Scotland Act 2012, the Scottish government can introduce 'new' taxes in Scotland. It should commit to publishing an assessment of the possibilities under this power. This assessment should include a review of the new taxes that could be introduced, together with an analysis of the potential scale of revenue and other consequences associated with each tax. The scope of the review should be bold, and include, for example, options for introducing Scotland-specific taxes on wealth or inheritance.

Notes

1. Budget 2019/20 speech by Scottish government Cabinet Secretary for Finance, Derek MacKay
2. There is a very active Scottish Women's Budget Group in Scotland: www.swbg.org.uk and Engender also conducts gender analysis of policies: www.engender.org.uk. Both groups also emphasise the expansion of the idea of infrastructure investment to include social infrastructure (such as childcare and social care).
3. See letter from Patrick Harvie to Nicola Sturgeon, February 2018: https://greens.scot/news/green-budget-deals-have-stemmed-local-austerity-it-s-time-to-empower-a-fairer-system-of-local-taxation
4. C Hughes and others, *Investigation of Potential Land Value Tax Policy Options for Scotland*, Scottish Land Commission, 2018
5. Under the Scotland Act 2012, the Scottish government can introduce new taxes in Scotland. The Welsh government has considered the possibility of introducing a social care fund. See G Holtham, *Paying for Social Care*, Welsh Government, 2018, available at https://gov.wales/paying-social-care

Twenty-two
A strategy for reform
Alan Buckle

Tax and poverty

'Taxes, taxes, taxes… all the rest is bullshit' (Rutger Bregman)

In a publication commissioned by the Child Poverty Action Group, we inevitably view the UK tax system through the eyes of the large and growing number of families who live in poverty. At the time of publication, 4.1 million children live in poverty in UK and this is rising fast.

Reductions in annual social security payments are planned to approach £40 billion, between 2015 and 2021. This has largely gone to fund tax cuts. Most of the reductions in social security have reduced the real income of working families.

Since the financial crash, the lowest income deciles lost a higher percentage of income than far better-off groups. Lone parents have been hit hardest, losing an average of £2,000 per year.

This book sets out a number of measures that can be taken in the short term to raise money to alleviate the impact of these cuts and longer term proposals to reform our tax system, in the hope that a more effective system can lead to ending child poverty in the UK. But as described below, it also argues for a fairer and more progressive tax system in its own right, including not only tackling vertical inequality between rich and poor, but also horizontal equity between those with and those without children, between women and men, and in a range of other ways as well.

The rich and diverse chapters of this book do not lend themselves to summary and they have their own recommendations for policy makers. In some cases, the recommendations of individual chapters may offer alternatives rather than a single strategy. This chapter draws out some overarching themes that should be pursued if we are to have an effective tax system that can fund the most pressing needs of our society.

The UK tax system now

This book sets out the weaknesses in our tax system:

- **UK tax is unfair with respect to the ability to pay.** Those in low-income decile groups measured by household income pay similar overall tax rates to those in high-income decile groups, the taxes that might be seen as playing the most progressive role by taxing wealth are easily avoided – capital gains tax and inheritance tax raise relatively little revenue – while corporation tax rates have continued to be cut. The plans to continue cutting corporation tax rates are striking. The UK already has a corporation tax rate lower than virtually all developed economies and is planning to reduce this further. We do not actively use the tax system to redistribute within couples – indeed, latterly we have done the exact opposite, through the marriage tax allowance, which rewards the higher-earning partner for having a lower-earning one. Neither does the tax system give sufficient attention to intergeneration imbalances.

- **The system is dominated by VAT, income tax and national insurance.** Income tax faces the risk of shrinking revenues as self-employment and incorporation grow. Employers have reduced costs in the so-called 'gig economy' by shifting from an employed workforce to self-employed workers, who are likely to pay less national insurance. Additionally, the personal allowance has been raised well ahead of inflation, reducing income tax and while this is presented as helping the lower paid, the benefit is greater to those people who pay higher rates of tax, and increasing numbers of people get no benefit as they are already paying no income tax because their income is below the threshold. VAT, which proportionately falls most heavily on those with lower incomes, has seen rates rise from 15 per cent to 20 per cent since 2010. The same is true of other indirect taxes, such as tobacco duty.

- **Taxation is ever more centralised.** The concept of local taxation is virtually meaningless, with tight controls over revenue-raising powers and the erosion of council tax, in part through the failure to rebase property values for council tax purposes. At a time when all political parties have spoken about transferring power away from Westminster, there has been an aversion to local tax raising. The exception is Scotland and, in due course, Wales

- **Political agendas have contributed to a serious erosion of the UK tax base.** Certain taxes raise high emotions, which perversely are stirred up by politicians. The revenue from taxes such as fuel duty have fallen dramatically, while inheritance tax has become more or less optional. These moves also tend to benefit relatively advantaged groups more than others, exacerbating inequalities.

- **The tax system is ineffective in taxing wealth.** Returns on wealth are taxed at far lower effective rates than returns on labour, inheritance tax can be escaped through lifetime gifts, and personal savings by way of pensions and other investments are heavily subsidised. In the case of personal pensions, tax breaks can be passed on to future generations.

- **The system is riddled with a plethora of tax reliefs.** There are more than a thousand tax reliefs and allowances, which reduce the tax take by many tens of billions of pounds and create an expectation that much of individuals' or businesses' taxes can be planned away. The current and previous governments have attempted to withdraw some of the allowances for the higher paid, but this has not significantly decreased the tax take from poorer families, and has complicated the system further, creating perverse cliffs and irrational higher rates for certain bands of taxpayers. The reduction in the tax total brought about by these tax reliefs, and the erosion of the tax base described above, result in less to invest in the benefits and public services disproportionately relied on by low-income families and women.

- **The system has taken some steps backwards recently in relation to independent taxation of women and men.** A transferable tax allowance for married couples and civil partners may currently be relatively small, but reintroduces the idea of directing support for someone outside the labour market via a main breadwinner.

- **The principle of horizontal equity in the fiscal system has taken a knock.** The high-income child benefit charge undermines the principle of horizontal equity in the fiscal system by charging additional tax on parents compared with others at the same income level if child benefit is not given up. The interdependence of partners thus created in the case of couples is another step backwards in relation to independent taxation.

In many ways, the system is simply out of date. There has been no overall reform of the tax system in a generation, but plenty of tinkering, which only increases complexity. The absence of radical thinking applies both to the taxes that are levied and the ways they are assessed and collected. The world has changed to be more global, more digital and highly unequal as regards super wealth. The tax system is largely unchanged.

There seems to be an increasing public awareness of problems in the tax system, with a greater readiness to highlight avoidance and support for campaigns against it. For example, the Fair Tax Mark campaign has seen a large number of companies recognised for doing the right thing.

A failure to act

So why are governments so reluctant to act?

In contrast to tax, the social security system has been completely overhauled twice in the last 20 years. The tax credits system, which was introduced in 2003, had its teething problems, before functioning effectively. Universal credit – which is now replacing a benefits and tax credits system which was working tolerably well – is many years behind schedule and far from being functional. Yet the government has pressed ahead in the face of increasing criticism, extreme hardship and large-scale injustice.

Despite an almost cavalier willingness to reform the social security system, there is a reluctance to reform the tax system. The original objectives of universal credit – reduction in the number of benefits, removal of perverse incentives, automation of payments – while not achieved, would apply far more readily to tax reform.

So why is tax reform so hard to get on the agenda? There are strong well-funded voices who portray tax as a burden while arguing that public services are by definition inefficient. Tax is highly complicated so that it is easy to blind campaigners with technicalities. A major overhaul would require a change in government processes and IT systems. Tax is emotive. Change to tax brings winners and vociferous losers.

An agenda for change

The preceding chapters set out a wide range of reform proposals, which are not easily summarised since the weaknesses in the tax system are so complex and diverse. However, it is possible to draw out themes which any reforming government should respond to.

- **Take short-term action to increase tax revenues and use this money to reduce child poverty.** While wider tax reform will take time, there are ample opportunities to withdraw, cap or reduce ineffective reliefs, freeze allowances, address differing VAT rates and reconsider the VAT registration limit. The preceding chapters give plenty of examples.

- **Make the system fairer.** Too little attention is given to the overall distributive effects of the tax system as a whole, rather than to income tax in isolation. The government should recognise that total tax rates (including indirect taxes) are barely lower for those in lower income brackets than for those in higher income brackets. Tax reforms and increases in child benefit are needed in order to ensure that higher taxes are paid by those who can afford to do so, and to ensure horizontal equity in the fiscal system at whatever income level.
- **Reform the system of more than a thousand tax breaks and allowances.** These should be systematically reviewed to ensure that they serve a valuable social and/or economic purpose and that there are no more effective means of achieving their social/economic purpose.
- **Tax wealth.** A road map should be developed to introduce effective taxes on wealth. Measures must address returns on wealth so that they are taxed at least as much as earnings, and there should be effective taxation of holdings of wealth and transfers of wealth between generations, so that, for example, lifetime gifts are taxed and beneficial tax reliefs (for example, within personal pensions) cannot be passed onto future generations.
- **Make council tax meaningful and progressive,** by replacing it with a local property tax based on current capital values and considering a local income tax.
- **Take action to secure the income tax base.** This would include ending its continual erosion through above-inflation personal allowance increases and working to align taxes for employed, self-employed and incorporated entities.
- **Support HM Revenue and Customs (HMRC).** HMRC has done much good work to improve the effectiveness of the tax system. However, at times progress is slow and resources have been squeezed. Consideration should be given to an ambitious expansion of both HMRC's operational and analytical resources.
- **Take unilateral action to reduce global tax avoidance.** For example, the proposed sales levy should be introduced more quickly, at a more meaningful level and with a wider breadth of application. And tax

deductions for interest should be limited. Corporation tax rates should be reviewed and rates should rise, unless there is clear evidence that having such low rates is good for the economy and society.

- **Increase transparency.** There is a need for information of the same quality and accessibility as HMRC's *Measuring Tax Gaps*,[1] which clearly shows the cost and benefits of all non-structural tax allowances and reliefs, so that they can be effectively managed.
- Combine this with a **public education campaign** to explain the purpose and benefits of taxes, the reasons for investing in social, as well as economic, infrastructure and the need for resources to do so, and the consequences of avoidance for the individual and society.

The specific recommendations in our individual chapters are set out in the appendix that follows.

Conclusion

We hope that this book will serve as a source of information and a stimulus for discussion, further analysis and fresh ideas. We hope that it will help others to fight against injustice. And most of all, we hope that it will spur this and future governments to ensure that the millions of families living in poverty will benefit from a change in direction, sparked by a realisation that poverty is a policy choice and not a societal necessity.

We believe that this book amply demonstrates that there is plenty of scope to free up funds to recommence the fight against child poverty which was effectively abandoned in 2010.

We dare to dream that politicians of all parties, those who influence them and those who campaign for and against them, will think and act differently having read this book.

Notes
1 HM Revenue and Customs, *Measuring Tax Gaps 2018 Edition: tax gap estimates for 2016/17*, 2018

Appendix
Summary of recommendations

This appendix summarises the recommendations from the preceding chapters. In some cases, these may overlap or offer alternative approaches as they arise in two chapters from differing perspectives.

Income tax (Chapters 5 and 6)

In the short term

- Abolish the high-income child benefit charge in order to reinstate child benefit as a universal benefit for families with children, reduce complexity and unfairness in the personal tax system, and reverse a breach of the principle of independent taxation.

- Introduce statutory Consumer Price Index-indexation of all tax thresholds, including those for withdrawing the personal allowance and for the additional rate of income tax, in order to establish a fair and coherent approach to determining the real-terms tax liability of individual taxpayers.

- Avoid above-inflation increases in the personal allowance and the introduction of new tax reliefs – to stop further erosion of the income tax base.

- Launch a public information campaign to promote the messages that: tax revenues fund public services and measures to combat poverty and other social ills; it is the duty of every citizen to pay their fair share of taxes; and high-quality public services are not compatible with low levels of personal taxation.

- Reinforce the above messages by adding 1p to each of the basic, higher and additional rates of income tax. The Institute for Fiscal Studies estimates that this could raise some £6 billion per year.

- Announce a consultation on the options to equalise the marginal rates of tax paid on income received from employment, self-employment and a personal service company.

In the longer term

- Introduce a package of measures (emerging from the consultation) to reduce or eliminate tax advantages attached to providing services through self-employment or personal service companies. This would help secure the personal income tax base.

- Consider turning the current personal allowance into a refundable tax credit against an individual's tax bill – recognising that this would be a complex change.

- Establish an independent commission to examine the evidence on the revenue-raising potential of different income tax schedules and their distributional consequences, and to make recommendations on the one most appropriate to the UK.

National insurance (Chapter 7)

In the short term

- Create more consistency in the application of income tax and national insurance contributions. In particular, undertake a review of the differing and diverging points at which income tax is paid and where national insurance contributions begin to be payable.

- Lift the upper earning limit. The relative regressivity of national insurance contributions arises from this. Lifting the limit could generate relatively large amounts of revenue – which, under current rules, would need to be spent on contributory benefits or possibly the NHS.

Taxation, couples and children (Chapter 8)

In the short term

- Abolish the transferable tax allowance for married couples and civil partnerships.
- Abolish the high-income child benefit charge and restore the real value of child benefit following the four-year freeze.

In the longer term

- Introduce improvements to parental leave payments and other non-means-tested benefits that replace earnings in order to provide more generous resources directly to non-earning individuals, including those in couples.
- Increase child benefit at least in line with inflation, and by more than this if personal tax allowances are increased by more.
- Consider other reforms to the tax system as a whole to make it more gender sensitive.

Tackling tax reliefs (Chapter 9)

- Provide much more published evidence and open discussion about the aims and achievements of the great range of tax reliefs: what they cost; how equitable they are; whether they provide value for money; and which should be kept or modified to reduce inequalities.
- Review and scrutinise spending through the tax system on a regular basis alongside public spending.
- Ensure more consistent treatment of tax reliefs and social security benefits.
- Switch as many tax allowances as possible to tax credits.
- Refund the national insurance fund for national insurance contribution exemptions on private pension contributions.

- Consider institutional changes, including the creation of an Office for Tax Responsibility and a Ministry of Taxation, to ensure greater accountability.

- More radically, limit the total tax reliefs for any one person, which could be reduced to a few thousand pounds above the personal allowance.

Tax and social security (Chapter 10)

- Improve the design of universal credit to provide better support for low-paid workers to progress and boost their pay.

- Restore the value of working-age benefits to ensure they do not undermine any improvement in incomes that the new financial incentives created by universal credit could bring. Optimising financial incentives to increase employment participation rates and encourage people to increase their earnings will be undermined if the generosity of the system fails to provide an effective safety net.

Direct taxes and cash benefits (Chapter 11)

- While we do not believe that a full basic income would work, a partial basic income might. However, it is likely that funds would be better spent on repairing the existing benefits and tax systems.

- Austerity has so much reduced the effectiveness of the existing means-tested and contingent benefits system that increased tax revenues should first be given to restoring the real value of payments prevalent before 2010 as a matter of urgency.

Taxing wealth: an overview (Chapter 12)

In the short term

- Communicate a clear intention to increase the share of the total tax revenues raised from taxes on wealth relative to the existing major tax bases of labour, income and consumption, and ensure that all taxes on wealth adopt a progressive rate structure.

- Publish a 'road map' for reform that specifies long-term targets (for example, a share of total tax revenues to be raised from taxes on wealth) and the initial policy focus – for example, reforms to allowances/reliefs for capital income and gains.

- Focus initially on reforms to taxes on *returns* on wealth, in particular through measures that increase alignment between effective tax rates on capital income/gains and effective tax rates (including national insurance contributions) on income from work.

- Prioritise reforms that would achieve both an increase in the redistribution of wealth (so increasing the overall progressivity of the tax system) *and* an increase in economic efficiency (by reducing existing distortions in investment decisions and associated opportunities for tax planning).

In the longer term

- Consider options for more extensive reform of taxes on *transfers and holdings* of wealth, including (for example) reforms to the tax base for inheritances and gifts, and the tax treatment of owner-occupied housing.

- Where the existing tax treatment has become 'capitalised' into asset prices or has otherwise generated legitimate expectations on the part of individual owners, implement the reforms gradually and according to a clear timetable.

Taxes on inheritances and gifts (Chapter 13)

In the short term

- Immediately abolish the current inheritance tax exemptions for unused private pension pots, and 'normal expenditure out of income' that would otherwise constitute a lifetime gift within seven years of death – ie, retain only the fixed annual exemption for gifts.
- Announce the gradual phasing out of the current inheritance tax reliefs for agricultural and business property. The phasing out of these reliefs should be accompanied by new measures to allow temporary deferral of the tax charge where necessary to avoid the break-up of small farms or businesses.
- Introduce comprehensive measures to prevent non-domiciled residents from avoiding inheritance tax on UK assets through the use of overseas companies and to prevent 'deemed domiciled' residents from avoiding inheritance tax on foreign assets through the use of non-resident trusts.

In the longer term

- Consider the options for replacing the existing donor-based inheritance tax with a recipient-based tax on inheritances and lifetime gifts. In particular:
    - Consult on the option of introducing a new lifetime receipts tax in line with Resolution Foundation proposals, with particular attention to resolving transitional and other administrative challenges.
    - Consult on the alternative option of taxing inheritances and gifts as income of the recipient, with particular attention to resolving challenges related to averaging and the 'lumpiness' of receipts.

Taxes on investment income and gains (Chapter 14)

In the short term

- Immediately abolish the separate tax-free allowances for interest, dividends, rent and capital gains, retaining a single personal allowance for all forms of income (including capital gains). A strictly limited exemption from the requirement to file a self-assessment return for small amounts of non-employment income could be retained for administrative convenience only.
- Immediately abolish the 'forgiveness' of capital gains tax on death. All transfers on death should be treated as disposals by the deceased for capital gains tax purposes.
- Review the current proliferation of tax preferences for ISAs, venture capital schemes, employee share schemes, entrepreneurs' relief, investors' relief and all other schemes supposedly justified as incentivising savings and investment. Any schemes that lack clear evidence of both effectiveness and value for money in achieving the claimed incentive effects should be phased out.
- Align tax rates on capital gains with the rates currently applied to savings income.

In the longer term

- Consider the options for increasing the effective tax rates on capital income and capital gains to align them with the effective rates currently applied to income from work including national insurance contributions. In particular:
    - Consult on the option of reintroducing an investment income surcharge on all sources of capital income and capital gains, at a rate equivalent to the effective rate of national insurance contributions (including employer contributions).
    - Consult on the alternative option of directly adding national insurance contributions (including a component equivalent to employer contributions) to all sources of capital income and capital gains, with particular attention to the implications for the contributory principle.

- Consider reforms to the tax base for capital gains tax, including the options of introducing an indexation allowance or normal-rate-of-return allowance, together with measures to take account of the taxpayer benefit on the deferral of tax on unrealised gains.

Taxes on property and net wealth (Chapter 15)

- Consider the options for more extensive reforms to the tax treatment of owner-occupied housing. In particular:
  - Consult on the option of taxing 'imputed rent' on owner-occupied housing under income tax, with particular attention to the challenges of deducting interest payments and fairness towards the asset-rich/cash-poor.
  - Consult on the alternative option of a separate tax (to replace or reform council tax) on the consumption of housing by both owner-occupiers and tenants, based on updated property values.
  - Consult on phasing out stamp duty land tax, but only in combination with the introduction of a progressive alternative to the taxation of housing (as above).
- Consider the option of introducing a net wealth tax. In particular:
  - Consult on the relationship between a net wealth tax and other reforms to the taxation of wealth, recognising these reforms as a connected system.
  - Consult on potential solutions to the challenges of regular valuation, especially for private businesses and other thinly-traded assets.

Value added tax (Chapter 16)

In the short term

- Lower the VAT registration thresholds to bring more activity into consumption taxation.

In the longer term

- Examine zero-rated and exempt goods and services on an item-by-item basis to establish whether a case still exists for their historic status in the modern setting.

- Re-examine the need to address regressivity directly within the VAT system to ensure that this element of the consumption taxation system remains the best way to achieve this policy objective amid other available approaches.

- Explore the opportunities leaving the European Union provides to re-imagine the role for indirect taxation as a local or regional tax.

Drinking, driving and smoking (Chapter 17)

- End the freeze on annual fuel duty increases.

- Use tobacco tax returned to the Treasury from low-income smokers to fund wide-ranging interventions to assist them to give up smoking.

Council tax (Chapter 18)

- Replace council tax with a new local property tax at a proportional rate of 0.5 per cent of the capital value of domestic properties. This would benefit the vast majority (80 per cent) of households. Include a mechanism to help the small number of cash-poor/asset-rich households affected and ensure it is kept up to date with regular revaluations using new technologies.

Taxing companies (Chapter 19)

- Commission a study of the impact of the reductions in corporation tax over the last 30 years. This would develop the government's 2013 study further and make more publicly available a justification for why the policy of operating very low rates of tax on corporate profits remains suitable in the current climate, and it would enable this policy choice to be more subject to public debate.

Escaping tax (Chapter 20)

In the short term

- Immediately remove or restrict tax incentives where there is little evidence that they achieve their behavioural objectives, or where they are simply not affordable. This might include: ending entrepreneurs' relief, the transferable tax allowance for married couples and civil partnerships, and any other reliefs that seem to serve little or no purpose; reducing the capital gains tax annual allowance to an administrative *de minimis* or merging it with the income tax personal allowance; and further reducing the value of the pension annual allowance and setting a far lower lifetime allowance.

- Introduce the sales levy that was heralded in the last Budget, but apply it to a wider range of companies that pay little or no tax because of their international and/or capital structure. Consider a 3 per cent rate (as proposed by the European Union), or a sliding scale of up to 5 per cent (as in France), rather than the UK's 2 per cent.

In the longer term

- Introduce a 'road map' and programme so that, during the life of the next parliament, each of the more than a thousand tax allowances is tested to ensure it meets its purpose and does this more effectively than alternatives, such as grants or behavioural 'nudges'.

- So far as possible, a 'spending department' should review each non-structural allowance, so that its effectiveness in achieving a policy objective is properly evaluated.

- In each case, consider alternative mechanisms – financial or other – to achieve behavioural change, and undertake a cost-benefit analysis of alternatives to tax relief. This might mean grants or behavioural 'nudges', rather than tax breaks.

- Where there *is* an economic benefit to a tax incentive, consider a lower annual and lifetime cap. For example, *if* ISAs are proved to encourage people to save for retirement (and are more effective than other methods), a limit of, say, £200,000 per person in total ISA protected savings might be sufficient.

- Any new reliefs deemed necessary in the future should be introduced with a 'sunset clause'.
- Consider setting an overall limit to the total reliefs that can be claimed in a single year, as opposed to the current regime where reliefs are accumulated by those with a wide range of significant income sources.
- Supplement the current HM Revenue and Customs (HMRC) tax report by a report of the same clarity, but which includes all tax expenditures and reliefs, so that the full cost of planning, avoidance and evasion can be seen. HM Treasury should be required to account for the economic benefit that has accrued from each tax allowance or expenditure.
- Publish the overall tax paid by income level in the population and accompany each Budget with an impact assessment by income level. This should sit alongside the impact of changes to social security and poverty levels.
- Communicate the fact that tax is a necessary component of civil life. The government should provide clear information about who pays specific taxes – wealth taxes and taxes of transfers are feared by the public at large, most of whom will in never pay them.
- Open up for public scrutiny the tax affairs of individuals who take public appointments or receive honours.
- Reinforce the progress made against aggressive tax planning by regulating tax advisers.
- Extend the register of beneficial ownership to non-resident trusts with UK resident beneficiaries.
- Restrict tax allowances for interest deductions, so that highly leveraged companies owned from low tax jurisdictions pay their fair share of tax.
- End non-domicile status. A wide review of tax status is overdue.
- Require all businesses, including sole traders, to ask their customers to pay them by bank transfer or, if they do not have a bank account, to provide a written receipt. It should be a criminal offence to offer discounts for cash payment.

- Align the taxation of the employed, self-employed and incorporated businesses as closely as possible to remove anomalies and prevent avoidance.
- Fully resource the HMRC programme to 'make tax digital'.

Devolved taxation: Scotland (Chapter 21)

In the short term

- Undertake a robust evaluation of the system of reliefs in non-domestic rates, in order to assess whether their benefits justify the £750 million opportunity cost.
- Commit to giving local authorities the ability to introduce taxes on workplace parking spaces and transient visitors, and ensure that these policies do not increase the funding disparities between economically stronger and weaker authorities.

In the longer term

- Commit to bring forward legislation to replace council tax by the end of this parliament, regardless of whether there is unanimous cross-party agreement on this.